SHAKESPEARE IN CHILDREN'S LITERATURE

Children's Literature and Culture
Jack Zipes, *Series Editor*

Retelling Stories, Framing Culture
Traditional Story and Metanarratives in Children's Literature
by John Stephens and Robyn McCallum

Pinocchio Goes Postmodern
Perils of a Puppet in the United States
by Richard Wunderlich and Thomas J. Morrissey

Little Women and the Feminist Imagination
Criticism, Controversy, Personal Essays
edited by Janice M. Alberghene and Beverly Lyon Clark

The Presence of the Past
Memory, Heritage, and Childhood in Postwar Britain
by Valerie Krips

The Case of Peter Rabbit
Changing Conditions of Literature for Children
by Margaret Mackey

The Feminine Subject in Children's Literature
by Christine Wilkie-Stibbs

Ideologies of Identity in Adolescent Fiction
by Robyn McCallum

Recycling Red Riding Hood
by Sandra Beckett

The Poetics of Childhood
by Roni Natov

Voices of the Other
Children's Literature and the Postcolonial Context
edited by Roderick McGillis

Narrating Africa
George Henty and the Fiction of Empire
by Mawuena Kossi Logan

Reimagining Shakespeare for Children and Young Adults
edited by Naomi J. Miller

Representing the Holocaust in Youth Literature
by Lydia Kokkola

Translating for Children
by Riitta Oittinen

Beatrix Potter
Writing in Code
by M. Daphne Kutzer

Children's Films
History, Ideology, Pedagogy, Theory
by Ian Wojcik-Andrews

Utopian and Dystopian Writing for Children and Young Adults
edited by Carrie Hintz and Elaine Ostry

Transcending Boundaries
Writing for a Dual Audience of Children and Adults
edited by Sandra L. Beckett

The Making of the Modern Child
Children's Literature and Childhood in the Late Eighteenth Century
by Andrew O'Malley

How Picturebooks Work
by Maria Nikolajeva and Carole Scott

Brown Gold
Milestones of African American Children's Picture Books, 1845-2002
by Michelle H. Martin

Russell Hoban/Forty Years
Essays on His Writing for Children
by Alida Allison

Apartheid and Racism in South African Children's Literature
by Donnarae MacCann and Amadu Maddy

Empire's Children
Empire and Imperialism in Classic British Children's Books
by M. Daphne Kutzer

Constructing the Canon of Children's Literature
Beyond Library Walls and Ivory Towers
by Anne Lundin

Youth of Darkest England
Working Class Children at the Heart of Victorian Empire
by Troy Boone

Ursula K. Leguin Beyond Genre
Literature for Children and Adults
by Mike Cadden

Twice-Told Children's Tales
edited by Betty Greenway

Diana Wynne Jones
The Fantastic Tradition and Children's Literature
by Farah Mendlesohn

Childhood and Children's Books in Early Modern Europe, 1550-1800
edited by Andrea Immel and Michael Witmore

Voracious Children
Who Eats Whom in Children's Literature
by Carolyn Daniel

National Character in South African Children's Literature
by Elwyn Jenkins

Myth, Symbol, and Meaning in Mary Poppins
The Governess as Provocateur
by Georgia Grilli

A Critical History of French Children's Literature, Vol. 1 & 2
by Penny Brown

Once Upon a Time in a Different World
Issues and Ideas in African American Children's Literature
By Neal A. Lester

The Gothic in Children's Literature
Haunting the Borders
Edited by Anna Jackson, Karen Coats, and Roderick McGillis

Reading Victorian Schoolrooms
Childhood and Education in Nineteenth-Century Fiction
by Elizabeth Gargano

Soon Come Home to This Island
West Indians in British Children's Literature
by Karen Sands-O'Connor

Boys in Children's Literature and Popular Culture
Masculinity, Abjection, and the Fictional Child
by Annette Wannamaker

Into the Closet
Cross-dressing and the Gendered Body in Children's Literature
by Victoria Flanagan

Russian Children's Literature and Culture
edited by Marina Balina and Larissa Rudova

The Outside Child In and Out of the Book
Christine Wilkie-Stibbs

Representing Africa in Children's Literature
Old and New Ways of Seeing
by Vivian Yenika-Agbaw

The Fantasy of Family
Nineteenth-Century Children's Literature and the Myth of the Domestic Ideal
by Liz Thiel

From Nursery Rhymes to Nationhood
Children's Literature and the Construction of Canadian Identity
By Elizabeth A. Galway

The Family in English Children's Literature
Ann Alston

Enterprising Youth
Social Values and Acculturation in Nineteenth-Century American Children's Literature
Monika Elbert

Constructing Adolescence in Fantastic Realism
Alison Waller

Crossover Fiction
Global and Historical Perspectives
Sandra L. Beckett

The Crossover Novel
Contemporary Children's Fiction and Its Adult Readership
Rachel Falconer

Shakespeare in Children's Literature
Gender and Cultural Capital
Erica Hateley

SHAKESPEARE IN CHILDREN'S LITERATURE

Gender and Cultural Capital

ERICA HATELEY

NEW YORK AND LONDON

First published 2009
by Routledge
270 Madison Ave, New York, NY 10016

Simultaneously published in the UK
by Routledge
2 Park Square, Milton Park, Abingdon, Oxon OX14 4RN

Routledge is an imprint of the Taylor & Francis Group, an informa business

Transferred to Digital Printing 2010

Typeset in by Minion by IBT Global.

Library of Congress Cataloging in Publication Data

Hateley, Erica.
Shakespeare in children's literature : gender and cultural capital / Erica Hateley.
p. cm. — (Children's literature and culture ; 58)
Includes bibliographical references and index.
1. Shakespeare, William, 1564-1616—Adaptations—History and criticism. 2. Children's literature—History and criticism. 3. Children's literature—Moral and ethical aspects. 4. Children's literature—Themes, motives. 5. Children—Books and reading. 6. Social values in literature. I. Title.
PR2880.A1H38 2009
822.33—dc22
2008017684

ISBN10: 0-415-96492-X (hbk)
ISBN10: 0-415-88888-3 (pbk)
ISBN10: 0-203-88924-X (ebk)

ISBN13: 978-0-415-96492-0 (hbk)
ISBN13: 978-0-415-88888-2 (pbk)
ISBN13: 978-0-203-88924-4 (ebk)

For my parents, Phillip and Sandra Edwards.

To my mentors, Alan Dilnot and Heather Scutter.

Contents

List of Figures

Series Editor's Foreword

Dedicated to furthering original research in children's literature and culture, the Children's Literature and Culture series includes monographs on individual authors and illustrators, historical examinations of different periods, literary analyses of genres, and comparative studies on literature and the mass media. The series is international in scope and is intended to encourage innovative research in children's literature with a focus on interdisciplinary methodology.

Children's literature and culture are understood in the broadest sense of the term children to encompass the period of childhood up through adolescence. Owing to the fact that the notion of childhood has changed so much since the origination of children's literature, this Routledge series is particularly concerned with transformations in children's culture and how they have affected the representation and socialization of children. While the emphasis of the series is on children's literature, all types of studies that deal with children's radio, film, television, and art are included in an endeavor to grasp the aesthetics and values of children's culture. Not only have there been momentous changes in children's culture in the last fifty years, but there have been radical shifts in the scholarship that deals with these changes. In this regard, the goal of the Children's Literature and Culture series is to enhance research in this field and, at the same time, point to new directions that bring together the best scholarly work throughout the world.

Jack Zipes

Introduction

> . . . his work has become deeply constitutive of all of us for whom the world is (to a greater or lesser degree) shaped by the English language . . . Through four hundred years of imperializing history our Anglophone cultures have become so saturated with Shakespeare that our ways of thinking about such basic issues as nationality, gender and racial difference are inescapably inflected by his writing . . . The question that needs to be resolved is not whether but how he should be taught. (Neill 184)

> A major industry has grown up to feed Shakespeare to the nursery and schoolroom, and it is on foundations acquired in childhood that the superstructure of much of our knowledge is built. (Bottoms, "Familiar" 11)

Contemporary culture circulates William Shakespeare, the man and his works, as a "privileged site of intersecting codes that reflect and effect discourse production and consumption" (Freedman 245). No longer is "Shakespeare" generally understood as the author of a stable body of unified texts, but rather as a complex signifier, not confined to 'high culture' but continually expanding through integration into popular culture, which "contributes to Shakespeare's status as a widely shared touchstone and thus sustains his cultural life and power, albeit in forms and with meanings that stand well outside 'proper' Shakespeare" (Lanier, *Shakespeare* 19). This book traces an aspect of this expansion by examining the discursive ends to which "Shakespeare" is put in contemporary children's literature. Following Neill, my question is not *whether* Shakespeare is being taught to contemporary children, but *how* he is being taught in a cultural rather than an institutional manner. When children's literature is Shakespeared it not only rewards cultural capital, but also inscribes gendered juvenile readers who are made subject to a literary culture within which the Bard functions as father figure to sons *or* daughters, rendering the expansion of "Shakespeare" an emphatically political act.

Children's literature as a discursive formation reflects and shapes normative models of being and knowing. That is, it prescriptively implies a "standard or pattern of social behaviour that is accepted in or expected of a group" ("norm"), and one of its primary functions is instruction:

> Writing for children is usually purposeful, its intention being to foster in the child reader a positive apperception of some socio-cultural values which, it is assumed, are shared by author and audience. These values include contemporary morality and ethics, a sense of what is valuable in the culture's past (what a particular contemporary social formation regards as the culture's centrally important traditions), and aspirations about the present and future. (Stephens, *Language* 3)

Thus children's literature is expected to further a child's understanding of both their society, and their place in that society, from two perspectives: 1) their accepted role as child; and 2) their projected role as adult. I am investigating what happens in contemporary children's novels when that which is marked as 'valuable' or 'centrally important' is Shakespeare, and what Shakespeare is in turn made to mean.

Children's literature achieves its formative function by serving two masters: education *and* entertainment, the latter often masking the former. This masking is a crucial aspect of the ways in which children's literature constructs readers:

> the child, finding within the book an implied author whom he can befriend because he is of the tribe as well, is thus wooed into the book. He adopts the image of the implied child reader and is then willing, may even desire, to give himself up to the author and the book and be led through whatever experience is offered [and this] works powerfully as a solvent, melting away a child's non-literary approach to reading and reforming him into the kind of reader the book demands. (Chambers 259)

In other words, literary 'solvent' masks a sustained discursive conditioning. Replace 'the book' with literary culture, and Chambers is demonstrating the formative power of children's literature: making over the implied reader into 'the kind of reader'—the kind of subject—contemporary culture desires. When narrational strategies encourage readers to 'desire to give themselves up to' this process, to participate in their own 'reforming', the critical project of uncovering the implicit cultural functions of children's texts becomes urgent. Indeed, Chambers's assertion must be expanded beyond the moment of reading: children's texts do not just *imply* readers, but actively *construct* subjects. This is not to suggest that children submit themselves without resistance to a text, rather that texts seek to shape the reader.

The competition between entertainment and education in children's literature becomes complex cooperation when Shakespeare is deployed, as he is perceived by 'adult culture' as serving both needs. Within (and beyond) the field of children's literature, popular uses of "Shakespeare" inherently signify tensions between education and entertainment, being caught between competing logics of Shakespeare's derivative entertainment value (plots) and Shakespeare distinct genius available for educational value (language), and are forced to negotiate the difficulties in communicating both: "Shakespeare's plays present peculiar problems for prose retellings partly because of the complexity of the plots and partly because of the semantic density of the language—the tangible features of the cultural capital which is 'Shakespeare'" (Stephens and McCallum, *Retelling* 259). In the intersections between education and entertainment in children's literature, then, and the equivalent intersections in "Shakespeare", appropriations must negotiate between the ideals of rewarding cultural capital and the realities of retaining the interest of their readers. Indeed, appropriations often reify these functions by constructing intratextual models of children consciously being entertained by, while unconsciously learning from, Shakespeare. In turn, these functions will ideally become extratextual realities for the implied child reader.

This ongoing tension between story and language as index of Shakespeare's value manifests predominantly in juvenile Shakespeare via a reproduction of plot (while effacing Shakespeare's own borrowing of plots), coupled with 'the idea' of Shakespeare's language as valuable, even where that language is rarely reproduced. Edith Nesbit's children's Shakespeare is representative then, when its preface states that "the stories are the least part of Shakespeare" (*Children's* 5), but the volume is comprised of plot-based reproduction of those stories. This is endemic to the genre, which has developed the perspective that, "the plots, previously criticised by scholars as Shakespeare's weakest point, have come to be seen as valuable in themselves because they are *his*" (Bottoms, "Familiar" 17, original emphasis). Today authors seemingly consider the language of Shakespeare's plays valuable but difficult, and settle instead for introducing juvenile readers to Shakespeare's plots, interpellating children as *future* readers of Shakespeare's plays.

These many questions of language/plot, literary/theatrical, authored/cultural, educational/entertaining are visually produced (although not resolved) in the work of Marcia Williams whose two books for younger readers, *Mr. William Shakespeare's Plays* (1998) and *Bravo, Mr. William Shakespeare!* (2000), consist of a comic-strip version of the plays' content and context. For example, Figure I.1. reproduces the final page of Williams's version of *The Tempest* and demonstrates her juxtaposition of linguistic registers, visual styles, and the intra- and extratextual elements of a Shakespearean play.

On her final page (n.p.), Williams's design incorporates and performs the central tensions of 'Shakespeare for Children' as a genre: plot versus language,

Figure I.1 Mr. William Shakespeare's plays. Copyright © 1998 by Marcia Williams. Reproduced by permission of Candlewick Press, Cambridge, MA, on behalf of Walker Books Ltd., London.

theatrical versus literary, and the plays as culture texts or authored products. Note the illustration of William Shakespeare in the bottom right corner; given picture-book literacy most often depends on a left to right, top to bottom apprehension, Shakespeare is given the last word of this text and uses it to express a hope for longevity. In this case, the reader is absorbing Shakespeare, and the *reception* of Shakespeare in the form of audience responses. Thus the child reader is inducted not only into a text-reader relationship, nor an approved understanding of socio-cultural values, but also into a vision of cultural capital that is accompanied by instruction on how such cultural capital should be absorbed and reproduced.

Although "Shakespeare" has been present within the field of children's literature for two centuries, and despite the growth of children's literature studies (or indeed the ubiquitous field of Shakespeare studies), there has been little critical work done on the intersection between them: appropriations of Shakespeare for children. Morse notes that,

> Shakespeare for children is, if not exactly undiscovered country, certainly an outlying province in the cartography of Shakespeare scholarship . . . unlisted in Shakespeare bibliographies, ignored in Shakespeare Studies and, with the honorable exception of the Lambs, largely unknown even in the annals of children's literature. Children's Shakespeare is equally absent from the burgeoning field of children's literature. (194)

There have been useful critical interrogations of the intersection, for example Frey's accurately titled "A Brief History of Shakespeare as Children's Literature" (2001), which offers an overview of the genre by identifying key texts from the nineteenth century through to the late twentieth century. Although the scope of the article demands brevity, Frey does note that "we need to consider carefully our purposes in sharing Shakespeare with such youth" (150). In terms of such consideration, beyond a handful of articles dealing with individual authors or works, the field is constituted by a monograph (Isaac 2000) and two collections of essays (Miller 2003; Chedgzoy et al. 2007). While these works necessarily form a valuable basis for the field and have been invaluable to my own research, they share a number of limitations. First amongst these is a lack of diachronic reading, a lack that ironically springs from an implicit aim of broad synchronic reading. That is to say that Isaac's text and Miller's edited collection each investigate a broad range of contemporary juvenile texts, but this admirable diversity leads either to limited in-depth investigation or broad generalisation at the expense of a genealogy of appropriation (although I should note that Isaac offers a brief account of nineteenth-century texts such as those produced by the Lambs and Nesbit). Such a genealogy is necessary to diachronically contextualise the methods and politics of the genre of Shakespeare for children, and to provide a long-view perspective on its changes and stagnations.

Megan Isaac's *Heirs to Shakespeare: Reinventing the Bard in Young Adult Literature* (2000) is a survey text intended for classroom teachers; its pedagogical focus means that its chapters deal usefully with a specific pre-text (*Hamlet, Othello, Macbeth* etc.), and offer the reader a cross-section of young adult (YA) texts that use these plays in some way. Isaac writes that the "purpose of this book is to illustrate explicitly how canonical literature, especially Shakespeare, informs the characters, plots, and interpretations of many recent books for middle- and high-school-aged audiences" (xi). Thus she admits a kind of 'fidelity criticism' approach to the works she is considering, but rarely considers the political or ideological implications of the YA texts' use of Shakespeare. Isaac's exclusion of contemporary adaptation theory (particularly Shakespearean adaptation theory) renders the text somewhat barren when read against the existing literature on uses of Shakespeare in popular culture, and her text reads as a catalogue rather than a critique of the field. To be fair, Isaac herself concludes that "[h]opefully, this book . . . will serve as an inspiration to seek [rewritings] out and explore how they add to Shakespeare's legacy and our interpretation of his plays" (146), and she thus knowingly gestures towards work to be done.

In comparison, the collection of essays edited by Naomi Miller, *Reimagining Shakespeare for Children and Young Adults* (2003), has a broader intended audience. The volume includes contributions from literary critics, authors of children's fiction, and pedagogical critics, who between them discuss no fewer than eighty-five texts for children that 'reimagine' Shakespeare in some way. This diversity is laudable, and obviously functions as a foundation of knowledge in the field. However, the sheer number of contributors and texts means that discussion of any one text is necessarily brief. So, for example, Mathur's essay on contemporary adaptations of *The Tempest* examines four texts in seven pages, leaving no room for historical context, or in-depth textual analysis. Mathur's reading of Leon Garfield's *The Tempest* (1996) concludes that it renders "a confusing, incoherent [version of the] play, which reinforces the cultural belief that for young audiences Shakespeare's work remains wholly impenetrable" (150), but never explains precisely what meanings 'should' be offered to young audiences beyond Shakespeare's "delightful and intriguing stories which invite the reader to revisit and rediscover the playwright's world" (152). In a sense Mathur is representative of the volume in that she implies that an adaptation can stand-in for its pre-text, and as a result imagines a child-reader being 'inspired' to *return* to Shakespeare's world and works after reading an adaptation.

Underpinning Miller's volume is the 'necessity' of passing on Shakespeare to the next generation, but the legitimacy of this presumption is never interrogated. So the introduction states that,

> by exploring many of the different "local habitations and names" through which it is possible for young people to meet Shakespeare, both within the classroom and without, the goal is at once to communicate and experience together the synergy of name and voice that composes the words, and worlds, of William Shakespeare. (Miller 3)

Similarly Marcia Williams asserts that "[u]nless we keep reimagining Shakespeare for a new audience, his works will be inaccessible to vast numbers of every new generation, and they will become the property of an academic elite" ("Bravo" 31). The 'hows' and 'whys' of this are never examined nor explained. Alone of the contributors, Howard Marchitello notes that "the politics of adaptation have generally remained undertheorized" (181), and suggests further that:

> professions of adoration of Shakespeare that frequently attend or preface adaptations of the plays for children and that serve as their justification derive from the romantic definition of Shakespeare as the repository of Western culture and aesthetic value—a conception that is increasingly difficult to maintain given the current critical re-evaluation of such issues as author/authorship, canon formation, and for that matter, the politics of cultural and aesthetic valuation itself. (185)

2007 saw publication of a collection of essays edited by Kate Chedgzoy, Susanne Greenhalgh and Robert Shaughnessy, *Shakespeare and Childhood,* a collection which saw itself as "the first definitive study of a surprisingly underdeveloped area of scholarly investigation, namely the relationship between Shakespeare, children and childhood" (blurb). Unfortunately, despite excellent essays on child characters in Shakespeare's plays, and indeed, children in Shakespeare's era, the book contains only one introduction and three essays dedicated to contemporary children's texts. There are essays which consider the use of Shakespeare in Victorian periodicals, and even the use of Shakespeare in the Terry memoirs, but few discussions of children's literature as we understand it today. Perhaps my greatest concern with the volume is that, despite Greenhalgh's observation that, "concepts of childhood, as well as of Shakespeare, are intrinsically bound up with questions of ideology, especially with issues of class, and economic and cultural privilege" (118), such questions are rarely addressed by the contributors, most of whom seem to have a fundamental faith in the value of "Shakespeare" and therefore are unlikely to question the circulation of the man or his works in children's culture.

This book aims to build on foundational critical texts such as Isaac's and Miller's in considering the field of Shakespeare for children broadly, but also to refine those investigations in terms of combining diachronic and synchronic readings with a politicised consideration of the cultural *functions* of appropriation. Hence, as critically important for me as these texts is John Stephens and Robyn McCallum's *Retelling Stories, Framing Culture: Traditional Story and Metanarratives in Children's Literature* (1998), in that it considers appropriations of Shakespeare (amongst other pre-texts) for children in the light of political understandings of the genre:

> Novelistic and prose retellings and reversions of Shakespeare's texts for children have three main interrelated cultural functions. First, they have a role in making Shakespeare accessible and popular. Second, they are instrumental in the continued cultural canonization of Shakespeare, and

> simultaneously, in the construction of a canon of Shakespeare's texts retold for children . . . And third, reversions of Shakespeare texts perform a key role in the transmission of the culture's central values and assumptions to children. The central assumption that underlies and links these three functions is that Shakespeare is cultural capital. (255–56)

It is therefore important that it is as much Shakespeare's cultural capital—particularly in terms of authorship—that originates the saturation of Shakespeare in Western culture that Neill refers to, rather than any inherent appeal of Shakespeare for the child reader that dictates his continued appropriation in children's literature.

More generally, adaptation studies necessarily engages with questions of intertextuality, and provides useful models for thinking about the relationship between appropriations and their pre-texts generally, and Shakespeare for children specifically. Robert Stam, writing about filmic adaptations of literary texts, and the dominance of fidelity criticism, notes:

> Much of the discussion of adaptation quietly reinscribes the axiomatic *superiority* of literary art to film, an assumption derived from a number of superimposed prejudices: seniority, the assumption that older arts are necessarily better arts; *iconophobia*, the culturally rooted prejudice . . . that visual arts are necessarily inferior to the verbal arts; and *logophilia*, the converse valorization, characteristic of the "religions of the book," of the "sacred word" of holy texts. (58)

Stam's notion of the 'inevitable supplement' (55) involved in adapting prose to film certainly applies to the adaptation from playtext to prose, where generic characteristics demand narrational representation. He notes the importance of taking account of such generic standards in both the pre-text and the adaptation, as they influence the production of meaning, but not to articulate these points of difference as an hierarchical relationship.[1]

Mitsuhiro Yoshimoto also critiques fidelity as an index of successful adaptation. Here he is specifically considering a Shakespearean pre-text, and suggests that fidelity criticism springs from an anxiety about degradation of cultural capital when Shakespeare is adapted:

> fidelity is a misleading and unproductive notion because it establishes a hierarchical relation between original and adaptation, and also because it assumes that there is some uniform set of standards for comparing two artworks in different media. What is ignored in both is not only the specificity of the adaptation but also that of the original . . . The original play by Shakespeare functions as the objectified cultural capital, which is appropriated by Kurosawa to make a new cultural product [*Kumonoso-Jo/Throne of Blood* (1957)]. What is transferred in this

> transaction is of course not any specific manuscript of Shakespeare as a material object but the text of Shakespeare titled *Macbeth* (or to be more precise, a Japanese translation of that text). But this does not fundamentally change the status of Shakespeare's text as the objectified cultural capital. It merely foregrounds the fact that the acquisition of cultural capital in the objectified state is not just the question of legal ownership but that of the ability to use that capital, that is, the embodied cultural capital. (25–60)

Given my critical interest in repetition and difference, my own analyses necessarily invoke a comparative reading strategy between the Shakespearean and appropriative texts, but I wish to avoid this manifesting as a hierarchy of fidelity. It is crucial to consider the relationships between appropriations, as well as their relationship with their pre-text, and I am more interested in considering the deployment and manipulation of cultural capital as a specifically (gendered) educative textual strategy used by children's authors, than 'ticking boxes' of Shakespearean fidelity. Children's appropriations of Shakespeare contribute to his cultural capital even as they draw on it, and although they may not change the 'actual' meaning of the Shakespearean playtext as 'objectified cultural capital', they have the potential to change ways of understanding or reading those plays.

The issue of agency, of what Yoshimoto calls the ability to use cultural capital, is in children's literature an idealised and imagined *future* agency. The presumption about the child as future adult corresponds to this future-readership, and depends on a model of subjectivity as stable, essential, and recognisable as unique. Shakespeare becomes a symbol of such stability, unified in his self and his work. Thus if criticism of Shakespeare in popular culture has sought to interrogate "how this 'Shakespeare myth' functions in contemporary culture as an ideological framework for containing consensus and for sustaining myths of unity, integration and harmony in the cultural superstructures of a divided and fractured society" (Holderness xiii), I am interrogating how the Shakespeare myth itself becomes a defence against fracture and division in children's literature. The primary component of this defence is a Romantic notion of authorship (where great individual genius leads to great individual works) retrospectively applied to Shakespeare, naming him as the patriarch of liberal-humanist culture, and as proto-modern subject.

Romantic visions of authorship create an obvious target for poststructural thinkers who proffer fracture and division as inherent in the subject and society. In the late 1960s, Roland Barthes and Michel Foucault each sought to problematise dominant conceptualisations of such an 'author', in order to extend their own theorisations of subjectivity and society. Barthes in particular initiated a challenge to traditional models of authorship and readership, the effects of which can be felt throughout literary culture today.

Roland Barthes's "Death of the Author" (1968), attempted to displace the idea that "[t]he *explanation* of a work is always sought in the man or woman who produced it, as if it were always in the end, through the more or less transparent allegory of the fiction, the voice of a single person, the *author* 'confiding' in us" (143). This move was made in order to invest the *reader* with agency in the production of textual meaning, concluding with the infamous polemic: "the birth of the reader must be at the cost of the death of the author" (148). While I would agree with the spirit of Barthes's definition of text as a "multi-dimensional space in which a variety of writings, none of them original, blend and clash" (146), at least as a pointer to intertextual functions of literature, I find his replacement of one source of meaning with another (reader for author) too limiting to be critically useful.

In comparison, Michel Foucault's "What is an Author?" (1969), rather than polemically replacing the author with the reader as primary source of textual meaning, offers a *discursive model* of meaning: the 'author function'. Foucault claims, "I am not certain that the consequences derived from the disappearance or death of the author have been fully explored or that the importance of this event has been appreciated" (117). The 'author function' becomes for Foucault a way of talking about the maintenance of authorship as an aspect of textual meaning, without privileging the author as sole Romantic source of such meaning. This idea simultaneously allows for 'groupings' of works, the attribution of literary value, and the privileging of certain authors within a culture:

> Discourse that possesses an author's name is not to be immediately consumed and forgotten; neither is it accorded the momentary attention given to ordinary, fleeting words. Rather, its status and its manner of reception are regulated by the culture in which it circulates . . . The function of an author is to characterize the existence, circulation, and operation of certain discourses within a society . . . a standard level of quality . . . a certain field of conceptual or theoretical coherence . . . a stylistic uniformity . . . the "author-function" is tied to the legal and institutional systems that circumscribe, determine, and articulate the realm of discourses; it does not operate in a uniform manner to all discourses, at all times, and in any given culture; it is not defined by the spontaneous attribution of a text to its creator, but through a series of precise and complex procedures; it does not refer, purely and simply, to an actual individual insofar as it simultaneously gives rise to a variety of egos and to a series of subjective positions that individuals of any class may come to occupy. (Foucault 123–31)

Foucault's author function therefore provides a useful taxonomy for discussing the discursive authority that Shakespeare has accrued over recent centuries, without necessarily subscribing to Romantic ideology. It has been noted that popular culture may deploy "contemporary scholarship which threatens to undermine its conception of the author, [but Shakespeare] the author emerges triumphant, more formidable after his encounter with the giant-killers of post-structuralism" (Kingsley-Smith 162). Indeed, while Barthes and Foucault offer ways of interrogating how authorship is constructed, it *seems* that Shakespeare *qua* author remains all-powerful. The Shakespeare offered to children is very much a Romantic author, but the fact that children's literature—itself a site for the production and circulation of discourse—routinely offers Shakespeare at all indicates that post-structuralism has saturated culture beyond the academy. Thus Foucault's notions of discourse and authority in cultural contexts are being deployed here in order to consider the ways in which contemporary children's literature uses Shakespeare both as a discursive formation and to legitimise discourses of gendered subjectivity.

The value of Shakespeare as Author for the implied reader is usefully measured in terms of cultural capital. Sociologist Pierre Bourdieu influentially theorised modes of capital available to the individual:

> the four types of capital which are by now almost synonymous with his approach, [are] social capital (power gained by the sheer number of family members, retainers or network of supporters), symbolic capital (reputation or honour—including intellectual honesty), cultural capital (distinction within the autonomous fields of art and science; intellectual or educational qualifications) and economic capital (ownership of stocks and shares, or, more generally of monetary awards). (Fowler 31)

Although these types of capital intersect and overlap, cultural capital is of interest here, particularly as it applies to "Shakespeare" as both embodiment and marker of its attainment. Bourdieu's notion of cultural capital—formulated most simply as the symbolic exchange value of approved modes of knowing and being—has been appropriated by critics as a model for reading the literary production of cultural value because literature can thematise and materially represent cultural capital. Bourdieu describes it as "a theoretical hypothesis which made it possible to explain the unequal scholastic achievement of children originating from the different social classes by relating academic success . . . to the distribution of cultural capital between the classes" ("Forms" 243).[2] I emphasise this origin for the concept as it demonstrates the extent to which a vision of childhood as a time or place where the foundations for social status and success are laid is dominant in contemporary culture. Bourdieu elaborated on multiple occasions that the *crucial* moment for the initiation of such capital is early childhood; it "always remains marked by its earliest conditions of acquisition" ("Forms" 245) insofar as:

> Total, early, imperceptible learning, performed within the family from the earliest days of life and extended by a scholastic learning which

> presupposes and completes it, differs from belated, methodical learning not so much in the depth and durability of its effects . . . as in the modality of the relationship to language and culture which it simultaneously tends to inculcate. (Bourdieu, *Distinction* 66)

Therefore, learned/inculcated dispositions and 'tastes' are rendered natural and normative within a framework of cultural capital, and are linked inextricably with a classified vision of society. Bourdieu argues that, "art and cultural consumption are predisposed, consciously and deliberately or not, to fulfil a social function of legitimating social differences" (*Distinction* 7). I am taking this proposition seriously in order to consider the ways in which the discourse of "Shakespeare" is put to work in literature for young readers to legitimate gendered difference. If "one can see how it is that the manner of using symbolic goods, especially those regarded as the attributes of excellence, constitutes one of the key markers of 'class' and also the ideal weapon in strategies of distinction" (Bourdieu, *Distinction* 66), it is arguably a first step towards contesting certain modes of distinction and difference, including dominant understandings of gender and gendered subjectivity.

However, where Bourdieu uses words such as "concealment", "diffuse", "disguised", and "risky" ("Forms" 254) to describe the transmission of cultural capital, it strikes me that in the case of Shakespearean children's literature the circulation of cultural capital is relatively obvious. It is my belief that concealment and diffusion come into play insofar as the process of inculcation and access to Shakespearean cultural capital are gendered within children's texts. It is my overarching contention that Shakespearean capital operates within a patriarchal model in contemporary children's fiction, and does so in order to privilege masculine cultural subjectivity and delimit feminine cultural subjectivity. Thus while Bourdieu is specifically interested in the extent to which the education system is complicit in the circulation and transmission of hierarchical cultural capital, I am interested in the inscription of children as the gendered future-bearers of cultural capital within their literature rather than their classroom.

Like the classroom, children's literature is a 'space' for children produced and supervised by adults. Indeed, children's literature *qua* commodity depends on an "asymmetry of communication" that is produced by the "assignment by adults of texts to children and young people" (E. O'Sullivan 14). Emer O'Sullivan identifies the comprehensiveness of adult mediation of children's literature when she writes that in "[p]roduction, publication and marketing by authors and publishing houses, the part played by critics, librarians, booksellers, teachers and others as intermediaries—at every stage of literary communication, we find adults acting *for* children" (14, original emphasis). This is made relatively obvious in the specific case of Shakespeare for children:

> The adults who buy the books, similarly, are buying into the belief that they are thereby giving their children access to something that is seen as the mark and property of the cultured and educated. Yet to who or what are these children being "introduced"? To a handful of stories about lovers and dukes and fairies; about girls who dress up as boys, and lords who commit murders to become kings? Or to the Shakespeare "myth," the figure obscurely robed in greatness—though divested of his original garments—who, to the sharp eye of childhood, turns out after all to be only the emperor who has no clothes? (Bottoms, "Tales" 73)

It is obviously as much for themselves as for their children that adults (consciously or not) maintain circulation of cultural capital, even when the child-figure is effaced. Indeed, there are cases when discussion of the function of high-culture references within a children's text reveal precisely how self-congratulatory the display of cultural capital can be. For example, in a reading of Disney's *The Lion King* (1994), an animated feature that clearly draws on Shakespeare's *Hamlet,* Smith writes that "while the kids enjoy the hyenas, at least some of the parents can enjoy a little nod of recognition of *The Lion King's* literary underpinnings" (K. H. Smith 139).[3] Ignoring Smith's construction of the Shakespearean pre-text as literary only, it appears inconceivable to her that Disney's use of Shakespeare could be for any implied audience outside the 'adult', hence she refers to a "sprinkling of '*Hamlet*-dust'" (139) taking place to legitimise adult consumption of an animated film. I am not suggesting that the film operates as an appropriation of *Hamlet*, merely that it may be short-sighted to assume the Shakespeare is only there for adults. When Shakespeare is interpolated into children's literature, the 'value' of literacy and cultural capital is performed in the present, but also projects a future 'high-literacy' and establishes the goal not just of future reading, but the future reading of Shakespeare. Thus present-adults produce and circulate qualities they consider inherently valuable, in order to create future-adults who share such views, not as Smith believes, purely for their own enjoyment.

It is not my goal, then, solely to identify the presence of Shakespearean cultural capital in children's literature, but to examine the ways in which the production and circulation of gendered subjectivity accompanies this cultural capital:

> To produce a gender habitus requires an extremely elaborate social process of education or *Bildung*. For Bourdieu, an important aspect of this process is the inscription of social power relations on the body: our habitus is at once produced and expressed through our movements, gestures, facial expressions, manners, ways of walking, and ways of looking at the world. The socially produced body is thus necessarily also a political body, or rather an embodied politics. Thus even such

> basic activities as teaching children how to move, dress, and eat are thoroughly political, in that they impose on them an unspoken understanding of legitimate ways to (re)present their body to themselves and others. (Moi 1030–31)

Children's literature functions as a tool of such social education in that it 'inscribes' children into 'ways of looking at the world' because "literary and cultural formations re-presented in retold stories are often apparent bearers of clear attitudes to such things as power (political, social, and personal), hierarchy, gender, class, and race" (Stephens and McCallum, *Retelling* 21). Appropriations of Shakespeare are thus politically motivated towards regulating the implied reader's body as well as mind. Thus, children's authors deploy Shakespeare, not just as cultural authority but as cultural authority *on gender*.

Moi's own feminist appropriation of Bourdieu leads, for the purposes of my project, to a consideration of children's literature as contributing to 'legitimate' models of gendered identity (habitus). Even as she acknowledges the lack of literary consideration in Bourdieu's own writing, Moi further demonstrates the use-value of his ideas for literary criticism:

> insofar as his is not a theory of textuality at all, a *purely* Bourdieuian reading is unthinkable. What his analyses may help us to see, however, is the way in which certain texts enter into field-related intertextual relations with other texts. Once we have perceived these relations, we may then go on to use them to produce new readings of the texts in question. (1040, original emphasis)

Specific to children's literature, Stephens agrees that "narrative representations of ideology and power can . . . be explored in texts which exist in explicit dialogue with other texts, especially re-versions and sequels" (*Language* 45). Thus in the relations between children's literature and broader literary culture, between "Shakespeare" and appropriations *of* Shakespeare, between past and present texts, gender emerges as a crucial formative discourse that, I will demonstrate, is made visible not only by a narrative's "operation of cause-and-effect and the movement towards closure; the representation of relations between characters, actions and outcomes . . . point of view and focalization; the subject positions constructed for implied readers; aspects of register chosen; and the effects of intertextuality" (Stephens, "Gender" 20), but also by Bourdieu's notion of cultural capital. Because children's literature is instrumental in the production of gender, and constructs it as central to agency and authority, my project is driven by a feminist politics of contesting the 'naturalised' patriarchal constructions of gendered subjectivity it produces: binary models of normative masculinity and femininity which are ascribed to the plays, and then re-circulated as "Shakespeare". In doing so, I share Skeggs's position that, "[g]ender operates as a hidden form of cultural capital, but also as a disposition, an asymmetric form of capital" (23)

My understanding of appropriation as a critical term is differentiated from adaptation insofar as adaptations of Shakespeare's works tend to retell the plot, or story, of one or more plays in a simplified format within short prose narratives. In comparison, appropriations of Shakespeare offer the implied reader not only an understanding of a playtext, but also a model for reading that playtext. That is to say that an adaptation of *Macbeth* would offer the reader the play's plot, where an appropriation of *Macbeth* would offer such understanding of the play, and contain instruction about how and/or why to read the play. I am offering a working definition of appropriation as follows: an intertextual usage that establishes a dialogue of interpretation to some critical end; it may take one of several modes (Lanier) but is recognisable as 'repetition with critical difference' (Hutcheon). The recognition of the intertextual appropriation will lead to a 'new' understanding of both the contemporary text and the original, and will in fact depend on, or reward, a level of reader competence to ensure the achievement of appropriation. In the case of Shakespearean appropriation, this often depends on an inherently circular logic of cultural value.

I agree that, "[i]ntertextuality has usefully directed attention to the relationship between texts: discourse moves us towards a clarification of just what kinds of relationships are involved" (Barker and Hulme 37). Thus I am further arguing that intertextual appropriations of Shakespeare for children serve to discursively reflect and produce normative behaviours (Stephens and McCallum) with specific reference to cultural and literary value, inculcating a sense of cultural capital (Bourdieu), while also inscribing specifically gendered positions (Butler, *Gender*) in relation to such capital generally and Shakespeare specifically. The achievement of such literary and cultural functions is both facilitated by and expected of the broad expectations placed on children's literature: education and entertainment.

Appropriation of the plays' plot, language, and characters, is (perhaps necessarily) accompanied by a simultaneous appropriation of the plays' (often misread) discourses of gender, or at least attributes gendered discourses *to* those plays. A discursive understanding of Shakespeare, appropriation, and gender, reveals that normative values of the social and the cultural become mutually authorising. Hence, within popular culture broadly and children's literature specifically, "Shakespeare" is deployed as cultural authority on gendered identity.

Chapter 1 considers the historical development of the literary production of Shakespeare for children by reading significant examples from the nineteenth century in order to map a trajectory of methodologies and concerns that continue to 'haunt' the genre today. The chapter establishes dominant models of reader and author, child and Shakespeare, and considers how these were absorbed into, and reproduced by, nineteenth-century Shakespearean children's literature.[4] It does so by reading three key authors of the genre through their versions of *Macbeth* (being the only one of my focus plays treated by all three): Charles and Mary Lamb, Mary Cowden Clarke, and Edith Nesbit, whose works "constitute a brief cultural history of the adaptability of Shakespeare's plots and characters to the social agendas of a century that took seriously its responsibility to edify and provide models of behavior for youthful readers while introducing them to the classics" (Rozett 153). Of course, neither child-reader nor Shakespeare-author were ever politically neutral subjects, but for the Romantics who deified these constructions and circulated them as transformational, they ironically come to function conservatively (at least in Shakespeare for children). The Lambs' *Tales From Shakespeare* is directly influenced by the Romantic political ideal, within which:

> 'Imaginative creation' can be offered as an image of non-alienated labour; the intuitive, transcendental scope of the poetic mind can provide a living criticism of those rationalist or empiricist ideologies enslaved to 'fact'. The literary work itself comes to be seen as a mysterious organic unity, in contrast to the fragmented individualism of the capitalist marketplace: it is 'spontaneous' rather than rationally calculated, creative rather than mechanical. The word 'poetry', then, no longer refers simply to a technical mode of writing: it has deep social, political and philosophical implications . . . Literature has become a whole alternative ideology, and the 'imagination' itself, as with Blake and Shelley, becomes a political force. Its task is to transform society in the name of those energies and values which art embodies. (Eagleton 17)

However, *Tales* also reflects the tension between such ideals and the realities of writing texts for children in terms of education and entertainment. The Lambs' paratexts reflect an intent of appropriation, but the texts are adaptations, thus I suggest that while the context of the Lamb text is Romantic, the content is conservative. Throughout the nineteenth century, this conflicted text accrued influence and authority such that even Sir Arthur Quiller-Couch could not avoid when producing his own juvenile adaptations of Shakespeare in 1899:

> Although in the following pages I have chosen those plays, or most of them, which Charles and Mary Lamb omitted from their *Tales from Shakespeare*, and although I have taken a title very like theirs, my attempt has not been to round off or tag a conclusion to their inimitable work. (Quiller-Couch vii)[5]

The later focus of this chapter is on two women writers who arguably did intend to extend the Lamb project: Mary Cowden Clarke and Edith Nesbit, who each acknowledge the Lamb legacy and in doing so, also acknowledge the conflicted politics of gendered Shakespearean readership. Given the genre's history of conflating 'ladies' and 'youths' as an implied audience, the female youth is (at least) doubly-othered by their cultural positioning: subordinate to adults (of both genders) and male children. Further, the female child is narrationally encouraged, even by women writers, to *participate* in their own othering and subordination. The repercussions for the mature female reader these girls will grow into are troubling indeed, for their maturing has been discursively pre-determined, always already subordinated to "Shakespeare" and the patriarchal culture he is made to represent. The chapter argues that the nineteenth century *actively* inscribed a female juvenile reader of Shakespeare *as* a strategy of cultural containment. Recognising the potential power of the female reader (the culturally informed, and thereby empowered, feminine subject), these texts deployed a circular cultural logic of Shakespearean value and authority: the female reader must at once recognise that value and authority while remaining subordinate within a patriarchal order, itself endorsed by Shakespeare, at least in the "Shakespeare" constructed by these texts.

Criticism of Shakespeare for children has tended to accrete around adaptations of the plays, works by authors such as the Lambs and Leon Garfield. However, with the exception of Chapter 1 which engages with such retellings as a way of historicising the genre, and indeed is a product of necessity due to the literary history *of* the genre, this book considers *appropriations* of Shakespeare and his plays for children. As a symptom of postmodern and poststructuralist culture, contemporary Shakespearean children's literature has tended towards more complex literary modes of rewriting, reflecting as surely as the nineteenth-century texts, their specific cultural context as part of a broader trend in children's literature which Nikolajeva suggests "today is evolving towards complexity and sophistication on all narrative levels" (Nikolajeva 207).[6] Although I believe such a model of literary development can be "deterministic and ultimately impoverishing" (E. O'Sullivan 27), it is nonetheless the case that when considering the appropriation of Shakespeare as a 'sub-genre' of children's literature, Nikolajeva's four-stages of literary development appear to apply:

1. Adaptations of existing adult literature . . .
2. . . . didactic, educational stories written directly for children . . .
3. . . . children's literature is established as a literary system with its different genres and modes . . . the *canon* of children's literature is created. . . .
4. Polyphonic, or multi-voiced, children's literature. (Nikolajeva 95–97)

It is certainly true that as the nineteenth century progressed, retellings of Shakespeare for children proliferated, participating in the first three 'stages' of adaptation/didactic-educational/canonical children's literature, often all three simultaneously as in the preface of Mary Seamer's *Shakespeare's Stories Simply Told* (1899):

> These stories have been put together in the hope that they may familiarize children with the works of our great national dramatist. Care has been taken to omit any expression which might be deemed unsuited to young readers, and to introduce all the familiar passages so aptly termed the "Beauties of Shakespeare". (5)

Having established then, a sense of historical context for the production of Shakespeare for children, Chapter 2 considers the shift from such approaches to the more complex Shakespearean children's literature of the late twentieth-century. While *adaptations* of the plays continued throughout the early twentieth century, it is predominantly in recent decades that *appropriation* has emerged within the genre. This increased complexity is demonstrated to be the product not just of the broad generic developments noted by Nikolajeva but also of a cultural context informed by anxieties about the shape and function of 'the author'. After the ideological assaults launched on traditional (Romantic) notions of authorship by critics such as Barthes and Foucault, Shakespeare can no longer be innocently promulgated as the first among many. Hence, a range of late twentieth-century Shakespearean texts for children do what the nineteenth-century examples never had to: install Shakespearean authority as legitimate and persuasive. In other words, Shakespeare's cultural capital is no longer assured, and must be established before it can be passed on. His authority is figured explicitly as paternalistic, and he is installed as a character who takes up the role of mentor-father. In that sense, these novels exemplify the notion that,

> In patriarchal culture the place of the big Other may be occupied by God, King, Pope, Lord, Father—placeholders who quilt a paternal allegory over a fundamentally antagonistic social formation and call things to order and account within it . . . By holding itself in reserve, the big Other allows the subject to fantasize a site—always elsewhere—of absolute knowledge, authority, and control which organizes the subject's narrative integration into the social order, assigning him or her, as it were, a place in the story. (Charnes, "Dismember" 2)

Perhaps unsurprisingly, then, a significant area in which Shakespeare for children of the twentieth century diverges from that of the nineteenth therefore is in the fictional presence of William Shakespeare as character. These novels engage in a nostalgic return to the past to ensure a simultaneous installation of the playwright alongside his plays.

Chapters 3 through 5 read appropriations of individual plays: *Macbeth, A Midsummer Night's Dream* and *The Tempest*. In order to track the ways in which adaptation has evolved into appropriation, and to consider how individual plays have been used in a variety of contexts, these chapters consider how the complexities of Shakespeare's playtexts are simplified in the service of cultural politics, even as they are invoked in the service of cultural capital.[7] In choosing pre-texts, I have been influenced both by content and circumstance. In order to maintain a strong focus and to enable diachronic and synchronic readings, these plays were chosen because of the number of appropriations of each with both masculine and feminine implied readers. Their popularity may stem from the dominance of fantasy within children's literature, particularly as *Macbeth, A Midsummer Night's Dream,* and *The Tempest* themselves contain elements endemic to fantasy (witches, ghosts, prophecies, fairies and magic). Hence, they provide a range of authoritative cultural reference points which can be deployed in the service of fantasy's obvious function: reifying that which can only be rendered as metaphoric or symbolic within realist genres. In addition to these generic qualities, *A Midsummer Night's Dream* and *The Tempest* are also thematically concerned with maturation, another key concern of children's literature. These plays then, are readily available to be attributed with the very politics of subjectivity they are used to reify and authorise within the children's texts I am reading.

These chapters not only reveal a continuing investment in normative gender roles facilitated by "Shakespeare", but also demonstrate that the production of this normativity is shaped by both the play's construction of gender, and the gender of the implied reader. So when aimed at girls, children's literature that appropriates *Macbeth* focuses almost exclusively on the figure of the witch and its 'necessary' containment, as an unacceptable model for femininity, but appropriations of *A Midsummer Night's Dream* tend to privilege a romance plot rather than any specific character, while uses of *The Tempest* are deeply concerned with feminine familial identity, and the subordination of the self to one's family obligations. In comparison, *Macbeth* for boys offers an idealised masculine role model in Macbeth, *Dream* focuses on the liberatory possibilities of identifying with Puck, and *The Tempest* becomes a narrative of 'necessary' separation from the father in anticipation of taking his role in the future. The consistently patriarchal models of gendered identity attributed to the Shakespearean pre-text reveal far more about contemporary anxieties about feminine autonomy than about gender in Shakespeare's own texts: juvenile readers are offered consistently hierarchical models of subjectivity within which gender informs (and it is argued limits) access to cultural subversion, sexuality, and autonomy/authority.

It is not enough to note that "Shakespeare has been established as a cultural icon for several hundred years, so it is clearly an advantage, even if only in terms of 'cultural capital', to have met him at an early age" (Lindblad 133–34): what the child reader is exposed to is not Shakespeare but "Shakespeare", a discourse fitted to specific contextual and ideological moments. The exposure is not only transmitting a form of cultural capital, but also a key to its meaning and value. In contemporary children's literature, "Shakespeare" has become the vehicle of naturalised, historicised and authorised discourses of normative gender, subjectivity and behaviour.

Chapter One
Romantic Roots: Constructing the Child as Reader, and Shakespeare as Author

By the nineteenth century a familiarity with Shakespeare was expected of every educated person; the sooner aspirant middle-class children could acquire such knowledge, the better. Shakespeare was thus forcibly transformed into a children's author. (G. Taylor 207)

Science has succeeded to Poetry no less in the little walks of Children than with Men. Is there no possibility of averting this sore evil? Think what you would have been now, if instead of being fed with Tales and old wives fables in childhood, you had been crammed with Geography & Natural History.? **Damn them.** I mean the cursed Barbauld Crew, those **Blights & Blasts** of all that is **Human** in man & child. (Charles Lamb writing to S. T. Coleridge, 1802. *Letters* 81–82)

As these epigraphs demonstrate, nineteenth-century Shakespeare for children no less than contemporary cases was imbricated with concepts of education and entertainment. The responses to these competing functions within dominant literary cultures of the nineteenth century, often marked temporally as well as ideologically—the (early) Romantic, the (mid-century) high-realist Victorian, and the (late) pre-Modern—can be mapped through major examples of Shakespeare for children produced under their auspices. A consideration of the cultural and critical contexts and content of Charles and Mary Lamb's *Tales From Shakespeare* (1807), Mary Cowden Clarke's *Girlhood of Shakespeare's Heroines* (1850–51), and Edith Nesbit's *The Children's Shakespeare* (1897) offers the opportunity to establish the foundations of today's appropriations of Shakespeare for children, and reveals attitudes both to children as reading subjects and 'Literature' in the form of Shakespeare. They establish the broad paradigms of appropriating Shakespeare (as Author) for Children (as Readers) that have continued throughout the twentieth century, and thus diachronically contextualise contemporary Shakespearean children's literature and the cultural forces reflected and reproduced by it. These forces include distinctions between Shakespearean plot and language; anxiety about Shakespeare's authority instructive or poetic; and most significantly for my purposes, the emphatic gendering of the genre and its implied readers.[1]

In the complex (and predominantly masculine) interplay of voices that enact and represent the height of English Romanticism at the turn of the nineteenth century, two significant discourses emerge which prove to be influential throughout that century and well in to the twentieth in terms of constructing Shakespeare for children: one of the great author-artist figure, another of the child as embodiment of Sublime innocence, and figure of natural truths. The intersection of these models—Shakespeare as Author and Child as Reader—produces a new site for the production of cultural meaning: the Shakespearean text for the child audience. However, where ideals meet social reality (commodified publication and real readers), negotiations must be made between the ideal and the real, which reveal the possibilities and limits of Romantic ideology as performed in Shakespeare for children.[2]

From such varied points of reference as Wordsworth's poetry, Coleridge's criticism, Burke's political philosophy, and Rousseau's model of child-rearing, an understanding may be drawn of Romantic ideals, and the specific models of author and reader that inform Shakespearean children's literature in the early nineteenth century. This plurality of voices is characteristic of the British Romantics who, "did not propound a 'theory' of Romanticism, as the Schlegel brothers and their circle did in Germany, but such a theory—although it is more like a series of working principles, which are often violated—may be evinced from their responses to Shakespeare" (Bate, *Shakespeare* 5). Thus, it is too simplistic to assert a single Romantic position, but it is possible to extrapolate a range of ideas based on dominant voices within the group.

The Romantic view of authorship—often figured through, though not exclusive to, Shakespeare—is most clearly articulated by William Wordsworth in the preface to the *Lyrical Ballads* (1802).[3] This preface is a long, and at times circular, manifesto, but it is worth quoting substantially as an accessible model of the Romantic author:

> All good Poetry is the spontaneous overflow of powerful feelings, but though this be true, Poems to which any value can be attached were never produced on any variety of subjects but by a man who, being possessed of more than usual organic sensibility, had also thought long and deeply . . . such habits of mind will be produced that, by obeying blindly and mechanically the impulses of those habits, we shall describe objects, and utter sentiments, of such a nature and in such connection with each other, that the understanding of the being to whom we address ourselves, if he be in a healthful state of association, must necessarily be in some degree enlightened, and his affections ameliorated. (62–63)

> The Poet, singing a song in which all human beings join with him, rejoices in the presence of truth as our visible friend and hourly companion. Poetry is the breath and finer spirit of all knowledge; . . . the Poet binds together by passion and knowledge the vast empire of human society, as it is spread over the whole earth, and over all time . . . Poetry is the first and last of all knowledge—it is as immortal as the heart of man. (76–77)

This model of authorship obviously functions as a strategy of self-canonisation, but this canonisation is also applied retrospectively to Shakespeare. Wordsworth refers to him throughout, and Shakespeare is established as the ideal figure through whom the privileged discourses of the Sublime, personal experience mediated through nature, and the individual as distinct from the idealised societies of the Enlightenment, may be written.

William Shakespeare, already identified as England's national poet—thanks in no small part to David Garrick's 1769 Jubilee—offered a model forebear in a self-legitimising genealogy.[4] It is important to note that the Romantics do not simply retrieve Shakespeare from an obscure past. Critics such as Gary Taylor, Michael Bristol, and Michael Dobson have cogently demonstrated that the seventeenth no less than the eighteenth century had embraced Shakespeare as "normatively constitutive to British national identity as the drinking of afternoon tea" (Dobson 7). It is this level of symbolic value that makes Shakespeare a worthy object of appropriation for the Romantics, who circulate imaginative cultural capital rather than knowledge-based cultural capital as is demonstrated in commentaries on Shakespeare and his works. In these commentaries concepts of creative authorship and national character coalesce. If at times this involved a degree of distortion, "the necessity outweighed the difficulty and the price of partial or distorted reading was one well worth paying, for the benefits of making use of Shakespeare, of making him contemporary" (Bate, *Romantics* 9). The distorted or remade Shakespeare as Romantic author and subject is crucial, not simply to nineteenth-century Shakespeare (for children or generally), but also to twenty-first-century understandings of "Shakespeare".[5]

If Wordsworth's model of poetry reveals, "how Shakespeare becomes an archetype of the creative imagination which was an essential element of Romantic literary theory" (Han 15), then Samuel Taylor Coleridge demonstrates the simultaneous privileging of the 'Romantic reader' within appropriations (in the sense of taking ownership) of Shakespeare:

> Another excellence in Shakespear, and in which no other writer equalled him, was in the language of nature, so correct was it that we could see ourselves in all he wrote; his style and manner had also that felicity, that not a sentence could be read without its being discovered if it were Shaksperian. (Lectures 521, original emphases)

> Thus is Shakspeare always master of himself and of his subject—a genuine Proteus: we see all things in him, as images in a calm lake, most distinct, most accurate—only more splendid, more glorified. This is correctness in the only philosophical sense. But he requires your sympathy and submission; you must have that recipiency of moral impression without which the purposes and ends of the drama would be frustrated, and the absence of which demonstrates an utter want of all imagination, a deadness to that necessary pleasure of being innocently . . . drawn away from ourself to the music of noblest thought in harmonious sounds. (Coleridge, *Literary* 249)[6]

In making Shakespeare a poet, Coleridge is privileging a literary rather than theatrical Shakespeare, in an example of the ways in which "the Romantics contend that the complexity and artistry of Shakespeare's texts are accessible only through imaginative reading, because the actor tends to degrade their literary and dramatic values for the sake of momentary theatrical effect" (Han 25). Such a privileging (which may also be seen in Lamb, "On the Tragedies of Shakespeare") not only makes Shakespeare an ideal author, but also necessarily implies and valorises an ideal reader, for Shakespeare; for Romanticism; for Romantic poetry; and for the Romantic circle's responses *to* Shakespeare. Coleridge explicitly made Shakespeare over into a Romantic poet-author most accessible to the Romantic reader, for whom "the romantic poetry—the Shakespearian drama—appealed to the imagination rather than to the senses" (*Literary* 35).

Just as Shakespeare became the figure of ideal authorship, the child became the figure of ideal readership as a result of discursive connections between innocence and the natural (potentially Sublime). This child, as the possible embodiment of Romanticism, was as heavily debated as authorship. In the eighteenth-century debate on juvenile development, a debate which consolidated early-modern constructions of childhood *as* a category of individual and social development, the concepts of John Locke (moral neutrality, or the *tabula rasa*), John Wesley (original sin), and Jean Jacques Rousseau (natural education) were in competition.[7] Although Locke and Rousseau differed philosophically, their mutual interest in the child as reader offered meat for the Romantics, who in negotiating between these thinkers located their "natural connection between children and higher truths [that] opened the way for a new means of communicating through fiction" (Thacker and Webb 16).

John Locke's *Some Thoughts Concerning Education* (1693) privileged reason as a precondition to moral good, and was deeply concerned with the child as the 'future adult'. Although Locke was primarily concerned with the development of good citizens, he also offered the proposition that "*Learning* might be made a Play and Recreation to Children" (208, original emphasis). Locke included specific pedagogical advice regarding reading materials for children:

> I think *Æsop's Fables* the best, which being Stories apt to delight and entertain a Child, may yet afford useful Reflections to a grown Man. And if his Memory retain them all his life after, he will not repent to find them there, amongst his manly Thoughts, and serious Business. If his *Æsop has Pictures* in it, it will entertain him much the better, and encourage him to read, when it carries the increase of Knowledge with it. (212, original emphasis)

The combining of entertainment and education here identifies Locke as a key precursor of dominant understandings of children's literature today, even though literature is of limited concern within his text.

In dialogue with Locke's *Education*, Jean Jacques Rousseau produced a semi-fictionalised polemic on child-rearing and education in *Emile: Or, On Education* (1762), where he took to task those who "are always seking the man in the child without thinking what he is before being a man" (34). Rather than reason, Rousseau identified instinctual feeling and sensory experience as the foundations of valuable childhood, suggesting indeed that the child "ought to receive [lessons] only from experience" (92): reason and morals are to be acquired as an adult. Within a framework of 'natural education', Rousseau posited childhood as a time where any outside/adult influence is potentially detrimental to the child, and such influence necessarily includes fictional narratives: "How can people be so blinded as to call fables the morality of children? They do not think about how the apologue, in giving enjoyment to children, deceives them . . . Fables can instruct men, but the naked truth has to be told to children" (112). Nonetheless, Rousseau used the book as metaphor when describing the child's 'instinctive' learning:

> He keeps in himself a record of the actions and the speeches of men, and all that surrounds him is the book in which, without thinking about it, he continually enriches his memory while waiting for his judgment to be able to profit from it. (112)

Rousseau's response to Locke "quickly attracted a band of ardent supporters in England—Rousseauphiles like Richard Edgeworth, Erasmus Darwin, Charles Lamb, William Hazlitt, Thomas Day, and Mary Wollstonecraft" (Cleverley and Phillips 36). Importantly these figures are not only followers of Rousseau in rethinking juvenile education, but are also proponents of a literature for children.[8] It is thus in the promulgation of a model of childhood drawing on both Locke and Rousseau—the reader who learns through entertainment and the child who instinctively 'knows' things—that the Romantics located the 'reading counterpart' to their 'writing genius'.

If the implication of Shakespeare in the construction of Romantic authorship, and "the idealized relationship between adult author and child reader, formed out of the Romantic aesthetic, which serves as a model for subsequent writing for children in English" (Thacker and Webb 13), it is surprising that only two examples of Shakespeare for children in English emerged in the early nineteenth century (and indeed only one that produced prose narrative for an intended child reader). These two examples however, Mary and Charles Lamb's *Tales From Shakespeare* and Henrietta and Thomas Bowdler's *The Family Shakespeare* (both 1807), are crucial to understandings of contemporary Shakespeare for children, and taken together reveal the gendered *goals* of adaptation that have been inherited as part of the genre. The Lamb and Bowdler texts speak simultaneously to the power and limitations of Romantic ideologies, for while they reify the Romantic faith in the author and the reader; they also implicitly represent the extent to which these are constructed discourses. That is, even as they inculcate Shakespeare as cultural authority—and in turn use that authority to naturalise gendered and national subject positions—they reveal that these discourses *need* to be inculcated.

Ideally, the child could be given the Shakespearean text 'as is' and draw from it the great truths so often attributed to Shakespeare. However, the Romantic understanding of Shakespeare implicitly acknowledges that the text is open to any number of interpretations. Enter the adapters, with an implicit faith in both the cultural capital of Shakespeare, and the value of transmitting that capital to a newly-invented market of child readers as future citizens. In the Lambs' preface, faith in Shakespeare's value as both cultural and moral authority is linked with the possibility of inculcating these values in the child through reading and assimilation:

> What these Tales shall have been to the *young* readers, that and much more it is the writers' wish that the true Plays of Shakespeare may prove to them in older years—enrichers of the fancy, strengtheners of virtue, a withdrawing from all selfish and mercenary thoughts, a lesson of all sweet and honourable thoughts and actions, to teach courtesy, benignity, generosity, humanity: for of examples, teaching these virtues, his pages are full. (*Tales* 17, original emphasis)

Not only does the preface produce a model of affective reading, whereby the genius of Shakespeare will have a direct impact on the child reader, but it also represents the extent to which Charles Lamb in particular, "like Coleridge and Wordsworth ... protested against the growing influence of utilitarianism on children's education, the early force-feeding with facts and classifications at the expense of more traditional imaginative reading" (Aaron 162). In this context, fancy and virtue are linked, and imaginative reading provides a nexus between the two.[9] The Lambs thus use their accrued cultural capital to at once designate and disseminate that which they perceive as being valuable: even as they contest didacticism, they didactically affirm the value of literary Shakespeare for cultural and personal improvement.

Siblings Charles and Mary Lamb were active in the literary society of early nineteenth-century London, as is evidenced by the fact that social philosopher turned publisher William Godwin, on the advice of his second wife, commissioned from Mary Lamb a series of children's tales based on the plays of Shakespeare. The resulting *Tales From Shakespeare* originates Shakespeare for children in English, and exemplifies the importance of context as well as content, in that it extratextually circulates Romantic discourses of authorship and readership, but intratextually reflects anxieties about normative gendered identities in ways which would seem to be counter to Romantic discourses of selfhood.

When first published in 1807, the *Tales From Shakespeare* were attributed solely to Charles Lamb, despite the original commission, and the fact that surviving letters of the siblings make clear that of the twenty stories, Mary was responsible for the fourteen comedies and Charles for the six tragedies (see Lamb and Lamb, *Letters* 223 and 256). This indicates that the text is at least co-authored if not positively a collaboration, as Marsden believes, between siblings for whom,

> writing was a communal process. They may have worked initially on separate sheets, but they then passed these sheets across a shared table. As a result it is difficult (if not impossible) to distinguish precisely where Mary's work stops and Charles begins; we know they began with different topics, but no significant distinctions exist in the finished product of collaboration. (50–51)[10]

The authorial attribution may be explained by "[r]emembering Mary Lamb's history, and the terrible death of her mother at her hand during an attack of insanity—[making it] evident why her name was not put on the title page [and further that] it is only within recent years that the full extent of [her] work has become known" (Thomson 27).[11] Marina Warner shares this position, when she writes in her recent introduction to the tales, that Mary's "name did not appear on *Tales from Shakespeare* because of her known record, not because women authors were sidelined (though they were)" ("Introduction" xxiv). However, I believe the attribution is due to more than Mary's personal history, which after all, did not prevent the original commission being made. The attribution to Charles not only 'protects' Mary, but also participates in a paternalistic model of artistic inspiration and transmission within which Shakespeare is the great father-figure of poetry. Within the Romantic model, Charles Lamb offers a more obvious and acceptable disciple of Shakespeare than his sister.

The rhetoric of the Lambs' preface promotes an ideal of sibling reading, which allows for both male and female children to be consumers of Shakespeare, but which designates the elder brother superior to his younger sister. A cultural hierarchy of reading is described, where female children are encouraged to read the adaptations (which does mark a progressive notion of feminine education) but male children are nonetheless encouraged to read the 'original' Shakespeare on behalf of their sisters (cf. Wolfson, "Explaining" 21):

> instead of recommending these Tales to the perusal of young gentlemen who can read them so much better in the originals, their kind assistance is rather requested in explaining to their sisters such parts as are hardest for them to understand: and when they have helped them to get over the difficulties, then perhaps they will read to them (carefully selecting what is proper for a young sister's ear) some passage which has pleased them in one of these stories, in the very words of the scene from which it is taken. (Lamb and Lamb, *Tales* 17)

In addition to Charles Lamb's infamous antipathy to theatrical Shakespeare then, it is also the case that the "scene of fathers reading to families [as in Bowdler's preface discussed below] or brothers reciting to sisters [Lamb preface] charts a narrow course between the licentiousness of the public theater and the self-indulgent solipsism induced by printed narrative" (Price 84). Price goes on to discuss the ways in which these texts make 'shared' domestic space into symbolic locations that negotiate between theatrical and literary consumption, and offer models of supervised reading to young women.

The Lamb preface renders their model of literary consumption as polite instruction, in language that makes clear their awareness of a lack in feminine access to Shakespeare and an implicit faith in the Shakespearean text:

> For young ladies too, it has been the intention chiefly to write; because boys being generally permitted the use of their fathers' libraries at a much earlier age than girls are, they frequently have the best scenes of Shakespeare by heart, before their sisters are permitted to look into this manly book; . . . and it is hoped they will find that the beautiful extracts, the select passages, they may choose to give their sisters in this way will be much better relished and understood from their having some notion of the general story from one of these imperfect abridgements;—which if they be fortunately so done as to prove delightful to any of the young readers, it is hoped that no worse effect will result than to make them wish themselves a little older, that they may be allowed to read the Plays at full length (such a wish will be neither peevish nor irrational). (17)

Thus while their preface may encourage the kind of intellectually-engaged sibling relationship that Mary and Charles Lamb appear to have themselves enjoyed, it nonetheless inscribes a passive female reading position in relation to Shakespeare. In other words, the *Tales* extratextually participate in a Romantic discourse, but intratextually construct patriarchy-friendly models of gendered subjectivity (a division which mirrors the paratext as appropriation and the stories as adaptation). The inscription of a gendered, passive audience marks clearly the Lambs' investment in patriarchal culture despite their Romantic context, and leads me to question if Mary Lamb, "even in her writing for children, [displays] a concern for the reader as an equal or a friend, and an anxiety with regard to any influence her position as writer may give her" (Aaron 5). Rather, the Lambs' production of feminised anxiety about children's status marks the *reproduction* of cultural values (in particular the equation of women with children) rather than a critique of them.

Indeed, the slippage in gendered authorship that is produced by the publication history of the *Tales* can be seen as symbolic of the slippage between gendered and neutral reading positions constructed by the preface. If Mary Lamb feels a symbolic equality with her child audience, this functions as an indictment of the position of women in the literary culture of early nineteenth-century England rather than as kudos for her authorial approach, because it links feminine and juvenile subjectivity, and renders both subordinate to masculine authority.

My own reading is necessarily affected by these lineaments of gender and cultural authority, because although I am convinced that Mary Lamb's authorship is central to the *Tales,* the fact that I am focussing on the Lamb "Macbeth" means that I may be closely critiquing the work of Charles rather than Mary. Of course, this fact exemplifies the 'elder brother' mediator of Shakespearean reading suggested by their preface insofar as Mary's authorship is both present and absent in and around the *Tales.*

If Charles *was* primarily responsible for the Lamb "Macbeth", the story is potentially disappointing to a reader familiar with his claim that Shakespeare's characters "are so much the objects of meditation rather than of interest or curiosity as to their actions" (C. Lamb 54), or his response to Shakespeare's *Macbeth* suggesting that "[t]he sublime images, the poetry alone, is that which is present to our minds in the reading" (55) of the play, for these elements seem to be effaced in the adaptation. The Lamb "Macbeth" simplifies the plot of Shakespeare's play, privileges action over meditation, and interpolates a clear moral trajectory leading to the conclusion that:

> Macduff, who, after a severe struggle, in the end overcame [Macbeth], and cutting off his head, made a present of it to the young and lawful king, Malcolm, who took upon him the government which, by the machinations of the usurper, he had so long been deprived of, and ascended the throne of Duncan the Meek, amid the acclamations of the nobles and the people. (Lamb and Lamb, *Tales* 131)

For the Lambs then, the play's resolution comes in the restoration of the rightful king and heir to the throne: a reinforcement of the social and cultural hierarchy invoked as an issue of gender in the preface.

The plot (narrative) may be readily made over into a normative trajectory, but rendering the characters and language of Shakespeare's tragedy in prose fiction (narration) appears to have made the Lambs (be it Charles, Mary, or both) sacrifice the 'beauties of Shakespeare' to an unambiguous account of the dangers of moral ambiguity. The preface's anxieties of gender mean that in the case of *Macbeth*, a greater challenge than the plot is going to be Lady Macbeth. Insofar as she presents an obvious challenge to normative femininity, the implied (mediated) girl reader must presumably be counselled *against* identification with Lady Macbeth. The extent to which the Lambs' narrational strategies perform this counsel implies that in this case, gendered morality has superseded imagination and fancy.

The simplification of the play's plot contributes in obvious ways to the containment of Lady Macbeth. So, for example, where in Shakespeare's play the reader is introduced to an unaccompanied wife who has immense confidence in her own powers, if not much faith in the determination of her husband, in the Lamb version she is contained and supervised at all possible times. Where Lady Macbeth's "unsex me here" soliloquy (Shakespeare, *Mac.* 1.5.40–54) quickly informs Shakespeare's audience of her independent character and determination, the Lamb text works hard to deny her agency. Their Lady Macbeth is never alone, and indeed any scenes which Shakespeare has featuring the Lady alone are either excised or conflated, structurally reinforcing the simplified reading of Lady Macbeth as "a bad, ambitious woman" (*Tales* 124).

Lady Macbeth *is* rewarded agency when it contributes to the removal of blame from Macbeth. Indeed her participation in Macbeth's crimes is rendered concrete in the Lamb version, including planning Banquo's assassination (an event she was ignorant of in Shakespeare's play) (*Tales* 127). Finally, the plot constructs her suicide as an unwifely, rather than an immoral, act. Her sleepwalking scene is erased, but it is later revealed that:

> While these things were acting, the queen, who had been the sole partner in [Macbeth's] wickedness, in whose bosom he could sometimes seek a momentary repose from those terrible dreams which afflicted them both nightly, died, it is supposed, by her own hands, unable to bear the remorse of guilt, and public hate; by which event he was left alone, without a soul to love or care for him, or a friend to whom he could confide his wicked purposes. (*Tales* 129–30)

Here then it would seem that Lady Macbeth's only purpose in the Lamb adaptation is to act as an initial spur and companion to Macbeth, to ensure that he is not entirely to blame for the course of action he chooses, and then to be quietly removed. In comparison with Shakespeare's Lady, the Lambs offer a one-dimensional character who never alters nor develops. Her sense of guilt is briefly mentioned in conjunction with anxiety of calumny, and then she is neatly erased.

It is in the specific use of language however, that the Lambs' moral vision of the play and of Lady Macbeth is reinforced. She has no direct discourse in the story, and is thus denied a speaking voice at the most basic textual level, a fact thrown into sharp relief when compared with Macbeth, Banquo, the Witches, and Macduff in the story, all of whom reproduce direct discourse from the Shakespearean text. In comparison, the reader is exposed to Lady Macbeth's infamous "I have given suck" (Shakespeare, *Mac.* 1.7.54–59) speech as descriptive prose and indirect discourse, when told that she "declared that she had given suck" (Lamb and Lamb, *Tales* 125). Moments like this obviously retain and reify the monstrous maternal while denying Lady Macbeth the rhetorical power of speech. This denial is revealed to be more than an anomaly, by the preface's claim: "those Tales which have been taken from the Tragedies, the young readers will perceive, when they come to see the source from which these stories are derived, that Shakespeare's own words, with little alteration, recur very frequently in the narrative as well as in the dialogue" (16).

It is true that the play's dialogue is used as narration in the story, but it is used in order to erase ambiguity. So Banquo's symbolic valuation of the king's gratitude (Shakespeare, *Mac.* 2.1.15) is quoted directly, but is made over into description, reified as literal truth, when the reader is told that Duncan "had sent a rich diamond to lady Macbeth, greeting her by the title of his most kind hostess" (Lamb and Lamb, *Tales* 124). Such rendering of metaphor as literal truth might seem innocuous, but the same strategy is used to reinforce the story's moral vision of Lady Macbeth. Her speeches are transformed into 'objective' narration, which identifies Lady Macbeth as aberrant woman. So where in the play she advises Macbeth to "look like th'innocent flower, / But be the serpent under't" (Shakespeare, *Mac.*1.5.66–67), the Lambs' version states that Macbeth "could look like the innocent flower, while *she* was indeed the serpent under it" (*Tales* 124, my emphasis). Narration, the necessary supplement in the transfer from drama to prose, reinforces the moral codings of the plot, even without obvious editorialising as in the case where Lady Macbeth "feared that the natural tenderness of his disposition (more humane than her own) would come between and defeat the purpose" (*Tales* 125).

There is little danger of the implied child reader's 'natural tenderness' defeating the purpose of the Lamb text. Lady Macbeth is unambiguously constructed as unfeminine, and dangerous. A reader unfamiliar with Shakespeare's play could be forgiven for thinking that Lady Macbeth has only a minor functional role in that text. My concern is that this model of subjectivity could be extrapolated to an understanding that women should play minor 'supporting roles' in their own society, as narratees rather than narrators of knowledge. The gendered moral is clear: transgressive women must be controlled or removed, and the most efficacious control is a denial of feminine agency or voice. As a cautionary tale, it offers an implicit model of the self-policing feminine so as to avoid Lady Macbeth's fate.

As a model of adaptation, the Lambs' text reveals both overt and covert moralising, interpretation disguised as abridgement, and the forcing of a unilateral meaning onto both the play and the designated audience. The third-person narrative is constructed so specifically as omniscient that no character is allowed to function as focaliser, either to offer an alternative perspective on events, or to offer the reader an opportunity to critique the authorial position. This appropriation of *Macbeth*, under the guise of simplistic retelling, actually recasts the play as a specifically moral fable, enforcing contemporary understanding of gender, education, and reading as timeless and authoritative. It seems then that the Lambs were reproducing, rather than "reacting to children's books' conventions of heavy moralizing and personification allegory" (Morse 195).

The silencing of Lady Macbeth within the Lamb text mirrors the silencing of Mary Lamb in its production, while also reflecting a broader nineteenth-century anxiety about Lady Macbeth as a dangerous example of excessive feminine anger and activity (see Ziegler) from which the Romantics were not exempt: "She is a great bad woman, whom we hate, but whom we fear more than we hate" (Hazlitt 14). Just as Mary Lamb represented the potential for violence and insanity in the middle-class woman, the Lady Macbeth of the Lambs' tale is implicitly unwomanly and inhuman and therefore necessarily removed from a central place in her culture. While several critics including Ziegler and Cilauro have noted a potentially subversive element to Mary Lamb's writing, the *Tales,* perhaps ironically given their Romantic context, have wielded an influence over subsequent Shakespearean children's literature as models of education rather than entertainment. Marsden's alternative proposition that Mary Lamb is a figure of cultural adherence is also too absolute, for Mary Lamb's achievements are marked by tensions between Romanticism and conservatism, challenge and conformity, and voice and silence, which are bound up in the cultural authority of the Lamb *Tales* even today.

Indeed, contemporary appropriations of Shakespeare for children reveal that the *Tales* were not only extremely commercially successful, in that the "first edition was nearly completely sold out on the first day" (Polowetzky 25), and "by 1900 Lambs' *Tales* had been reprinted some seventy-four times, including translations into French, German, Spanish and Swedish and 'an Indian imitation' in Bengali" (Thompson and Roberts 50), but discursively successful. Still in print, the Lambs' *Tales* have achieved a foundational authority in the field. Thus, although the limited and limiting model of feminine readership may appear to be safely historical, I will demonstrate that it remains the norm of contemporary feminine readership in Shakespeare for children.

The continuing influence of the Lamb strategies is thrown into sharp relief by the Bowdler *Family Shakespeare* that also appeared in 1807. While this text does not *rewrite* Shakespeare's plays into prose narrative, it is noteworthy as a manifestation of the broad cultural context, which produced the Lambs' text, and similarly promulgates Shakespeare as the great Author and the Child as

Reader, but does so in a reactionary sense. I will not engage with the Bowdler *Family Shakespeare* in any great detail here, as it constitutes neither adaptation nor appropriation, but it is nonetheless worth considering briefly as a contextual counterpoint to the Lamb text.

The Bowdler family's approach to textual editing is so well-known as to have spawned the term, "bowdlerize, *v. trans.* To expurgate (a book or writing), by omitting or modifying words or passages considered indelicate or offensive; to castrate" ("bowdlerize"). Henrietta Bowdler indeed expurgated, often on the basis of religious or moral rather than sexual indelicacy, twenty of the plays, which were published anonymously as the *Family Shakespeare* in 1807. Once Thomas Bowdler's name was added in 1818, and the plays presented expanded from a selection to the canon, Henrietta's achievement was subordinated to her brother's name (as with the Lambs). Noel Perrin has suggested that she may have "wanted to avoid the odium of admitting that she, an unmarried gentlewoman of fifty, understood Shakespeare's obscenity well enough systematically to remove it" (76) but it offers another gendered example of culturally acceptable Shakespeareana, within which the masculine voice is authorised.

The 1807 preface to *The Family Shakespeare* argues that:

> While few authors are so instructive as Shakespeare . . . his Plays contain much that is vulgar, and much that is indelicate [. . . this edition is intended for those] who wish to make the young reader acquainted with the various beauties of this writer, unmixed with any thing that can raise a blush on the cheek of modesty [. . . it is] intended to be read in private societies, and to be placed in the hands of young persons of both sexes. (cited in Thompson and Roberts 47)[12]

Clearly, literature is understood here as affective and able to morally influence its young readers. Much as the Lambs valorise their own sibling relationship in their preface as a model for gendered Shakespearean instruction, so too do the Bowdlers seek to (re)produce a very specific filial model of literary instruction. In a footnote to the first edition's preface (reprinted here in the fifth), Thomas Bowdler recalls:

> My first idea of the FAMILY SHAKSPEARE arose from the recollection of my father's custom of reading in this manner to his family. Shakspeare (with whom no person was better acquainted) was a frequent subject of the evening's entertainment. In the perfection of reading few men were equal to my father; and such was his good taste, his delicacy, and his prompt discretion, that his family listened with delight to Lear, Hamlet, and Othello, without knowing that those matchless tragedies contained words and expressions improper to be pronounced; and without having reason to suspect that any parts of the plays had been omitted by the circumspect and judicious reader.

Figure 1.1 "Shakespeare reading *Hamlet* to his family, 1597." Courtesy of George Eastman House.

> It afterwards occurred to me, that what my father did so readily and successfully for his family, my inferior abilities might, with the assistance of time and mature consideration, be able to accomplish for the benefit of the public. I say, therefore, that if "The Family Shakspeare" is entitled to any merit, it originates with my father. (Bowdler xviii) [13]

The implicit faith in Shakespeare as improver here clearly mirrors the Romantic faith in Shakespeare the great paternal author-figure, but is tempered with an anxiety about the malleability of the young reader exposed to the Bard uncensored. Expurgation necessarily marks absence, and thus clearly displays its politics, or at least that there are politics present (to the reader unfamiliar with Shakespeare). Arguably then, the politics of the Bowdler text are resistable, while the Lamb text, as prose adaptation, reveals the potential difficulty in resisting politics embedded in a text where wholeness is implied by both form and content, regardless of the preface's urging of later complete readings of the plays.

Both the Bowdler and Lamb texts engage in simplification as explication so as to render Shakespeare transparently valuable, accessible, and legible to young audiences, even to young girls. Thus it may be that "the achievements of Henrietta [Bowdler] and Mary [Lamb] proved the female participation in the Romantic intellectual movement towards giving priority to the readability of a Shakespeare play" (Han 47), but the critical heritage and reception of their texts also demonstrate the far-reaching discursive authority of a patrilineal genealogy of Shakespearean authorship central to Romanticism (see Figure 1.1.).

If the paratextual and contextual issues in each suggest anything, it might be argued that Henrietta Bowdler and Mary Lamb just as readily prove the extent to which feminine subjects can become self-policing as much as policed within discourses of patriarchal authority.

Both the Lambs and the Bowdlers offer a top-down model of literary reception wherein the adapted text becomes a substitute masculine mediator between Shakespeare and the child as *tabula rasa*, the blank slate onto which can and should be written approved cultural values. These texts enact a negotiation between the early nineteenth-century ideals of Shakespeare, text, and child reader. Each of these discourses had shifted in terms of 'ideals' by mid-century, as the Victorian "Shakespeare" reached its zenith.

With the rise of scientific discourse, a consolidation of a textual Shakespeare, and a notion of the child as an 'origin' in a telescoped version of evolution, Victorian Shakespeare for children represents a site of contestation between 'romance' and 'science' with reference to both Shakespeare and the child. For, while the didactic function of children's literature was firmly entrenched,

> [t]he implication that a spiritual knowingness in childhood, forgotten or hidden in adult life (and perhaps, recoverable in a childlike perspective), is replaced by a sense of seeking the beginnings of the adult self in the child that adult once was. Many Victorian novelists exposed this search through fiction in various ways . . . focus[ing] on the childhoods of their characters as a way of 'explaining' their adult actions. (Thacker and Webb 51)

This psychologising of the individual marks a pseudo-scientific notion of individual development, effectively set against Rousseau's natural child. Children's literature specifically, while still encompassing notions of entertainment as well as instruction, experienced a similar shift in focus:

> By the end of the [1840s] a new kind of children's literature was beginning to appear—serious, but not as explicitly didactic as earlier writing, increasingly alert to the needs of the child, imbued with a sense of responsibility and duty, but with an increasing capacity for warmth and laughter and imaginative enjoyment too. (Butts 101)

Like the Victorian Child, the Victorian Shakespeare was the site of ideological struggle between 'romance' and 'science', as "the Victorian era underwent a significant cultural divide as opinions varied over how to apply the era's notable scientific and technical advances within the literary sphere" (Grady 276). The debate would culminate in the competition between Frederick Furnivall and A. C. Swinburne. Founder of the 'New Shakespere Society' (1873), Furnivall's aims included the identification and cataloguing of Shakespearean technique through verse-tests. In comparison, Swinburne's *A Study of Shakespeare* (1880) "took aim in the name of art and intuition against the scientific versification analyses of Shakespeare" (Grady 276) in its use of Romantic discourses. In a similar approach, Edward Dowden's *Shakespeare, his Mind and Art* (1875) "attempted to deduce the man from his work by treating the plays as chapters in a sort of spiritual autobiography, whose hero gave vent to tragic expression when sad and to late romance in a mellower mood" (Levin 226). As Lootens suggests, this Victorian Shakespeare, caught between the scientific and the idealised, is at once the untouchable literary saint of Carlyle's rhetoric and a textual body to be scrupulously catalogued and perfected as part of the nineteenth century's "explosion of bibliographic, scholarly, and curatorial activity, all aimed at establishing or preserving textual accuracy" (9). This competing sense (and sensibility) of Shakespeare laid the groundwork for the split between professional and popular Shakespeare in the twentieth century.

Mary Cowden Clarke emerged in the mid-nineteenth century as a foremost Shakespearean scholar, combining linguistic and character-based appreciation of the plays. Altick has argued of Cowden Clarke's life that it "affords a revealing instance of how the romantic ideal, somewhat vulgarized, was subtly and gradually transformed into the sentimental outlook so characteristic of the mid-Victorians" (x–xi), and her children's Shakespeare is often read as a textual example of this transformation. It is true that Cowden Clarke reimagined the child reader, and in elaborating on the Lamb project, enacted the evolution from a Romantic Shakespeare and Child Reader, to a Victorian Shakespeare and Child Reader. However, while the *Girlhood of Shakespeare's Heroines* (1850–51) maintains a didactic function, its mode of storytelling is that of imaginative extrapolation rather than retelling, and is appropriation rather than adaptation.

Cowden Clarke, like the Bowdlers and the Lambs, held a notable position in the literary culture of nineteenth-century England. Born in 1809, she was raised in an intellectual environment that was populated by the Leigh Hunt Circle (Keats, Byron, the Lambs etc.). Where Mary Lamb had to depend on access to a neighbour's library and her brother's good will for a literary education, Mary Novello (later Cowden Clarke) benefited from an active education. The Novello family valued education for all their children who, regardless of gender, were home-schooled by their parents and a series of excellent tutors. Later in life Cowden Clarke remembered her mother as the source of "a love for all that is good and beautiful, and who therefore may well be said to have originated my devotion to Shakespeare" (Cowden Clarke, *Complete* ix). Further, Mary Novello was taught Latin *by* Mary Lamb, and was to reminisce: "[t]he echo of that gentle voice vibrates through the lapse of many a revolving year, true and unbroken, in the heart where the low-breathed sound first awoke response; teaching, together with the fine appreciation of verse music, the finer love of intellect conjoined with goodness and kindness" (Cowden Clarke and Cowden Clarke, *Recollections* 179). Cowden Clarke then, grows up with a vision of women as instructors, including the Lamb *Tales* and their female author, and in remembering Mary Lamb's voice links the oral and the literary.

In privileging feminine influence over masculine, Cowden Clarke potentially embodies a resistance to the textual emphasis on a patrilineal inheritance of Shakespeare such as that emphasised by the Lambs and the Bowdlers. Certainly, Cowden Clarke's output designates her commitment to Shakespeare: her *Complete Concordance to Shakespeare* (1844–45) initiated a career in which 'fancy' and 'virtue' manifested. If Wolfson believes that "Clarke was one of the girls for whom the Lambs wrote, and her subsequent mediation of Shakespeare for juvenile instruction repays her debt" ("Shakespeare" 215), I am suggesting that Mary Cowden Clarke is *the* success story of the Lambs' preface: as a careful reader of Shakespeare, she was to follow up the *Concordance* with *Shakespeare's Proverbs; or The Wise Saws of our Wisest Poet Collected into a Modern Instance* (1847–48); *Shakespeare's Works* (1859–60) (the first of several editions) and with her husband, *The Plays of Shakespeare* (1864) and *The Shakespeare Key* (1879); alongside numerous essays, reviews, and opinion pieces. In producing her own juvenile Shakespeare, I would suggest that Cowden Clarke is the inheritor of the Romantic 'spirit' of Shakespeare for girls rather than a direct product of the Lamb preface: her remembrance is of Mary Lamb's voice rather than her writing, and the tensions which characterised Mary Lamb's text are thematised within Mary Cowden Clarke's.

Cowden Clarke's position as "one of the first women to make writing on Shakespeare her profession" (Thompson and Roberts 81), and thus of access to writing and publishing, may go some way to explaining her choice, in producing a Shakespearean text for children, not to 'rewrite' or adapt the plays in the style of Mary Lamb (having alternate outlets for such interpretive writing). Rather, she imagined the childhoods of some of Shakespeare's heroines, and applied a Victorian logic of child-to-adult psychological development, in order "to place the heroines [of Shakespeare's plays] in such situations as should naturally lead up to, and account for, the known conclusion of their subsequent confirmed character and after-fate" (Cowden Clarke, *Girlhood* iv). The choice of heroines, rather than the plots that contain them, indicates an interest in feminine agency:

> The subjects of Mary Cowden Clarke's *The Girlhood of Shakespeare's Heroines* may be paragons of womanhood even more exalted than Anna Jameson's—their histories are repeated demonstrations of their moral

> purity in the face of male assaults—but Clarke's format emphasizes still more insistently the immortal vitality of the heroines that overwhelms their role as moral vehicles ... Through these imagined biographies, which fall somewhere between the spiritual history of the bildungsroman and pre-Freudian case history, we learn the origins of their character, the why of their heroinism ... Clarke frees the heroines from the boundaries of their plays, endowing them with rich lives of their own whose autonomy is impinged on by neither Shakespeare nor the man his play will make them love. (Auerbach 211–12)

Auerbach, like the feminist critics who make claims for Mary Lamb's active subversiveness, seems too ready here to posit Cowden Clarke as a pre-feminist critic of Shakespeare's treatment of women, but her stories do demonstrate that Shakespeare's women at times 'need' explaining, or in other words, are *not* the simplified moral symbols of the Lamb text. What I find truly subversive about Cowden Clarke's contribution to the genre is her notion that Shakespeare is to be a topic of discussion, debate, and exchange *between women*. Indeed, she went so far as to identify Shakespeare himself as feminine in her account of him as valuable for self-instruction:

> For moral introspection and self-culture Shakespeare is a grand aid, as well as for mental discipline; and, perhaps, peculiarly so, as regards women: since he, the most manly thinker and most virile writer that ever put pen to paper, had likewise something essentially feminine in his nature, which enabled him to discern and sympathise with the innermost core of woman's heart. ("Shakespeare" 562)

Addressing a juvenile audience, Cowden Clarke imagines a matrilineal inheritance of Shakespeare that simultaneously invokes and inverts the filial models of reading offered by the Lambs and the Bowdlers:

> Happy she who at eight or nine years old has a copy of "Lamb's Tales from Shakespeare" given to her, opening a vista of even then understandable interest and enjoyment! Happy she who at twelve or thirteen has Shakespeare's works themselves read to her by her mother, with loving selection of fittest plays and passages! Happy they who in maturer years have the good taste and good sense to read aright the pages of Shakespeare, and gather thence the wholesomest lessons and choicest delights! ("Shakespeare" 564)

Less than questioning the suitability of Shakespeare as an object of reading then, it seems more accurate to describe Cowden Clarke as questioning the suitability of some young women as readers, not constitutionally as in the early nineteenth century, but intellectually. Shakespeare for Cowden Clarke, while obviously the foremost of authors, is also a figure who wields great influence over the active reader and is interpolated as an instructional text to aid in a child's personal progress. Rather than the Lamb model of explanatory reading, however, Cowden Clarke constructs an implied independent, *critical* reader, and her *Girlhood of Shakespeare's Heroines* thematises the question of how to read.

In 1850 to 1851, Cowden Clarke published a series of fifteen stories that were later collected and republished in three- or five-volume collections. The stories read fourteen plays (*Twelfth Night* occupies two stories), and offer explanations for 'later' events. The preface invokes and denies romance, and thus marks the ambiguity of the implied reading position: "[i]f it be borne in mind that all *climax* in incident and sentiment was to be carefully avoided throughout these stories—inasmuch as they are merely preliminaries to catastrophes already ordained—the obstacles in the way of giving them startling features of romance will be understood" (*Girlhood* iii-iv, original emphasis). Cowden Clarke may efface her entertainment function and implicitly encourage an analytical reading of the stories *as* preliminary to Shakespeare's plays, but her heroines' early years quickly develop into incident-filled narratives, resonant with Shakespeare's plays, and certainly describable as climactic romance as Cowden Clarke deploys it (replete with moral). Thus the reader is encouraged to read *against* paratextual advice, as is true in a more complex sense of Cowden Clarke's 'anxious' caveat within the preface: "an explanatory word concerning the design of the work, and an exculpatory word touching the choice of its subject . . . I beseech my readers to believe that love, not presumption, prompted the subject of this series of stories" (*Girlhood* iii–iv). The very existence of the stories, however, indicates that Cowden Clarke has identified gaps in the Shakespearean text.

The *Girlhood* preface concludes with citations from both Shakespeare and Jonson, the master and the disciple, implicitly positioning the tales in a genealogy of Shakespearean reception, but importantly, the preface refuses to inscribe an exclusively juvenile audience, or an adult mediator. Where both the Lambs and the Bowdlers address their textual apparatus to an adult mediator for the child reader, Cowden Clarke's text represents one of the earliest deployments of Shakespeare for children as a polyphonic (or double-address in Wall's terminology) text, at once addressed to a child and adult reader.[14] Within this text Cowden Clarke is both pupil and teacher. In extension, it is potentially the case that she also encourages the reading of her stories and Shakespeare's plays in concert, as the *Girlhood*'s paratexts include a concordance of references to the heroine's childhood in the Shakespearean text, which encourages Cowden Clarke's own readers to become Shakespeare's readers, and contradicts her claimed motivation of 'love' of Shakespeare's plays. It seems clear to me that Cowden Clarke's broader motivation is to inspire future feminine readers of Shakespeare; indeed this extratextual model is thematised intratextually as protagonists negotiate their reading-selves.

Cowden Clarke's appropriation of *Macbeth* is the second of her fifteen tales and is the only one not to be named after its heroine. Tale II, "The Thane's Daughter", opens with a description of a violent storm, obviously appropriating the storm imagery of the play itself, against which a child is "born into the world, destined to read a world-wide lesson, how unhallowed desires and towering ambition can deface the image of virtue in a human heart, and teach it to spurn and outrage the dictates of nature herself" (*Girlhood* 93–94). The story is prefaced with a quotation from the play—"I would not have such a heart in my bosom, for the dignity of the whole body" (93)—and concludes with an explicitly moral quotation about "will becom[ing] the servant to defect" (168). Therefore, Cowden Clarke would seem to have a clear vision of Lady Macbeth as other to the natural or acceptable feminine subject (the Victorian woman): the opening of the story ascribes a moral to the tale about to be told (and implicitly to its pre-text), focuses on Lady Macbeth as the central figure of the play, and seemingly renders her as an overtly cautionary figure for an implied reader. However, I would suggest that as the tale progresses, the reader is encouraged to consider the ways in which Lady Macbeth's otherness is produced, rather than dismiss her.

The narrative of this child's birth gives way to a retrospective story of how its mother came to be called "the dark lady". The Lady Gruoch exhibits a sustained perception of her husband that anticipates Lady Macbeth's insults to Macbeth's honour in Shakespeare's play, thinking him "bland . . . misplaced . . . weak . . . unmanly" (*Girlhood* 99). Rather than embrace her role as wife, Gruoch instead nurses her unfulfilled ambition into hatred of her husband and her determination to encourage masculine traits in her daughter. The problematic elements in her daughter's (also named Gruoch) character are notionally ascribed to this early conditioning, and after her mother's death, explicitly attributed to her own failure to fulfil filial duties and her father's ineffectiveness as a "kind-meaning, but weak parent" (118).

The tale contains multiple precursors to Shakespeare's Lady Macbeth, and obvious indications of personality, such as when Gruoch (the future Lady Macbeth) has trouble sleeping after sending a romantic rival to her death: "[t]he waking soul roused the sleeping body, and constrained it, still sleeping as it was, to perform the deeds of waking" (*Girlhood* 145); her frequent nights spent observing her own father sleep; and her Machiavellian notions of the desired ends justifying any means. In comparison, Macbeth is represented as a noble and honourable soldier, absolutely loyal both to his king and the codes of his culture. As the tale progresses, Gruoch is seen to manipulate him, offering this trait as explanation for the action of Shakespeare's play. Cowden Clarke goes so far as to have a Highlander tell the 'weird' of Gruoch—in an obvious foreshadowing of Shakespeare's witches—as the crown obtained through blood (153) in a sustained portrait of "the wilful child [who] became the determined woman" (126).

Cowden Clarke also engages with the play as historical document by giving Gruoch and Macbeth a child, specifically a son, and describes the child's death as fateful:

> To inherit their present growing dignities—and that crowning one which might be in store for them, a son was born to them; and Macbeth beheld the beauty of his mother, while she beheld the representative of his father's honors, in the infant Cormac, who thus enhanced the joy of both parents (*Girlhood* 161) . . . But fate has decreed that the boy shall not live; the little Cormac yields to the disease, and is carried off in his infancy. (166)

This event is used to justify Macbeth's interest in the throne, fill the infamous gap of Lady Macbeth's maternity in Shakespeare's play, and remove any remaining sense of social obligation she may have felt as a mother. Also, the son's death can be read as simultaneously being a punishment for Gruoch's earlier treachery, and a spur to her future actions, as it leads directly to her spoken intent to assist Macbeth to the throne whatever the cost. Given the constant intertextual referencing to motifs and language of Shakespeare's play, it would be easy to read Cowden Clarke's tale as a simplistic reflection of Shakespeare's Lady Macbeth. However, just as the collection's paratexts encourage critical reading, Cowden Clarke embeds within this narrative an element that engages with concern with the possible function of juvenile narratives such as the one she is producing.

A small but significant element of the tale thematises the possible effects of exposing the young to inappropriate narratives, and engages directly with questions of girlhood (feminine development), authoritative narrative, and affective reading. As a child, Gruoch is often distracted from bad behaviour by stories: Bethoc, her nursemaid, "sought to detain her within the women's apartments by tales and legends that she thought might amuse her fancy" (*Girlhood* 112). However, despite Bethoc's attempt to confine Gruoch within the realm of acceptable femininity, the child's favourite story is that of "Fenella, the lady of Fettercairn" (113), a bloodthirsty story of a woman who violently avenges the death of her son through an elaborate death-trap for her enemies. As with Shakespeare's *Macbeth*, the story of Fenella finds its roots in Fordun's fourteenth-century *Chronicle of the Scottish Nation*:

> The daughter of Cruchne, Earl of Angus, who was named Finele . . . her only son having formerly been ordered to be put to death by the king at Dunsynane . . . caused to be made . . . a kind of trap [. . . which] had attached to it on all sides, crossbows always kept bent by their several strings, and fitted with very sharp arrows; and in the middle thereof stood a statue, fashioned like a boy, and cunningly attached to the crossbows; so that if any one were to touch it, and move it ever so little, the

> bowstrings of the crossbows would suddenly give way, and the arrows would straightway be shot forth, and pierce him through. (166)[15]

With "treacherous words" (Fordun 166), Fenella lures the King to her home, where he falls prey to the trap, and "was shot through arrows sped from all sides, and fell without uttering another word" (167). Importantly, Fenella escapes punishment because royal soldiers are unable to find her after they discover their king's body. In the version of this story that Gruoch hears in Cowden Clarke's tale, the means of death is cross-bows, but there are additional details/changes, including Fenella's being "sleepless in devising means for the compassing of her revenge" (*Girlhood* 113), a statue in the "likeness of the king himself" (113), and her playing at hostess: "she entertained him in sumptuous manner, and after meat she led the king to behold the chamber within the tower" to see "a gift for him" (113). Given these exciting elements, it is hardly surprising that Gruoch asks to hear the story repeatedly, and as the narrative obviously offers points of identification with Shakespeare's Lady Macbeth, it would seem a case of a child being influenced by inappropriate stories.

Metafictionally, however, the story of Fenella arguably functions as a case-study of juvenile feminine readership, and is made over into metareading.[16] The Fenella episode engages with a fundamental concern of writing for children: the split between education and entertainment. Bethoc's aim to amuse Gruoch's 'fancy' mirrors Charles Lamb's emphasis on imaginative reading, but it may also have offered her an inappropriate model of feminine identity to emulate. Bethoc has clearly failed to tell the story of Fenella in a sufficiently cautionary tone, an error that Cowden Clarke seemingly avoids in her own tales insofar as she does not simply produce a text-to-be-read, but a vision of reading itself. However, Cowden Clarke does not produce a simplistic model of 'bad teller' equals 'bad girl'. Indeed, challenging authorial authority, the narrative is liberated from the teller: "Bethoc would shake her aged head, and speak of leaving vengeance in the hands of Heaven; but *the story went on to say*, that the Lady Fenella . . ." (*Girlhood* 113, my emphasis). Thus, despite the intentions of the teller, the story functions autonomously, and the reader/listener Grouch, attributes her own 'moral' to the tale: "she gained her end!" (114).

Nor does Cowden Clarke opt for a simplistic (proto-Barthesian) reader-as-producer-of-meaning conceptualisation of 'reading': Gruoch's father tells her: "You look as Fenella of Fettercairn might have looked, child, when she led my royal ancestor to the fatal tower-chamber . . . she was an ancestress of your mother's; but don't let us think about Fenella—it's a dark story" (*Girlhood* 120–21). Thus Gruoch learns that she is descended from Fenella (and indeed Fenella's victim) which raises, for Cowden Clarke's reader, the question of nature versus nurture in a child's development. It would seem that Gruoch's nature responds not only to Fenella's story, but secret knowledge of that story:

> Gruoch held down her head, and thought within herself that Bethoc had already told her the story, so that she need not care for her father's evasion. She felt that he had put her off with this slight answer, and she therefore indulged the triumph of knowing that his attention was foiled by her previous acquaintance with the tale he would have concealed. (*Girlhood* 121)

It is ultimately this 'triumph of knowing' without self-reflexivity that is Gruoch's greatest flaw: she lacks empathy.

Cowden Clarke's representation of Lady Macbeth is as aberrant; however, in terms of critical response, "The Thane's Daughter" is less a critique of Lady Macbeth as aberrant, than an attempt to explain how such aberrance might be produced. Set amongst implicit ideals of femininity, marriage, and parenting, Cowden Clarke's heroine emerges as a victim of 'masculinist' treatment, and as a failed reader. It may be true that Gruoch and the other heroines "must step into their comic and tragic roles and live out the endings Shakespeare wrote for them" (Rozett 167), but I believe implied readers are encouraged to question their own 'future endings'. The stories affirm a normative model of femininity, but do not link such normativity to passivity. Rather, critical, self-reflexive reading of Shakespeare is produced as a tool for self-development, and thus Cowden Clarke disrupts the patrilineal model of cultural inheritance of the Lamb and Bowdler texts.

Cowden Clarke's focus on the personalities of Shakespeare's characters anticipates the character-criticism that dominated Shakespeare studies in the late nineteenth and early twentieth centuries. Although the late nineteenth-century approach to Shakespeare may be tracked through its "investment in scholarly apparatuses of various kinds: libraries, editions of Shakespeare, dictionaries, concordances, data banks, scholarly societies, bibliographies, checklists, and so on" (M. Taylor 1) it is also true that the end of the century produced a man whose 'character criticism' was known popularly, and which remains influential today. A. C. Bradley, whose lectures on Shakespeare dominated reception of Shakespeare at the time of Edith Nesbit's literary output for children, produced moral readings of Shakespeare's plays, and read characters as representations of moral conflict.

The very reasons for Bradley's success offer insight into Nesbit's success as a children's author. Each of them deploys a reader-friendly style that masks politicisation. Michael Taylor argues that Bradley produced:

> literary criticism that sounds like a story. Bradley's tendency to write his essays in the form of narrative, often of an overheated kind, combines with other friendly characteristics of style and rhetoric . . . Calm, magisterial, confident, reasonable, and orderly—and yet passionate also—it's the voice of the authoritative pedagogue . . . There is something peculiarly comforting about the way Bradley writes and, more importantly, in

> what it is he wishes to convey. The message as well as the medium is one of reassurance, a gospel of good news. (41)

Similarly, there is 'something comforting' about Edith Nesbit's narratives; best-known for children's novels like *Five Children and It* (1902) and *The Railway Children* (1906), she also produced adaptations of Shakespeare for children. Wall argues that,

> Nesbit deliberately made the relationship between adult narrator and child narratee a dominant element in her books. Although superficially her narrative manner seems light-hearted and playful, her address to her narratee casual and familiar, in reality she treated child readers with a new seriousness, for she placed them first, and in doing so gave the act of communicating with children, of writing *to* them, a new significance. (148)

Nesbit thus takes her juvenile audience seriously, and although she clearly inherits the Romantic child, she nonetheless attempts to render the child as an active subject in the transmission of Shakespeare. Like Bradley, she retains an interest in the characters of Shakespeare's plays as points of identification for a modern reader. At the same time, the function of Shakespeare is marked as not only contributing to individual development, but also aiding socio-cultural development and maintenance.

The publication history and variant editions of Nesbit's adaptations illustrate shifting notions of Shakespeare for children from the nineteenth to the twentieth centuries. In 1897, Nesbit published *The Children's Shakespeare* which inherited the Lambs' strategies of adaptation, but combined them with Nesbit's style of narration. The first version featured retellings of twelve plays, but this was expanded to twenty stories (of the same twenty plays the Lambs retold), and published as *Twenty Beautiful Stories from Shakespeare: A Home Study Course* in the United States in 1907. This publishing history marks a shift from an entertainment function to one of education. Nesbit's biographer may describe the Shakespeare stories as part of Nesbit's early "hackwork . . . lack[ing] distinction" (Briggs 185), but these texts mark Nesbit's participation in a nineteenth-century genealogy of Shakespeare for children; simultaneously, the expanded edition performs a fundamental shift within the genre as it leaves the nineteenth century and enters the twentieth.[17]

In the brief preface to *The Children's Shakespeare*, anxieties about rewriting, the intent of juvenile education, and the division between Shakespeare's plots and his language can be traced. Taking place on an evening by the fireplace, this preface establishes a feminine oral tradition as the origin of this collection of stories. The narrator, possibly Nesbit, tells the reader that "we had been that day to see Shakespeare's house, and I had told the children all that I could about him and his work" (*Children's* 5). As she sits dreaming by the fire, these children who are specifically named and identified as female, Iris and Rosamund, express frustration at reading Shakespeare's *A Midsummer Night's Dream* until their adult companion offers to *tell* them the story. This narrator has "the recollection of Lamb's [sic] tales" (6) and clearly views them as a model, establishing a genealogy of retelling Shakespeare for children. That the female narrator views this as the source text rather than the play itself marks the possible cultural success of the Lambs' aim that "[f]or young ladies too, it has been the intention chiefly to write" (*Tales* 17), while also replicating its gendered model. However, where the Lambs invested themselves with the role of transmitters of Shakespeare's stories to an essentially unknowing audience, Nesbit establishes the child reader as the impetus: her narrator is responding to the juvenile audience's 'request' for Shakespeare for their own benefit. Unlike the implied audience of the Lamb text, Nesbit's implied reader already appreciates the inherent value of Shakespeare:

> "You see he did not write for children."
>
> "No, but you might," cried Iris, flushed with a sudden idea. "Why don't you write the stories for us so that we can understand them, just as you told us that, and then, when we are grown up, we shall understand the plays so much better. Do! Do!"
>
> "Ah, do! You will, won't you? *You must!*"
>
> "Oh, well, if I must, I must," I said.
>
> And so they settled it for me, and for them these tales were written. (*Children's* 6)

In comparison, the later version of Nesbit's text, *Twenty Beautiful Stories From Shakespeare: A Home Study Course*, paratextually performs a top-down model of didacticism. Edited by E. T. Roe, this version included the twelve plays from the 1897 edition, an additional eight plays, an editor's preface, a Shakespearean biography, a pronunciation guide, and a collection of quotations from Shakespeare's plays. Thus, where the 1897 text privileges entertainment, the 1907 version clearly privileges education as its primary function.

Removing Nesbit's cosy fireside chat, the 1907 text is prefaced by "A Brief Life of Shakespeare". Written by F. J. Furnivall, its content remains of interest as it retains a heavy focus on the life of Shakespeare as a child, presumably to establish a point of identification for the child reader. It also offers an implicit defence of adaptation via its explanation of the ways in which Shakespeare himself worked as an adapter:

> very soon after arriving in London he began that work of adaptation by which he is known to have begun his literary career. To improve and alter older plays not up to the standard that was required at the time was a common practice even among the best dramatists of the day . . . When the alterations in plays originally composed by other writers became very

> extensive, the work of adaptation would become in reality a work of creation. (Nesbit, *Twenty* 10–11)

The adaptation of *Macbeth* added to this edition is clearly marked as such a case of creation through adaptation, in that its opening lines immediately draw a distinction between the "two stories" (*Twenty* 153) of Macbeth, one historical, one imaginative. Although the reader is told "you shall hear" (*Twenty* 153) the latter, (invoking an oral storytelling tradition), the adaptation actually mixes historical and Shakespearean versions of Macbeth's story. Even as the adaptation notionally presents "Shakespeare", Nesbit seems unconvinced by his depiction of Lady Macbeth; history supersedes imagination in the story primarily to justify the actions of Lady Macbeth. Like Cowden Clarke, she draws on earlier narratives in an implicit challenge to Shakespeare's construction of femininity.

Unlike the Lambs, Nesbit seems less interested in a moral interpretation of the play than in retelling as much of the plot as possible. In a much shorter tale than the Lambs', Nesbit nonetheless takes the time to gloss meanings of Shakespearean language, and offer the following introduction for Lady Macbeth: "the grand-daughter of a King of Scotland who had died in defending his crown against the King who preceded Duncan, and by whose order her only brother was slain" (*Twenty* 156). When compared with the Lamb version, Nesbit's Lady Macbeth is more active, has regular direct discourse, and perhaps most significantly, where Lady Macbeth's death is an 'off-stage' event in the Lamb version, Nesbit's story offers an account of Lady Macbeth's decline and death:

> Retribution was working, for Lady Macbeth was mad. She walked in her sleep amid ghastly dreams. She was wont to wash her hands for a quarter of an hour at a time; but after all her washing, would still see a red spot of blood upon her skin. It was pitiful to hear her cry that all the perfumes of Arabia could not sweeten her little hand.
>
> "Canst thou not minister to a mind diseased?" inquired Macbeth of the doctor, but the doctor replied that his patient must minister to her own mind. This reply gave Macbeth a scorn of medicine. "Throw physic to the dogs," he said; "I'll none of it."
>
> One day he heard a sound of women crying. An officer approached him and said, "The Queen, your Majesty, is dead." "Out, brief candle," muttered Macbeth, meaning that life was like a candle, at the mercy of a puff of air. He did not weep; he was too familiar with death. (*Twenty* 164–65)

This excerpt is representative of several of Nesbit's techniques: she often retains scraps of the Shakespearean language, but glosses a meaning (or even an interpretation) for it, and quickly summarises entire scenes in brief paragraphs. The conjunction of Shakespearean and contemporary language leads Peter Hunt to comment that the "modern reader, then, has to make some allowances for the curious linguistic byways into which Nesbit has strayed—and to sympathize with her when the subsequent development of the language has left oddities stranded, as it were, on the linguistic beach" (Nesbit, *Best* 108). This claim limits the tensions in the text to language choice, when the historical development of the genre suggests the tensions may be far more complex negotiations between gender, reading, and cultural authority.

Compared with the overtly happy ending of the Lambs' version, Nesbit's concluding line, "[s]o Malcolm reigned after Macbeth; but in years that came afterwards the descendants of Banquo were kings" (*Twenty* 167), appears to display a greater level of fidelity to the moral ambivalence of Shakespeare's ending, in that it is expository where the Lambs' conclusion is overtly moral. This may be a product of Nesbit's inclusiveness, for where the Lambs actively pruned their narratives, retaining only those elements they perceived as central to the moral drive of the narrative, Nesbit seemingly seeks to include all possible detail in as short a time as possible. Her ambivalence regarding the moral trajectory of the play would appear to be a product of 'her time' as much as the Lambs enact their own cultural context. This moral ambivalence may be interpreted as an attempt to extricate her text from the overtly didactic modes of Victorian writing.

Although Nesbit appears to share Bradley's insistence on the Shakespearean text as accessible for the 'average person', she does not seem to share his insistence on moral readings. So where Nesbit refuses a moral reading of Macbeth as character in favour of his historical fate, Bradley claims that:

> To the end he never totally loses our sympathy; we never feel towards him as we do to those who appear the born children of darkness. There remains something sublime in the defiance with which, even when cheated of his last hope, he faces earth and hell and heaven. (305)

Ironically, Bradley, as a kind of descendant of the Lambs here, produces the type of reading which dominated the twentieth century in popular and critical texts, while Nesbit's approach—even as it marks a paradigm shift in children's Shakespeare—has been absent from future texts. This may be because, in a functional shift from entertainment to education, Nesbit's strategy of 'writing *to* children' seems to disappear. Therefore, where Bradley's occupation of two moments in one insofar as his "work stand between the truly Victorian belletristic criticism and the truly modern academic research" (Cooke 80) guarantees his texts longevity, Nesbit appears to be a victim of paradigm shift, at once of and alien to two moments. Her Shakespeare stories are *not* the children's literature for which she is remembered today.

Where the Lambs and Cowden Clarke understood a moral effect for reading Shakespeare (an explicit mode of improvement), Nesbit's audience is constructed as already understanding that in order to be fully rounded adults they will need to be familiar with Shakespeare, but that familiarity is an end in itself. If Nesbit's tales seem to lack passion when compared with those of the Lambs and Cowden Clarke, it may be because she lacks any goal *beyond* the retelling of Shakespeare and does not seem to overtly share their faith that models for behaviour can be found *within* Shakespeare. Exactly one century after the Lambs' *Tales* are published, Nesbit brings to a close the nineteenth-century model of British writing of Shakespeare for children and shifts it to North America, where, along with Commonwealth countries, the majority of Shakespearean children's literature was published throughout the twentieth century. These shifts not only necessarily implicate concerns of national and cultural identity, but also implicitly—as evidenced by the differences between Nesbit's 1897 and 1907 texts—raise concerns about the adaptation of Shakespeare for children as entertainment or education.

Given that literary texts are discursive artefacts, Butler's argument that if "a performative provisionally succeeds . . . then it is not because an intention successfully governs the action of speech, but only because that action echoes prior actions, and accumulates the force of authority through the repetition or citation of a prior and authoritative set of practices" ("Burning" 205) becomes useful as a way of thinking about this nineteenth-century cluster of texts. Just as the Lambs drew on an authoritative set of practices of Shakespearean commentary and dissemination to construct a new genre, and call into being new and future readers of the plays, their models of paternal authority and gendered juvenile readership have become authoritative praxes in themselves. Romantic models of authorship and readership remain a point of origin for contemporary Shakespearean children's texts, even as strategies of rewriting have shifted from adaptation (Lambs and Nesbit) to appropriation (Cowden Clarke and beyond).

Chapter Two
Author(is)ing the Child: Shakespeare as Character

> Today, many Shakespeareans have moved away from the concept of the plays as Works. They see the plays as free of the processes of filiation and (again to cite Barthes) read them "without the father's signature." (Mowat 137)

> Unlike contemporary criticism, popular culture remains invested in authorship and particularly in Shakespeare the author, even though its Shakespeare is patently a fiction. Pop depictions typically locate the meaning of Shakespeare's works firmly with the man himself, in his personal life or his individual genius rather than, say, in the source texts which he imitated, the collaborative conditions of the playhouse, or his posthumous reinvention by posterity. In fact Shakespeare is popular culture's favourite symbol for the principle of literary authorship (Lanier, *Shakespeare* 114)

Mowat and Lanier capture the tensions here of late twentieth-century academic and popular receptions of Shakespeare. For the former, post-structuralist theory rendered the Romantic author obsolete; for the latter, Romantic authorship became increasingly central to understanding Shakespeare as the *paterfamilias* of Western culture. For academics then, "Shakespeare" is a signifier or a discourse that continues to inspire the production and reception of biography, but whose personal history and experience are fundamentally irrelevant to the Shakespearean play. In contrast, within the popular cultural imaginary, Shakespeare is first and foremost the man whose plays *reflect* his personality and experience. To briefly use the Barthesian model referenced by Mowat, one might suggest that the academy sees the plays as texts where popular culture sees them as works (see Barthes, "From"). It makes sense then that contemporary children's literature has often reflected and responded to such tensions by inscribing Shakespeare as a character in concert with appropriations of his plays.

The appearance of Shakespeare as character marks, perhaps ironically via its implied absence, a kind of longing for the sureness with which the nineteenth century viewed Shakespeare as the Romantic Author. If contemporary fictional "treatments of Shakespeare the man . . . dwell in the long shadow of nineteenth-century conceptions of Shakespeare, in particular the outsize mythos surrounding Shakespearean authorship which had its roots in the cult of Romantic genius" (Lanier, "Shakespeare™" 100), then this is not to suggest that such treatments seek to move out of this shadow. Rather, fictional accounts of Shakespeare's life function as both an acknowledgement of the erosure or poststructural complications of Romantic Shakespeare, and a somewhat desperate nostalgia for a return to a post-Elizabethan but pre-postmodern time, when children could be told that Shakespeare was a genius without threat of a lapse into poststructuralist relativism. This is certainly true in recent novels for young readers by Gary Blackwood, Peter W. Hassinger, and Grace Tiffany, all of which construct to the point of overdetermination a quintessentially Romantic, albeit human, William Shakespeare. As these novels depict this Shakespeare acting as father to child protagonists, so the reader is encouraged to view the Shakespearean playtexts as artefacts of paternal advice from the Father of Western Culture: If the protagonist can literally bond with Shakespeare, the contemporary reader can symbolically bond with him by reading his work. Thus Barthes's trope of filiality whereby an "author is reputed the father and the owner of his work" ("From" 160) is central to the ways in which contemporary children's literature imagines Shakespeare as both father and author in relationship to child protagonists. The child reader invited to identify with that protagonist is, in some sense, simultaneously interpellated as reader-offspring of Shakespeare when those protagonists become Shakespeare's "children". Lanier has noted that, "in children's literature Shakespeare's cultural authority quickly becomes intertwined with fantasies of the father which serve as agents of socialization" (*Shakespeare* 117), but I would like to extend this point to note that the paternal fantasies circulated within contemporary Shakespearean children's literature are emphatically gendered. Shakespeare functions as symbolic author-father for masculine protagonists, but feminine characters are excluded from symbolic relationships with the playwright often, paradoxically, by virtue of being Shakespeare's actual daughter. Even further, not only is feminine subjectivity depicted as ideally separate from Shakespeare, but "Shakespeare" is also made a resolutely patriarchal discourse which is, in part, made possible because of its difference and distance from femininity. This marks a clear shift from the nineteenth-century texts which sought explicitly to address a feminine reader.

In terms of genre, Shakespeare can only logically appear as a character in historical or time-slip fiction. And indeed, if one were to identify 'Shakespeare as Character' as a sub-genre of children's literature, one would have to note that there is really only one plot in which he appears: a child travels in time (time-slip) or space (historical) and comes to be employed either by William Shakespeare or his theatre; in the course of that employment, the child forms a new sense of family, belonging, and identity.[1] The relationships established between Shakespeare and the adolescent protagonists offer the implied reader a template for their own potential reading relationship with the works of Shakespeare, and to become the inheritors of liberal-humanist Western culture. Insofar as competencies acquired by protagonists for the stage are seen to reflect their developing relationship with Shakespeare and may be made over into maturation, the implied reader learns that approved consumption of Shakespeare can be made over into their own maturation: ways of reading become ways of being. Thus the presumed embodied cultural capital borne by Shakespeare himself is made over into objectified cultural capital available to readers.

My focus here is historical fiction because where in time-slip fiction protagonists tend to have at least some pre-existing knowledge of Shakespeare as a significant cultural figure, in historical fiction, protagonists tend to recognise the value of Shakespeare independently. This may seem a fine distinction, but time-slip novels value Shakespeare because of his plays, whereas historical novels value the plays because of Shakespeare himself. In time-slip fiction the implied child reader is made subject to clearly pre-existing orders of cultural value and authority, whereas in historical fiction that implied reader is encouraged to identify with a protagonist who notionally *originates* an order of cultural value and authority which becomes uncontestable. In extension, and when combined with reader identification with the protagonist, although both time-slip and historical novels reproduce the circular logic of Shakespearean capital they are dependent on, in their differing emphases rest differing politics of juvenile cultural agency. In a sense this is indexed narrationally, as where the shift from the third-person narration of the Lambs gives way to first-person or heavily focalised narration might seem in contemporary fiction to guarantee juvenile agency, in fact, it works to produce identification strategies whereby the implied reader is aligned with the discovery or foundation of Shakespearean value, and have few positions from which they can contest that value or their own complicity in it.

Given "the essentially humanistic ideology of children's historical fiction, with its concern to foster a sense of wholeness and purpose" (Stephens, *Language* 204), it makes sense that when William Shakespeare appears as a character, he is endowed with an idealised ahistorical sensibility, except when some form of historical difference can usefully be mobilised in order to signify Shakespeare as a man who 'learned' to transcend his own time, and who can provide insight into our own. The absence of exhaustive or comprehensive biographical detail about Shakespeare's life operates, perhaps ironically, in the service of patriarchal agendas because what few details can be confirmed may relatively easily be combined with popular myths of Shakespearean biography, mapped on to simplistic readings of Shakespeare's context and work, and in turn, used to authorize hierarchical gender relations. More insidiously, insofar as "historical fiction encompasses not only an understanding of contemporary society but also an interpretation of history that makes such an understanding possible" (Schwebel 197), an aesthetic of pastness in Shakespearean children's literature is used to justify patriarchal models of gendered subjectivity and agency by representing them as ahistorical and natural. So, historical authenticity is pressed into service in order to authorise the exclusion of actresses from the Elizabethan stage, but is nowhere to be seen when orphan boys gain work as Shakespeare's personal assistant. Further, authenticity in these texts is usually a montage-citation of popular metonyms for Shakespeare's "extraordinary and dangerous times" (Rosen 16): filth, boatmen on the Thames, London bridge, heads on pikes, bear-baiting, disease (usually plague), spies, theatres, puritans, and the woman for whom the age is named, Elizabeth I. Often, the disparity between her constructed image and the corporeal reality of Elizabeth in the 1590s is commented on, and is equally often linked with a positive notion of performance 'natural' of both Elizabeth and the culture she embodies, as in Osborne's *Stage Fright on a Summer's Night* when Shakespeare tells a young girl, "[t]he queen pretends to be young and beautiful. Just as *you* pretended to be a boy, and the bear pretended to be an actor. You see, all the world's a stage" (M. P. Osborne 61). Elizabeth as figure of authority and identification reaches a zenith in Anthony Horowitz's *The Devil and his Boy* (1998), wherein the orphan protagonist Tom discovers that Elizabeth is his grandmother, a plot development based on Horowitz taking seriously the infamous rumours about the young Elizabeth's relationship with Thomas Seymour. Such is Horowitz's construction of Tom as the origin of Shakespearean value that he stages the boy conversing with Elizabeth about the playwright, albeit for his own gain:

> "There's a man I met. His name is William Shakespeare . . ."
>
> The Queen nodded. "Yes. I've heard of him. I'm told he's rather good."
>
> "I met him when I was trying to get into the Rose Theatre. We got on quite well and I'm sure he'd help me if . . ."
>
> "I'm not sure I approve of players," the Queen said. "They're a rowdy lot at the best of times. But if you're sure that's what you really want . . ."
>
> "It is. More than anything in the world."
>
> "I'll have a word with Master Shakespeare." (183)

Such links between gender, performance, Shakespeare, and Elizabeth could be deployed to historically authorise performative models of gendered subjectivity, but are usually used to affirm understandings of identity bordering on essentialist. Conceptualisations of performance are only rendered performative in terms of developing gendered subjectivity when linked with masculinity. In extension, there is *never* any suggestion that Elizabethan theatrical culture is linked with any sexual identity or behaviours other than heterosexual. That this is true regardless of the gender of the primary focaliser or protagonist (or implied reader) demonstrates both the continuing hegemonic authority of heteronormative patriarchy as a structuring discourse for contemporary Western culture, and some of the mechanisms by which such discourses are inscribed on juvenile reading subjects.

The specific sub-genre of Shakespearean historical fiction for younger readers analysed in this chapter finds its roots in Geoffrey Trease's well-known *Cue For Treason* (1940), which establishes a gendered template for the Shakespeare-as-character historical novel for children, and forms a bridge for the genre leading from the nineteenth to the late twentieth century. *Cue for Treason* tells the story of Peter Brownrigg, a farmboy who must leave his Cumberland home, falls in with a group of travelling players with whom he travels to London where, in turn, he becomes Shakespeare's apprentice. A fellow runaway, Kit, undertakes this journey with Peter and acts as his confidante and companion. Kit is unsurprisingly revealed to be a girl dressed as a boy, and as friend and love-interest, she helps Peter foil a plot to assassinate Elizabeth I. Pinsent accurately notes that this novel's publication date, "the year of Dunkirk", informs the text's overall concern with "Britishness" and its "patriotic message" (118); a concern made obvious when Peter must kill a stranger in order to save his own life, and in consequence, save the life of Elizabeth and perhaps even England (Trease 174). Beyond and within such patriotism, however, the novel also produces an explicitly gendered understanding of natural and acceptable behaviours. Peter's own developing acting skills (which literally save the day on a number of occasions) are applauded, where Kit's acting ability—logically confirmed by her successful 'passing'—is undermined as the natural ability of a young woman. Thus, despite gestures towards complicating gender stereotypes, as when Peter tells the reader that Kit can run nearly as fast as he can (187), the novel depends on patriarchal gender relations, and even renders them as constituent of British national identity.

Although *Cue for Treason* valorises Shakespearean texts, the theatre is marked as an unusual site that can be occupied temporarily but which must be curtailed by a return to 'normal' culture. This may be an extension of the novel's metaphoric representation of wartime England, but it also informs the permissibility of transgression of gender norms. The theatre provides a space where both Peter and Kit are allowed to engage in aberrant behaviours because of the extenuating or exceptional circumstances of national threat; so Kit can cross-dress and Peter can abandon his farming duties. However, even as the novel celebrates this theatrical space, it just as carefully represents as necessary Peter and Kit's departure from this space after Elizabeth's life has been saved. The final chapter of the novel affirms normative social values, as is reinforced by the self-conscious shift from a retrospective first-person account by Peter, to Peter reporting "what happened as it was later described to us by Shakespeare and our other friends in London" (Trease 230). Thus, although Peter narrates the conclusion, his own perspective is subordinated to Shakespeare as narrative authority and Elizabeth as social authority. The novel's affirmation of heteronormative gendered behaviour is produced by the closing lines:

> What else is there to tell? Only that the Queen proved a shrewder prophet than we, and lived to send us [Peter and Kit] a wedding gift. As I lay down my pen, I look through the fine glass window across the silver mirror of Ullswater, and hear from the garden the shouts of laughter as Kit shows my sons how to climb the apple-tree. (Trease 239–40)

Kit may retain some semblance of tomboyishness here as she climbs a tree, but this tree is contained within a rural garden, and she is the seen and discussed rather than the seeing and speaking. That Peter refers to "my" rather than "our" sons only confirms the patriarchal ideology that transcends even Elizabeth's rule. Although the novel celebrates performance and juvenile agency, each of these categories is ultimately circumscribed by normative gender roles: Peter is to be a farmer-father-writer, Kit is to care for Peter's children.

As inheritor of Trease, Gary Blackwood's *Shakespeare* trilogy exploits similar plots and politics in order to articulate the psychological and social development of its masculine protagonist. The implied reader is overtly rewarded a level of cultural capital and an understanding of its value, even as this capital and its value are circulated within a patriarchal hierarchy of gender.

Blackwood's novels, *The Shakespeare Stealer* (1998), *Shakespeare's Scribe* (2000) and *Shakespeare's Spy* (2003), depict a young Yorkshire orphan boy, Widge, travelling to London in the late sixteenth century. The primary narrative of the trilogy recounts Widge's personal trajectory of Shakespearean maturation that takes him from spectator, to actor, to author. This development is marked most overtly by an increasing mastery of language, particularly urban and theatrical language, and is affirmed by privileged access to the theatre, performance, and of course, Shakespeare himself. Problematically, this development is emphasised by juxtaposition with simultaneous narratives which enact the othering, exclusion, and objectification of feminine subjects in relation to these same markers of value: Shakespeare, the theatre, linguistic authority, and performance.

When *The Shakespeare Stealer* opens, Widge is apprenticed to Dr Timothy Bright, the author of *Characterie: An Arte of Short, Swift and Secret Writing* (1588), and is trained in the art it describes: an antecedent of shorthand.[2] Widge has, therefore, a functional literacy, which allows him to transcribe the words of others without necessarily understanding or analysing them. Bright sells Widge to a man-in-black, Falconer, who has acquired Widge to attend a performance of *Hamlet*, transcribe the dialogue, and sell it to a rival company of players.

Widge quickly evolves from an unthinking to an engaged receiver, as his first encounter with performed Shakespeare has an immediate effect:

> I began to think of these people not as players mouthing speeches but as actual persons, living out a part of their lives before me . . . I no longer noticed the press of the crowd, nor its unwashed smell for I was no longer there among them, but in a castle in Denmark. (*Stealer* 49–50)

The transformative and improving power of Shakespeare's language is demonstrated clearly when, inspired by the performance of *Hamlet*, Widge opts to join the company rather than steal from it. In establishing the theatre as a haven for Widge, Blackwood celebrates it as microcosm, embracing the Globe's motto: "*[t]otus mundis agit histroniem*" (*Stealer* 47). The valorisation of the theatrical space is, in a sense, the greatest anachronism of the trilogy. Blackwood's privileging of "the Bard" above any anxieties Elizabethans may have had about the theatre effaces the extent to which playhouses'

> [p]rosperity was not based upon any tangible commodity, and was inherently divorced from and opposed to the ideally ordered world which contemporary theory demanded. The theatres and those who worked in them earned their income from the presentation of an alternative world to that which existed outside their walls—a world which drew those who should be working away from their work and which provided a focus for other outsiders who preyed on society and threatened good order—prostitutes, pickpockets, and those eager for a fight. In the alternative world within the playhouse walls prevailed an anarchy which was threatening to external society. (Wilson 38)

In effacing such anarchy Blackwood participates in an homogenising of Elizabethan theatrical culture, ironically using it to construct precisely the kind of ordered, patriarchal world it historically challenged.

Such patriarchal order rules inside and outside Blackwood's theatre. Widge tells the reader, "I realized now that I was being offered something more than just a career as a player, acting out a variety of roles. I was also being offered a chance at a real-life role, as a valued member of the Globe family" (*Stealer* 211). The erasure of his orphanhood provides reader satisfaction, but Widge's acceptance into this family comes at the expense of those will not or cannot adhere to normative gendered behaviours. Two peers in particular, Nick and Julian, represent gender aberration, and their removal facilitates Widge's personal development. That the implied reader is encouraged both to identify with and approve of this development aligns them with the normative against any alternatives.

Nick, the senior-boy of the company, functions as a threat and rival to Widge, and occupies an uncertain space between boy and man: he is dissatisfied with playing female roles and yet is not deemed experienced enough to play male roles. Throughout *Stealer*, explicit links are made between Nick's on- and off-stage lives, which inform and represent each other and are explicitly gendered:

> "He's been a prentice for six or seven years, and now he'll have to begin playing a man's part."
> "On the stage, or in life?"
> "Both, I suppose." (*Stealer* 88)

When given the opportunity to play an adult male role, Nick squanders it by getting drunk and failing to make curtain. He further betrays the company by agreeing to steal the book and sell it to Falconer, the very act of course which Widge refused, and which facilitated his entry *into* the company. Nick fails to learn the lessons of dramatic development, and refuses to take responsibility for his actions. His problems are theatrically described as being "as though he had taken on a role he was not prepared to play, not only on stage but in life, and was looking for someone who would tell him what to do next" (*Stealer* 154). Nick has failed to transform his performance into performativity: he has not used the experience of the theatre to effect his own transition to mature masculinity. The message for Widge and the implied reader is clear: The necessary journey to adult subjectivity may be difficult, but is of value to one's self and one's community. Perhaps more importantly, a successful journey is likely to be that which follows the socially endorsed route.

At the opposite end of the behavioural spectrum from Nick is Julian, a conscientious apprentice who seeks to improve his own skills while contributing the playhouse's overall success. Julian continually attempts to befriend Widge, offering him advice and modelling appropriate behaviours. Towards the end of *Stealer*, Julian is injured protecting Widge from Nick. When first-aid is administered, Julian is revealed to be Julia, a young girl who has disguised herself as a boy so that she might act. She is henceforth banned from the stage, but remains with the company to perform acceptable feminine functions such as money collecting. Her frustration with this marginalisation leads her to emigrate to France. While it is historically accurate to remove Julia from the stage, the novel implicitly suggests that had she never cross-dressed she would not harbour resentment later at the loss of her masculine privileges. Her performance cannot become performative: She cannot—through a repeated series of gestures and statements—change her material or social reality. As with Nick's failure, Julia's inability functions as an example for Widge, revealing the hierarchies of his social context.

Julia's removal is both historical and ideological. Arguably, one inescapably problematic aspect of this otherwise privileged cultural and historical context for modern audiences is the exclusion of women from the pre-Restoration stage. Blackwood appears to circumvent this problem by using the (frankly Shakespearean) motif of cross-dressing to 'insert' a woman on the stage, thereby acknowledging the problem and implicitly critiquing its legitimacy. The novel seems to negotiate between the generic requirements of historical fiction and contemporary sensibilities by imagining a utopic end for Julia as a legitimately female actor on the French stage. However, this solution carries some highly problematic implicit loadings:

> The English equation of actresses with whores was also common in France and Italy, but this was not seen as an impediment to their performing in plays . . . The problem of female chastity was sufficiently resolved, officially at least, in French and Spanish theatres merely by requiring that the actresses be married. (Orgel 1–2)

The solution to Julia's exclusion from the English stage is therefore covertly a move which makes her subordination to normative models of domesticated feminine subjectivity a prerequisite to participation in an alternate version of the very discourse which guarantees her male peers maturity and legitimacy. In fact, beyond a vague sense of outrage on behalf of Julia, the broader experience of young male players performing female parts is limited to the carefully circumscribed space of the stage, and is subsumed into a rite-of-passage to manliness: the actors play female parts, not only as a product of their physical youth, but as a kind of apprenticeship. This establishes an hierarchical trajectory of gender in which the feminine is symbolically passed through in order to reach the masculine. It could be argued that this is a physically necessary trajectory in the Elizabethan playhouse, but this apprenticeship as training for 'real' life as well as the stage is emphasised when we consider the exemplar characters of Julian and Nick, whose experiences clearly mark a subordination of the feminine to the masculine, and aberrant masculinity to approved masculinity. Julian is too masculine (for a female), and Nick fails to learn the lessons of gendered maturity this apprenticeship is supposed to teach, either on or off the stage. The real feminine is thus excluded and confined while the symbolic feminine is subsumed as a stage in the development of masculine subjectivity.

The symbolic contribution of Nick and Julia to Widge's own development is made explicit when their absence ensures that Widge gets the chance to play Ophelia in a Royal Command performance of *Hamlet*. His successful performance not only demonstrates the lessons he has learned from Nick and Julia's failures, but also allows him to experience subjectively the transformative power of Shakespeare's language. The shift from consumer to consumer-producer enacts Widge's comprehensive entrance into the company, and is the commencement of his own performative journey towards adult masculinity:

> Through some miraculous process, I ceased to be Widge, and became Ophelia, except for some small part of myself that seemed to hover overhead, observing my transformation with amazement. The lines flowed from me as though they had just occurred to my brain and not been penned by Mr. Shakespeare a year earlier. (*Stealer* 180)

Widge is conflated here with Shakespeare as the conduit for great language; his understanding of, and identification with, the Shakespearean material connects him with the playwright's cultural authority. And, of course, he embraces the experience of playing a girl's part. *Hamlet* not only enables this connection but also provides a thematic intertextual reference for the novel overall as a play explicitly concerned with father-son relationships (see Rasmussen). Just as the play explores filiality through several pairings (Hamlet-Hamlet, Laertes-Polonius, Fortinbras-Fortinbras) and indeed adopted filiality (Hamlet-Claudius, Fortinbras-Norway), Widge is seeking a trustworthy father-figure: enter William Shakespeare.

Despite the title and setting, Shakespeare makes relatively few appearances in *The Shakespeare Stealer*. He is the spoken about rather than the speaking, and more exposition is given to historical context than either the man or his plays. What glimpses the reader catches of Shakespeare carefully inscribe him as a participant in the theatre's culture, an active writer, and an implicitly heterosexual man suffering anxieties about his inability to fulfil his actual paternal role: sacrificing his family in Stratford for the family of the theatre. Although he writes a great deal in the novel, and the textual products of this writing are fetishised, Shakespeare speaks very little. Blackwood revealed his anxiety about 'making Shakespeare speak' in *Stealer*:

> Probably the most intimidating task I faced was that of making Shakespeare himself speak. I copped out a bit in the first book, by keeping his appearances to a minimum. But in the sequel it was crucial for the reader to see him and hear him at some length—and not just in everyday conversation, either, but in the throes of creating a new play. ("Speaks" 78)

Shakespeare's absence from *The Shakespeare Stealer* has considerable effect on Widge's and the reader's sense of connection to the playwright. Widge is told early on that "You won't see much of Mr. Shakespeare. He's a private man, and a very busy one" (*Stealer* 79). Through Widge, however, the reader is exposed to stories *about* Shakespeare; that his father was "a glover" (77), that he "was the ghost in *Hamlet*" (80), and that his son "grew ill and died while Mr. Shakespeare was here in London. I doubt that he's ever forgiven himself" (151–52). These details signal both Shakespeare's position within the company and the novel's implicit construction of Shakespeare's position within Western culture: the absent father.

Just as Widge "could not see Mr. Shakespeare's face directly, only his reflection in the glass" (*Stealer* 115), the reader is encouraged to see reflections of Shakespeare in his writing. Although theatrical performance enacts Widge's personal development in accordance with the novel's general privileging of theatrical culture, *The Shakespeare Stealer* simultaneously—and somewhat anachronistically—privileges the textuality of Shakespeare and print culture. Clear distinctions are made between those who read books, and those who merely own them as assets. So villainous Simon Bass owns "more books that I would have suspected existed in all England" (28–29), whereas Widge has *read* and remembered Holinshed and Raleigh (7) and like Shakespeare is associated with an active print culture throughout. Widge encounters a "bookseller's stall [. . . where] displayed prominently were a number of plays by 'Wm. Shaksper'" (94). The novel does acknowledge that this creates a cultural tension between the plays as theatrical and literary texts, particularly given the competitive sense of ownership the company has in relation to Shakespeare's plays:

> We generally delay publication as long as possible. Some companies care little for registrations or rights, and to print the play is the same as saying 'Here it is, and welcome to it.' Yet if we *don't* publish it ourselves, someone will sell a pirated version. It's a tricky and an unfair business. (*Stealer* 200–01, original emphasis)

This tension not only reflects historical context, but anticipates the eventual limitation of Shakespeare's availability to the public *or* the playhouse as a textual artefact, and Heminge and Condell's advice to the readers of Shakespeare that:

> it is not our province, who onely gather his works, and give them you, to praise him. It is yours that reade him. And there we hope, to your divers capacities, you will finde enough, both to draw, and hold you : for his wit can no more lie hid, then it could be lost. Reade him, therefore; and againe, and againe : And if then you doe not like him, surely you are in some manifest danger, not to understand him. (n.p.)

As with these first editors of the plays, Blackwood's canonisation of Shakespeare offers a form of *textual* relationship with Shakespeare which implies that the adoption of Shakespearean discourse (via acting or reading) can materially aid the journey from adolescent to adult. The relationship that Widge forms with Shakespeare can be replicated by the implied juvenile reader willing to form a self-reflexive reading with Shakespearean texts.

The cultural logic which affirms Widge's development depends not only on the cultural capital of "Shakespeare" but also on a patriarchally-informed binary whereby the exclusion or subordination of femininity to masculinity legitimizes the accretion of such cultural capital by the masculine subject. This is a logic repeated and confirmed throughout the trilogy literally and symbolically. Widge's trajectory of development is linked with valorised discourses of the theatre, performance, linguistic authority, and cultural filiality as embodied by Shakespeare. This trajectory is repeatedly juxtaposed with feminine experiences which both enact and naturalise exclusion from these discourses, and which also find an embodiment in Shakespeare. Feminine subordination indexes Widge's increasing maturity just as surely as increasingly sophisticated participation in cultural production does. Hence the feminine as competition or equal is repudiated in *The Shakespeare Stealer*, absent from *Shakespeare's Scribe*, and reconciled as necessary to social subjectivity, but just as necessarily separate from the theatre, in *Shakespeare's Spy*. This is emphasised thematically and intertextually, as the key Shakespearean intertexts shift from *Hamlet*, to *All's Well That Ends Well*, to *Timon of Athens*.

The paradoxical absence of Shakespeare from *Stealer* is immediately challenged in *Shakespeare's Scribe*, where passivity and silence are displaced by activity in every sense: "[t]hen Mr. Shakespeare strode into the room, bearing a fistful of crumpled papers, which he held out to me. 'Can you copy these out in the form of sides, Widge?'" (*Scribe* 5). Here, Shakespeare interpellates Widge as his scribe, the mediator of his words, and Widge advances his literary development, moving from recognising himself as individual masculine subject to social masculine subject. As the novel's title indicates, Widge now belongs to Shakespeare, and is explicitly linked with the world of Shakespearean *writing*. Shakespeare's cultural capital as a *literary* figure demands not only that Widge be increasingly implicated in literary culture, but also that Shakespeare be present as *author*.

As the novel progresses, Widge develops as individual, as writer, and as actor: modes of being which become increasingly intertwined. In *Scribe*, Blackwood reverses the journey of discovery that Widge took from Yorkshire to London's playhouses in *Stealer*, and sends the company on a tour of northern England when the plague shuts down London's theatres. Widge's self-knowledge is furthered by this journey as he must now reconcile his belonging to a family and the resulting levels of social participation and responsibility. If the crisis of subjectivity to be resolved in *Stealer* was filial belonging, then *Scribe* considers the rights and responsibilities such belonging might render. Entering into a socially-embedded maturity necessarily means engaging with people beyond the playhouse while ideally retaining the security of the company. In becoming Shakespeare's scribe when Will breaks his arm this secure movement beyond the familiar is achieved as Widge symbolically moves to the centre of the company while the company itself moves away from the playhouse. Scenes in which Widge takes dictation for Shakespeare enact his apprenticeship and offer complex sites of the production of cultural authority and meaning. Shakespearean cultural capital is both articulated and problematised when Widge notes of his first encounter with the Shakespearean manuscript:

> A good half of [the lines] had been crossed out. In addition, there were black blotches everywhere, as though an ink plague had struck the paper.
>
> "They tell me," said Mr. Shakespeare, "there's a rumor about London to the effect that I never blot out a line. Obviously it isn't so." He sighed and added ruefully, "Would that it were." (Scribe 74)[3]

This scene is so heavily loaded as a point of Shakespearean appropriation that it begs the question of reader competence, for here Blackwood negotiates between prevalent myths about Shakespeare that a juvenile reader is unlikely to be aware of. As a result, the novel becomes overtly didactic precisely as it would seem to be marking instability. Blackwood *temporarily* debunks the notion of Shakespeare as a vessel for plays to pass through unproblematically when Widge notes, "I had supposed that composing plays was an effortless task for a man of Mr. Shakespeare's gifts. But he was behaving as though it were something to be dreaded, as though it required a degree of fortitude or courage he was not sure he was possessed" (*Scribe* 88). In comparison, the writing of a play at royal command causes pain:

> "Her Majesty finds that such fare as *Hamlet* and *Caesar* puts her in a melancholy humor. She prefers something more . . . lightweight." The pained expression Mr. Shakespeare now wore was, I fancied, due to more than just the swollen arm. (*Scribe* 72)

The Shakespearean reputation is preserved by the revelation that the play being worked on is *Love's Labour's Won* (one of the 'lost' plays), and thus the troubled production of the play does not affect Shakespeare's cultural capital even as it identifies cultural production as a form of labour. Even so, this scene is only a temporary disruption, and the novel soon returns to Shakespeare as inspired Romantic genius: "One might have thought the words were already fully formed in his head, and he was merely reading them off" (*Scribe* 90). Even when Shakespeare questions his ability, the reader shares Widge's inner repudiation of such claims:

> "They always betray you. When you're only imagining them, they seem so ideal, so full of promise and possibility. Then, when you try to get them down on paper, they turn on you and refuse to live up to your expectations."
>
> One of the uncanny qualities about Mr. Shakespeare's words, I had learned, was that, however general they might seem, at the same time they

> somehow managed to speak directly to each individual who heard them, and to address his particular plight. (*Scribe* 174)

This repudiation is confirmed by the action of the novel itself, as Shakespeare and Widge's writing relationship is mirrored in their respective negotiations between literal and symbolic family: each of them has to choose between an actual family member and the theatrical family. Shakespeare's brother Edmund (Ned) has joined the company and consistently fails to meet his obligations.[4] Shakespeare continues to support his brother, even as he disapproves of his behaviour, and his advice to Widge that "we must make allowances for family" (*Scribe* 195) is pointed given that Widge believes he has found his biological father in York: an ex-musketeer and Catholic, Jamie Redshaw. These emotional trials feed directly back into the play being written (crucially re-titled *All's Well That Ends Well*, thereby reinstating it in the Shakespearean canon) as Shakespeare appears to be creatively responding to Widge's struggles, and later, Widge identifies directly with Helena: "I felt a kind of kinship with her. Like me, she was an orphan; like me, she had been taught the rudiments of medicine; like me, she had offered her loyalty to a soldier and been rejected" (*Scribe* 255). Within a model where reading involves self-reflexive identification, Helena offers Widge strategies for dealing with the failure of his attempts to form a relationship with his biological father. The play stands in for paternal advice from Shakespeare, suggesting the instructive possibilities of Shakespeare's plays to the contemporary reader, and in turn, affirms the superiority of Shakespeare's symbolic paternity to any biological paternity.

Although *All's Well That Ends Well* performs a significant intertextual function in *Scribe*, it does not guarantee the kind of instant recognition that *Hamlet* might as it is not one of Shakespeare's more popular plays:

> Throughout its critical history [*All's Well's*] inversions of the normal patterns of romantic comedy—its sympathy with an older generation who are usually right to circumscribe the freedom of the younger, the relentless pursuit of the play's heroine of a love she knows to be unrequited, and the general atmosphere of disenchantment, loss and mourning within which her plot unfolds—have made readers happier with Shakespeare's more festive comedies uncomfortable. (Dobson and Wells 11)

It is arguably those very qualities Dobson and Wells identify as discomforting about the play which make it amenable to the normative development privileged by Blackwood (and very often by conservative children's literature generally), not least of which being the rightness of authority figures. As the trilogy deploys lesser-known intertexts, the ascribed value of "Shakespeare" becomes more general.

There are, of course, overt intertextual functions the play performs for knowledgeable readers despite the fact that Blackwood provides little in the way of specific linguistic competency in the play itself. Like Widge, Helena in *All's Well That Ends Well* is tormented by the loss of her father: "the remembrance of her father never approaches her heart but the tyranny of her sorrows takes all livelihood from her cheek" (Shakespeare, *AWW* 1.1.45–47). The play also overtly considers symbolic versus literal family relationships: "Tis often seen / Adoption strives with nature, and choice breeds / A native slip to us from foreign seeds" (*AWW* 1.3.139–41). *All's Well* privileges honourable behaviour and symbolic family relationships over literal filiality when it is undermined by dishonourable actions. The play's Countess, who views Helena as her own child, renounces her son Bertram when she learns of his appalling behaviour while away at war: "He was my son, / But I do wash his name out of my blood / And thou [Helena] are all my child" (*AWW* 3.2.66–68). Widge must learn to appreciate the more productive relationship he enjoys with Shakespeare as symbolic father, rather than the destructive relationship he experiences with Jamie Redshaw. In comparison, the reader must appreciate *that* the play is useful and important rather than *how* or *why* it might be.

Although one of Widge's major challenges is negotiating between biological and cultural paternity, he is unable to frame the issue in these terms, even as he acknowledges the competition between the groups these father-figures metonymically represent:

> After living most of my life without family or friends, I had only lately begun to learn about loyalty, so I did not yet know all it entailed. I wished to be faithful to my father, but if he had committed a crime I was not sure I still owed him any loyalty. Besides, what about my obligation to the Chamberlain's Men? In the hierarchy of loyalties, which one came first—family or friends? (Blackwood, *Scribe* 217)

The reader has modelled for them a concept of family which is not biological but social. The idea of family *loyalty* is never threatened by these novels, but rather the constitution of family is as Widge learns that you can indeed 'choose your family'. The resolution of these issues is marked by Widge's successful playing of Helena in *All's Well That Ends Well.* His ability to perform on the stage with absolute emotional authenticity is made possible by his achievements off-stage, with particular reference to social responsibility, filial loyalty, and self-reflexive reading. When he defeats an acting rival, Salaviel Pavy, in an acting duel Mr Armin tells him: "You know," he said, "when an actor truly shines in a role for the first time, we say that he's found himself. Well, it seems to me that you've found yourself. How does it feel?" (Blackwood, *Scribe* 265). Performance of identity, thematised throughout the trilogy, could be read as a simplified form of Butler's notions of performative subjectivity, and the young reader learns that the self is constituted through roles and repetitions, obviously on-stage, but also off-stage. It should not necessarily be surprising that this very fluid and performative notion of subjectivity is available to the masculine subject in Blackwood's novels if Stephens is correct in his account of the links between performance and masculine subjectivity in juvenile fiction:

> Performance as role-play, disguise, or play-acting might be expected to displace, at least temporarily, the notion of an essential and coherent self which predominates in junior fiction, but this is not the case. Rather, it serves as a process of self-definition, a staged rite of passage which erases feelings of marginality, fragmentation, and subjective dispersal which are typically presented as a lack in a character's material circumstances, and in their place imparts a sense of agency. ("Page" 40)

Widge being voted superior to Pavy affirms his individual and social value, but this social space is emphatically homosocial. Having achieved socio-cultural agency, Widge is in some sense free to move beyond the playhouse walls to make use of it.[5]

A reader could be forgiven for not noticing the absence of femininity from *Shakespeare's Scribe*. However just as Shakespeare himself was the absent-present in *The Shakespeare Stealer* but was central to *Scribe*, so too does femininity return to the trilogy in *Shakespeare's Spy* in order to demonstrate Widge's continuing personal development. Having cemented his place within the Chamberlain's Men, Widge's values are tested and expanded in the final novel when he must leave his own company and join another as a spy (on Shakespeare's orders) when it becomes clear that the playwright's works-in-progress are being stolen by or for these rivals. Widge must finally integrate his individual and social subjectivities into a coherent and mature whole.

In terms of symbolic spatial representation then, Widge moves to the periphery of the playhouse and the reader's exposure to the world of Shakespearean theatrical context is narrowed to the interpersonal relationship between Widge and Shakespeare. In turn, this seeming liminality provides a space where Widge can engage with femininities without ever threatening the overdetermined homosociality of the playhouse itself. As Widge becomes more fully a writer rather than an actor, his personal development is mapped as a successful move from consumer to producer which foresees a level of control over the sphere that the trilogy has used as index and marker of individual and socio-cultural achievement: the stage. This is cultural capital in action: readers have demonstrated for them Shakespeare's value and an illustration of the mechanisms by which such value is produced and maintained. At the same time, the precise nature of that value remains elusive and somewhat obscure as is indicated by the key intertext for this final novel: *Timon of Athens*.

It would seem that Blackwood negotiates his anxiety about using "Shakespeare" by using increasingly obscure plays the more heavily implicated Widge is in their production. The genealogy of *Timon* offers certain safety nets to

Blackwood's construction of Shakespeare's genius and authorship in that it is commonly thought of as problematic:

> ever since Charles Knight in 1838 argued that *Timon of Athens* was a reworking by another dramatist of a tragedy originally by Shakespeare, there have been theories that the state of the text could be explained if it was held *either* that Shakespeare was working over a play by another . . . *or* that another . . . was revising a play by Shakespeare. Such theories always began with the assumption that the play as it stood was unworthy of Shakespeare and that the poorer parts must be attributed to an inferior hand. (Shakespeare, *Tim.* xxii)

The novel's deferral of this playtext to Widge therefore simultaneously saves Shakespeare from this play, and safely interpolates Widge in the Shakespearean textual tradition. Where the earlier novels effaced Shakespeare's dependence on pre-texts, attention is overtly drawn to the 'borrowed robes' of *Timon* when Shakespeare tells Widge:

> "Take the story of Timon, for example. I found it in Plutarch's 'Life of Antony.' Come, now; you needn't look so dismayed. Don't you know that there are no new ideas in the world? Every story has been told—and lived—a hundred times before. The best we can hope for is to find some new way of telling them." (Blackwood, *Spy* 122)

Shakespeare loses interest in the story of Timon, and hands his notes to Widge. In accepting them and opting to complete the play, Widge becomes a playwright, completing his journey through cultural production, and absolutely marking his final rejection of his biological father Redshaw, who "had instilled in [Widge] a fierce resolve not to follow in his footsteps" (*Spy* 156). In working on the play, Widge is forced to consider how meaningful relationships are formed as he analyses his own relationships with other in order to write about how people form friendships (emphasising yet again a post-Romantic conception of authorship). The thematic concerns attributed to *Timon* are offered as a series of morals or lessons to Widge and by extension the reader; in particular, the play's concern with the quality of friendship, and the dangerous influence money can have on perception and behaviour. More explicitly, Timon as misanthrope or figure of self-imposed exile, functions as a cautionary tale for Widge.

Widge cannot live entirely within the walls of the playhouse. Unsurprisingly Shakespeare offers literary and embodied advice to Widge on how to negotiate between one's personal and professional theatrical lives and families. The relative absence of gender as a relational aspect of identity in *Stealer* is inverted in *Spy* where the forced reconciliation between the theatre and the real, as previously separate in an idealised and idealising way, is figured through the intrusion, literal and symbolic, of key female characters: Judith Shakespeare and Julia. Each of these young women openly articulates aspects of Widge's identity, and forces him to cohere the theatrical and real worlds, worlds which Widge realises Shakespeare has kept apart in order to achieve success: "Mr. Shakespeare's world was divided into two hemispheres. One, centered around his hometown of Stratford and his family, the other around London and the theatre, and the two seldom intersected" (*Spy* 48). Women are explicitly (and problematically) associated with reality, and in their relationships with women and the real, the male characters are marked as failures or successes. Readers must have 'explained' to them that, while literary culture is valuable, it is not autonomously valuable, but must be integrated in to a sense of self that functions in, and contributes to, the real world.

The return of the feminine to the novels coincides with Widge's burgeoning sexuality, and therefore functions heteronormatively in the broadest sense, while the two characters who represent the feminine here also function as symbolic markers of Widge's ongoing maturing process. At the opening of *Shakespeare's Spy*, Widge notes, "Most of the stories we acted out were rife with romance, but in our ordinary lives it was sadly absent, and no wonder. Since women were not permitted to appear upon the stage, all the parts were played by men and boys" (3). Here, the exclusion of women from the stage is marked as a loss to the (implicitly heterosexual) male players, rather than marking any sense of deprivation for women. In keeping with the broader gender politics of the trilogy, the presence of Judith and Julia serves to suggest, "that 'obligatory heterosexuality' is built into male-dominated kinship systems" (Sedgwick 3). Femininity then, functions not as a valuable subject position, but as a necessary and useful marker of the playhouse as emphatically homosocial but *not* homosexual space.

The heteronormative inscription of theatrical space is demonstrated by the careful policing of its borders against infiltration from Judith Shakespeare, and the containment within its borders of Julia. The policing of femininity in this final novel is as important as Widge's development into author in terms of shaping the trilogy's privileged mode of masculine subjectivity.

Judith Shakespeare, William's younger daughter, arrives unexpectedly in London in an attempt to forge closer familial bonds with her father. The challenge she poses to the symbolic filial relationship developing between Shakespeare and Widge is emphasised by and mirrored in the fact that her arrival coincides with that of a renegade Jesuit priest, the hiding of whom threatens the company as a whole. That Judith is continually and wilfully excluded from both the playhouse and from her father's company might seem to indicate that Blackwood is extending the political-cultural critique initiated by Virginia Woolf in *A Room of One's Own* (1929). In Woolf's well-known thought experiment, Shakespeare's "sister", Judith, travelled to London to participate in her brother's theatrical world and "stood at the stage door" (62) but was only useful as a sexual object, and ultimately "killed herself one winter's night" (62).

Where Woolf mobilised the figure of Shakespeare's sister in order to critique both the historical and ongoing exclusion of women from valorised cultural spaces, Blackwood mobilises Shakespeare's daughter in order to justify and authorise such exclusion.

Judith Shakespeare is an obvious mirror of Widge in several ways and serves to cement his interpersonal relationship with Shakespeare by a process of juxtaposition. She knows that her "father's name and work are well regarded all over England" (*Spy* 65), and views this success as proof that, if "you work hard and use your wits, you can make of yourself what you will" (65). Of course, Judith must learn that such social mobility as a product of labour is available only to men. Although she aids Widge's personal development, Judith is excluded from the cultural production that Widge participates in. Her relationship with Shakespeare is seen to fail because of her own inappropriate behaviour rather than any paternal lack on Shakespeare's part. This may explain Judith's indulgence of a common orphan fantasy when she says to Widge: "I mean, if you don't know who your parents are, then they might be anyone, mightn't they? Who knows, perhaps you're the illegitimate son of some great lord with piles and piles of money" (*Spy* 64). This is a fantasy of projection, for Widge has a more productive (albeit symbolic) filial relationship with William Shakespeare than Judith ever will.

Judith cannot reject her biological family in favour of the theatre because her biological father *is* the theatre. She, like her uncle Ned, must necessarily be rejected by Shakespeare in order for him to continue writing his plays. Such a model of Shakespeare's 'Faustian pact' (see Lancaster 72) whereby Shakespeare must sacrifice his literal paternal role in order to become the symbolic father of Western culture is a common enough trope. Although he is shown by Blackwood as regretting the loss of his son (Blackwood, *Stealer* 152), the rejection of his daughter is constructed as an action necessary to ensure his cultural a necessary action. Even this rejection, however, is displaced from Shakespeare onto Mr Pope, who informs Widge that Shakespeare has written his opinion of Judith into *Two Gentlemen of Verona*:

> He shifted uncomfortably in his seat. "How shall I put it? Well, you recall the duke's description of his daughter in *Two Gentlemen*?
>
> "No, trust me: she is peevish, sullen, forward,
> Proud, disobedient, stubborn, lacking duty;
> Neither regarding that she is my child,
> Nor fearing me as if I were her father." (*Spy* 86)

Later, Pope more explicitly states, "I rather suspect that Judith is less her father's daughter than she is her mother's" (117). The construction of Judith as lacking in responsibility and respect is confirmed when she suddenly returns to Stratford and thus fails to meet Widge for an assignation. However, this becomes a spur to write a play, and is thus a blessing rather than a hardship for Widge. Given her lively personality, it is not surprising that Widge finds himself attracted to Judith. However, the trilogy's carefully constructed categories of value would be upset by a romantic relationship between them. The oppositional values of the theatre vs. the real, the symbolic family vs. the real, and the masculine vs. the feminine would be irretrievably destabilised, just as Judith's arrival in London literally disrupts the theatre.

In comparison with Judith's refusal to respect the boundaries between theatrical and domestic spaces, Julia (who was excluded from the theatre in the first novel) learns to respect these boundaries as necessary to her individual and social status. Widge succinctly notes:

> Like me, she had found a family in the theatre. Unfortunately, membership in that family was limited to men and boys, at least in England. I only hoped that, across the Channel in France, she had managed to find a more permanent place for herself. (*Spy* 105)

The reader learns about Julia's experiences in France through Widge's reportage of letters she has sent:

> Every few months a French sailor turned up bearing a letter from her. These were usually brief and disappointingly impersonal, devoted mainly to what roles she was playing at the Théâtre de Marais. But now and again she let slip some line that made me suspect she was not as happy with her lot as she would have us think. (*Spy* 14)

After Judith's departure from Widge's life, we learn along with him that the source of Julia's implicit unhappiness is sexual threat:

> What she had never revealed in her letters was that most of the public still regarded female players as degraded and immoral, little better than women of the streets, and treated them as such ... with each month that passed [the Comte's] attentions grew more and more ardent, and the more she resisted them the more insistent he became, until at last he declared that if she would not come to him willingly, he would take her against her will. (*Spy* 248–49)

Having learned that even when allowed to act, being on the stage situates her as the apparently acceptable object of sexual violence (which not incidentally also serves to legitimise exclusion of women from the English stage), Julia returns to London and accepts her culturally-approved liminal role in the theatre, after realising that, the "only love I've ever felt is for the theatre, and it was not returned" (258). Rather than railing against her situation, Julia willingly joins Widge's offstage adoptive family where, Widge tells the reader, "she lent her efforts to the cause. She also cooked meals and cared for the younger orphans" (252). Julia's rejection of her biological family in preference to the symbolic family of the theatrical world is rewarded by the implication that she will eventually marry Widge. He realises that "given the choice between her happiness and mine, I preferred hers. Perhaps that is the true measure of love" (270). This telling development is emphasised by the revelation that Julia's true biological father is no less than Essex (258), which in a sense fulfils Judith's fantasy about special (but non-Shakespearean) origins. However, Julia does not need such origins in the way that Judith does; her biological origins cannot guarantee her a place on the stage, and she has no need to become Shakespeare's symbolic rather than literal daughter when she can be Widge's wife. Such a marriage will suture Julia into the theatrical world and its family without undermining Shakespeare's cultural paternity nor the homosocial integrity of the playhouse.

While Judith and Julia are learning or enacting their necessary distance from the stage, Widge's trajectory of personal development continues unabated. His success is onomastically performed by the selection of a pen-name which combines the names of biological and adoptive fathers: James Pope. The cultural activity this name will be used for, however, nominates William Shakespeare as his 'true' father. In learning to speak and write the language of the stage—and therefore of maturity—Widge enters a world of cultural authority. His closing statement to himself and the reader idealises the coalescence of self and text:

> I could not be certain what sort of part Fortune had written for me; all I could do was to play it out to the best of my ability. I had the feeling that it would prove to be rather like the script for Timon of Athens—far from perfect, but full of promise. (*Spy* 279)

Thus the reader has moved with Widge from spectator, to actor, to playwright. This trajectory valorises the literate subject in a liberal humanist fantasy, deploying "Shakespeare" as the ultimate discourse of cultural capital. The ideally literate subject, however, is emphatically masculine. Tropes of Shakespearean authority are reified in an interpersonal relationship implicitly available in the real world to the readers of his plays. Given however the links between interpersonal relationships with Shakespeare the man in the novels and a reading relationship with his plays outside the novels, it must be noted that circumstances or events which are productive in the trilogy for the masculine subject (Widge), such as disguise, altered naming, confused paternity, creativity, acting, literacy, and of course the direct relationship with Shakespeare, are explicitly unavailable or non-productive for Judith and Julia. In extension, the implied extratextual cultural value of Shakespeare is unavailable to feminine subjects. The inherently circular logic of Shakespearean cultural authority in Blackwood's novels does not allow any point of intervention for the female reader.

If the position of cultural privilege is occupied by symbolic sons of Shakespeare, it would seem an obvious counter-position to imagine as culturally privileged their opposite: Shakespeare's actual daughters. Indeed, two recent novels appear to do just this: Tiffany's *My Father Had a Daughter: Judith Shakespeare's Tale* (2003), and Hassinger's *Shakespeare's Daughter* (2004). These historical novels imagine relationships between William Shakespeare and his daughters, Judith and Susanna. Rather than contesting the gendered logic of Blackwood's trilogy, these novels actually reproduce a necessary separation of Shakespeare and the feminine. The female protagonists actually instigate this separation when they realise that in order for them to have a familial relationship with Shakespeare, he would have to sacrifice his genius. In turn, the implied reader, if female, must identify against the focalised feminine position if they are to imagine a productive reading relationship with Shakespeare.

In 2003, Shakespearean critic Grace Tiffany published the young adult novel *My Father Had a Daughter: Judith Shakespeare's Tale* which would appear to offer a point of comparison with Blackwood's trilogy. In Tiffany's novel, Judith Shakespeare offers a first-person historicised narrative of her family life in Stratford, and the changing terrain of her relationship with her father, William Shakespeare. As the novel's title and epigragh indicate, *Twelfth Night* is appropriated alongside Shakespeare. This is significant because the play arguably offers a narrative of temporary gender disruption subsumed into patriarchally-sanctioned social structures. Thus, despite the claims that, "In both her fiction and her scholarly work, Tiffany celebrates Shakespeare, embracing the themes of gender confusion, spiritual growth through roleplay, tragic choices, redemption, and ultimate forgiveness that are central to his work" ("Author"), which might lead one to anticipate a text which challenges the 'norms' of contemporary historical Shakespearean fiction for young readers, Tiffany's novel actually deploys tropes similar to those of Blackwood. Insidiously, Tiffany uses aspects of *Twelfth Night* and strategies of focalisation and reader identification (narrative and narration) to encourage female readers to participate in their *own* cultural marginalisation. When they are raised, issues of 'gender confusion' and 'roleplay' serve as temporary disruptions which are, like those in *Twelfth Night*, subsumed into a normative patriarchal social model. Readers travel along Judith's path of development which includes the initial recognition of the value of her father's professional work, the presumed legitimacy of his absence from the family home, her own attempts at professionalisation, and the presumed legitimacy of her own replacement in the domestic sphere of Stratford.

To connect Judith with Viola, Tiffany emphasises a narrative of guilt and mourning alongside a focus on symbolic doubling, mirroring, and reflective links with water. At the novel's opening, Judith notes of her and her twin brother's reflections in the river, "When Hamnet and I looked together, and stayed still enough, it was easy to imagine that I was he and he was I, and that truly we were four" (Tiffany, *My* 1). After Hamnet dies, Judith suffers from extreme feelings of guilt which she displaces into anger at her father, when she believes he is using the family tragedy as a fodder for a new play. In order to structure the text around guilt and displacement, Tiffany has to take poetic license with the cause of Hamnet's death. Where the historical record lists Hamnet Shakespeare's cause of death as unknown, in *My Father Had a Daughter* Hamnet drowns while on a midnight jaunt with Judith which establishes feelings of responsibility on her part (49–50).

Prior to this death, Judith has had a mostly productive albeit limited relationship with her father. He shares his new writing with her, and teaches her to read. Where the historical Judith Shakespeare is widely believed to have been illiterate Tiffany's Judith is a voracious reader. This seemingly revisionist nature of Tiffany's novel only establishes a filial relationship between Judith and William far enough to legitimise a patriarchal discourse. A focus on literacy initially enables a symbolic connection between father and daughter, as throughout the novel Shakespeare is shown reading as often as he is shown writing. Indeed, the two acts are closely related for the playwright. As often as he is depicted at work, Judith notes that his desk is covered with "Books, books, and more books, piled on shelves and on the floor. The Gospels. Plutarch's *Parallel Lives.* The poems of Ovid. *The Canterbury Tales.* A half-burnt candle" (Tiffany, *My* 168). While these books are obviously sources of inspiration for Shakespeare, he is also portrayed as a kind of autobiographical writer, who transforms his personal experiences into plays. When Judith suggests that the plays, were his real children, after all" (59), she calls up the trope of Shakespeare's cultural paternity in favour of his biological paternity.

Although Judith reads her father's plays voraciously, doing so is constructed as a form of denial of their familial relationship rather than a reinforcement of it. In imaginatively removing herself from a relationship with Shakespeare she effectively becoming analogous with a contemporary reader:

> And I read them, those plays of his, that were now printed and sold in the bookstalls in Stratford High Street. I read to lose myself in their high adventure, and I thought no more of the shadowy man who had conceived them, bending ardently over a tabletop in our parlor or a desk in a London room. I didn't want to think of that man, or to be that father's daughter. I only longed to drown myself in the words of the magical beings who had sprung from his pen. (Tiffany, *My* 59)

Judith is unable to sustain a division between her status as daughter or reader when Shakespeare's private and creative lives seem to coincide in his writing of *Twelfth Night*, which Judith views as a comedic rewriting of her personal tragedy. She discovers rough notes for the play in Stratford: "My father had doubled my own sorrow and my own self, and then chopped me into pieces of verse. *Why?* For money" (Tiffany, *My* 66). Seeing Viola as a version of herself,

Judith becomes a kind of Viola when she decides to dress as a boy, gain access to Shakespeare's theatre and disrupt the proposed production of *Twelfth Night*. Prior to cross-dressing, Judith's awareness of gender roles is fairly limited, and although she registers that her elder sister Susanna occupies time flirting with males of the town, her sense of personal sexuality is equally limited. Shortly after adopting the dress of a male, she believes masculine behaviour is "unaccountably easy" (93) to imitate, and even attributes an autonomous existence to her costume: "the words had jumped out of my mouth as though my boy's disguise had a life of its own; as though I was now not a boy but a particular boy, a rather rascally and witty and bold one" (83). Rather than expanding her sense of selfhood, however, after spending several weeks dressed as a boy Judith realises that "Not only could I not properly play a boy, I could not properly play a girl" (142). Dressing as a boy has disrupted her sense of stable femininity, but has not offered a productive nor useful understanding of subjectivity in its place.

Once Judith enters the theatre, she is transformed by its power, and rather than wanting to destroy the production of *Twelfth Night*, she covets the role of Viola. Deciding to travel to London and confront her father on his terms means that she finally understands the legitimacy of her father's lengthy stays in London and concomitant absence from his family in Stratford. Judith does get the opportunity to play Viola; however, the achievement of this goal is complicated as development by it being both the cause and result of sexual activity. Nathan Field, the company's lead boy actor slated to play Viola, discovers Judith practising Viola's lines and blackmails her into having sex with him to protect her secret. This secret was known to Nathan "at the first" (Tiffany, *My* 131), erasing any sense of homoeroticism, and enforcing heteronormative physical relationships. Initially, Judith tells the reader "I did not put much store by virginity" (137), and indeed voluntarily has sex with Nathan in order to protect her identity. Later she feels "shame" at the conclusion that "I had sold my body like the whores" (150). It is Judith herself who imposes such a reading on her behaviour, making the female subject self-policing with regard to sexuality. Her father is therefore only one of the men who functions as an antagonist to Judith's personal development, but it is Judith herself who willingly adopts the discourses of femininity defined in opposition to those men. Nathan becomes a double for Judith somewhat like Hamnet: as she is playing a male role, Nathan plays female roles on the stage. Their shared development in their brief sexual relationship at once marks a kind of physical progression into adulthood, and cements their gendered identities, as from that point on Nathan can no longer play women on the stage, and Judith *does* play a woman on the stage. Much later in life, Judith recognises this shared identity: "I had me a brother . . . But *you* were my true twin, Nathan. Is't not so?" (266). Just as she offers no sustained challenge to her father's theatre, Judith offers no challenge to heteronormative patriarchal politics.

Judith does achieve personal development by close engagement with Shakespeare's play, a function that is affirmed by Shakespeare who is depicted as wanting and encouraging critical reading of his plays even as he offers his own interpretation. Hence, after asking an actor if they understand *why* (Tiffany, *My* 118) their character behaves a certain way, he describes Olivia as "just the sort of melancholy and self-absorbed young lady who would fear [hell]" (119). Just as Judith achieves self-examination by participation in the production of *Twelfth Night*, implied readers are encouraged to read Shakespeare's plays closely, to consider the relation to their own lives, and to learn more about themselves through role-play. However, while Nathan, like Widge in Blackwood's trilogy, moves ever forward as a subject developing cultural literacy and agency, Judith is unable to. For her, reading is *temporarily* constructed as a way of both working through the grief over her brother's death, and renegotiating her relationship with her father before returning to a domestic life in Stratford. It is linked then, to adolescence and change. This is unsurprising given the target audience of the novel, but does not offer the feminine reading subject a role beyond adolescence. Given the inherent connections between London—"the city of my father's dreams" (235)—the theatre and Shakespeare, it is telling that Judith claims but does not question of the city that "'Tis a wondrous place for man or boy . . . But it affords little scope for a woman" (187).

Moreover, although Shakespeare encourages a kind of 'reading' of his plays from his actors, he explicitly cautions his daughter against reading them: "Do not [read them]. 'Tis not by my will they're in print. They are only poor mirrorings of what I read, and what I see" (Tiffany, *My* 179). With this instruction Shakespeare cuts off the final symbolic link between Judith's and London, and Judith's attempts to reclaim such a life demonstrate the limits of cross-dressing when, after her uncle Edmund Shakespeare dies, Judith again dons men's clothing and goes drinking in neighbourhood pub. This time she narrowly avoids rape, and while recovering realises, "I needed to do something with my hands and my brain besides weeding and folding and counting and cooking and reading. If I didn't I might go stark raving mad" (211), but cannot disobey her father by reading his plays. Reading is now aligned in Judith's mind with the masculine and public: its status falls simultaneously with cross-dressing, as a precursor to danger. What the implied feminine reader is supposed to make of this trajectory in the novel is difficult to judge: the novel's Shakespearean cultural capital is consistently evoked only to be removed from the feminine reader.

Another intertextual function exemplifies the gendered discourse of cultural value and consumption that pervades Tiffany's novel. Judith tells the reader that she has been reading the "Book of Judith" of the Old Testament. In this text, Judith actively takes advantage of existing models of the feminine in order to infiltrate the camp of her enemy Holofernes, and having done so, the men of the camp believe "Never was a woman such as this so fair to look upon, so wise to listen to" ("Judith" 13:19). Ultimately, she engages in an activity which disrupts traditional patriarchal notions of the feminine:

> With that, she went to the head of the couch, and unfastened the scimitar that hung there; unsheathed it, and caught the sleeping man by the hair; Lord God, she said, strengthen me now! Twice the scimitar fell on his neck, and cut clean through it; down came the canopy from the pillars, down fell the headless body to the earth, and ere long she was at the doors, giving the severed head to her maid-servant and bidding her thrust it away into the wallet she carried. Then they went out, both of them, right through the camp, as if bound on their customary errand of prayer; but this time they took the winding path along the valley, right up to the city gates. (13:8–12)

Judith is remembered as a heroine by her people, "All the while she lived, and long after her death, was never enemy that disturbed the peace of Israel. In the Hebrew calendar, a day of rejoicing commemorates her victory; in such honour have the Jews held it from that day to this" ("Judith" 16:30–31). Tiffany's Judith enjoys this narrative, but does not seek to replicate Judith's defiance of gender expectations. She is becoming more fully a daughter than a reader.

The Book of Judith's exclusion from the Protestant canon is mirrored by Judith Shakespeare's own life story in the novel. Just as Judith's biblical tale has become apocryphal, marginalised because of its unsuitability for patriarchal discourse in Protestant England, so too does Judith Shakespeare effectively inhabit, and produce, an apocryphal life story: one which appears to challenge the patriarchal *status quo*, but which actually—by participating in its own marginalisation—acquiesces to patriarchally normative models of feminine identity. Judith Shakespeare reads of, and admires, the biblical Judith, but like the fate of that Judith's story in the Protestant canon, she is marginalised within her culture.

Recognising the cathartic function of her father's writing, Judith begins writing her memoirs (presumably the content of the novel), however just as Shakespeare earlier advised her against reading his plays, he now advises her to stop writing. Where Shakespeare functions as creative mentor/father-figure in Blackwood's novels, in Tiffany's novel it seems as though Judith must learn about her father's importance in London, in order to accept his neglect of her *qua* daughter. Shakespeare now fulfils an instructional role, not as father, but as a person whose behaviour and experiences are *not* to be replicated. Throughout the novel, both Judith and others recognise strong correspondences between her father and herself, but her lesson is to not live as her father has done: "I'll never live torn in two as he does, betwixt country and city. Whate'er I do, I *will* find a way to be whole" (Tiffany, *My* 265). Just as she cannot be reader and daughter, nor can Judith be writer and daughter.

Again then, Virginia Woolf's Judith Shakespeare creates a triangulation of intertextual reference. Even as Tiffany appears to be replicating the silencing of the feminine in Renaissance culture which is critiqued by Woolf's parable, she appears to also be unfortunately replicating an element of Woolf's text which Coiro describes as "worrisome" in that it "romanticizes, and thereby eradicates, the possibility of Shakespeare's sister's writing voice" (360). Similarly, Tiffany's novel romanticises Judith's adventures, while eradicating Judith's creative possibilities, a move which is naturalised by recourse to historical context but which is offered to modern readers almost ahistorically.

It is from her father's mouth (therefore extratextually authoritative as well) that Judith learns her lesson: "[i]t takes real courage to promise thy care and life's company to another" (Tiffany, *My* 287). She marries Thomas Quiney in order to please her father, and after years of marital comfort (if not happiness) she realises her father was right to privilege the everyday and the solid over the written and the ephemeral. Tiffany not only has Judith willingly submit to a domestic feminine role, but depicts Shakespeare repudiating his own plays in favour of having Judith marry. Shakespeare may be the authority figure, but Judith's authoritative speaker becomes her mother, who tells her that "sometimes a woman must make her life apart from what men do, or alongside it" (199), a claim the novel never questions.

Like *Twelfth Night*'s Viola, Judith loses a brother to water, cross-dresses, is integrated into a 'foreign' culture, goes to work for a dominant male, and falls in love. However, unlike Viola's projected return to "woman's weeds" (Shakespeare, *TN* 5.1.271), the reader sees Judith's return to domestic normativity. This return, marked by marriage and motherhood is sanctioned by Shakespeare. Of course, Shakespeare himself has returned to his domestic life in Stratford by this point, and although he dies with a quill in his hand, he is no longer writing plays but is instead authoring Judith's life. Hence, even where the novel is invested in the cultural value of Shakespeare's plays, it is Shakespeare the father rather than Shakespeare the playwright who is useful to Judith. Reading this back into *Twelfth Night,* then, the novel is arguably offering an interpretation of the play that extrapolates a conservative, patriarchal conclusion for Viola, marked by a *temporary* model of feminine subversion or rebellion. The sense in which Judith's "father had a daughter" manifests as her ability to remember the past while moving forward into a domestic life, certainly not a public, creative inheritance. Judith, and the implied reader, affirm Shakespeare's cultural capital by not participating in it.

Similar cultural and political work is being performed in Peter W. Hassinger's *Shakespeare's Daughter* (2004) which takes as its protagonist Shakespeare's eldest daughter, Susanna.[6] Again, the death of Hamnet, here the product of a fever contracted after jumping into the Avon (Hassinger 52), creates an emotional and psychological void in the heroine which she attempts to fill by travelling to London. Unlike Tiffany's novel, however, Shakespeare is almost irrelevant to proceedings, and although readers are offered a model for autobiographically reading the plays, they are given little sense of *why* the plays should be read at all.

Hassinger has an historical advantage in deploying Susanna rather than Judith as a character, due mostly to her epitaph, the opening of which famously reads:

> above her sex, but that's not all,
> Wise to salvation was good Mistress Hall.
> Something of Shakespeare was in that, but this
> Wholly of him with whom she's now in bliss. (Dobson and Wells 419)

The epitaph offers a (gendered) model for Susanna's character as being witty, intelligent, and perhaps most importantly, like her father. From the beginning of the novel, Susanna is constructed as an active reader and storyteller. Indeed, once she is in London, her father acknowledges her as a superior reader of his own plays. The following exchange exemplifies this, but also draws on an autobiographical model of writing for Shakespeare, and confirms the connection between father and daughter suggested by the epitaph:

> "I think your kings are like poets. Richard [II] is paralyzed. He is so enthralled with the idea of kingship that he can't act like one. And his very inaction leads to his downfall. But Prince Hal has a different problem. He's so busy acting unkingly that he can't see his true nature, which is to abandon youthful folly and be a king. Or a poet, in your case."
>
> Her father was impressed, nodding his head slowly at her critique.
>
> "Susanna, you are wise beyond your years."
>
> "I am my father's daughter," she said simply. (Hassinger 176–77)

This exchange, however, while encouraging critical reading of the plays (but limiting it to autobiographical reading), also has Susanna herself denying autonomous intelligence as inherited from her father. This takes the notion of likeness to an extreme where any remarkable insight or knowledge is attributed *to* such likeness.

Throughout the novel, Susanna is constructed thus: physically active, but intellectually passive except where she has inherited wit from her father. Extrapolating a model of reading Shakespeare for the implied reader, then, the juvenile female is arguably encouraged to read the plays in order to learn more about the playwright and engage with superior language, but not necessarily to learn more about themselves, or to take up an active discursive or critical role in the public/critical sphere. Susanna's primary cultural activity throughout the novel is the appreciation and singing of devotional music, a distinctly aural and oral activity when compared with the literate occupation of her father. Indeed, the split between literacy and orality is emphasised by a music instructor: "Read it?" he said with a hint of impatience. "I want to know if you think you can sing it" (Hassinger 280). This is clearly opposed to the literacy she acquired only to understand a comment of her father's: "mind the books," [Shakespeare] admonished them. "The future of the race depends on them." Susanna, intrigued, took that to mean that they contained some secret information and was determined at an early age to learn to read, so that she could decipher them" (158). It must be noted however, that while Susanna is literate, she gains little benefit from her literacy throughout the novel. Although she is an approved consumer of Shakespeare's plays, she does not engage in a reading process that accrues cultural capital nor cultural authority.

Following the febrile death of her brother, Susanna decides to travel to London in order to spend time with her father, and to resolve feelings of guilt and grief. Unlike Judith in Tiffany's novel however, Susanna does not cross-dress in order to travel to London. Although she wishes to be a singer, and knows this is a profession for men only under English law, she nonetheless maintains her gendered identity. Travelling alone as a woman, however, leaves her open to sexual danger, and she is almost kidnapped by a vagrant man until a carriage arrives and rescues her. The carriage is owned by Emilia Lanier (née Bassano) and they travel together for a visit to Lord Hunsdon's estate where Susanna masquerades as Lanier's maid, and falls in love with Tom Cole, a chorister who is performing at the estate. Having found a situation in which she can travel safely as a female, Susanna has no need of cross-dressing, and so never experiences her culture (even temporarily) as a male. It is also worth noting that although she wishes to see her father's London life, unlike Julia in the Blackwood novels, or Judith in Tiffany's text, she has no desire to perform on the London stage. Hence, she poses no threat to the gendered circumstances of the theatre world, nor to existing categories of gender or gendered behaviours.

Certainly, Emilia does not appear to offer any alternative notions of feminine behaviour. Hassinger focuses on Emilia's musical ability and sexuality, effectively the discourses of identity which Susanna embraces. The novel also implies what several critics since A. L. Rowse have vigorously debated: that Emilia Lanier is the "Dark Lady" of Shakespeare's *Sonnets*. Sonnet 147, "My love is as a fever, longing still", is cited briefly when Susanna discovers drafts of poems on her father's desk (Hassinger 200), but beyond noting that the poems she reads offer a "rather bleak" view of love, Susanna's greatest problem seems to be "reconciling the poem with the Will and Emilia she knew" (200). Clearly then, the sonnet is about Lanier, and the scene thus reinforces an autobiographical model for Shakespeare's creativity; more importantly, it also reduces Emilia to a poetic device.

If Hassinger did not depend on maintaining a space between the feminine and the literary, Emilia Lanier might have offered a strong model for Susanna in terms of negotiating between expectations of feminine behaviour and an independent intellect. Emilia is, I believe, more characterised than Shakespeare is in the novel, functioning as a maternal mentor, but with less direct reference to historical fact. Hassinger focuses primarily on the details of her life which fit the novel's model of femininity, primarily her sexuality. In doing so, Hassinger replicates the work of critics like Rowse, whose interest in Lanier is as the possible sexual object and other of the *Sonnets*, and the historical lover of the Lord Chamberlain, Henry Hunsdon: "When the girl was got with child she was married off . . . The child she bore was called after the Lord Chamberlain, Henry—as he had been called after his mother's lover, Henry VIII" (Hassinger xl). Because her symbolic function is to affirm Shakespeare's status as "even more than normally heterosexual, for an Englishman" (Rowse, *Homosexuals* 46) in her capacity as the "Dark Lady", Aemilia Lanier cannot be a poet. For her to take up the pen would, in a manner potentially threatening to constructions of Shakespeare's sexuality, masculinise Lanier or at least undermine her femininity. Thus for Hassinger, as for Rowse, Lanier's function must only be that of lover, not writer.

In fact, of course, Lanier was herself a published poet. In 1611, *Salve Deus Rex Judaeorum* was published in London, and in it:

> Lanyer is beginning to work on and within the image of the professional author, an image evolving in literary culture at the time she wrote, and that her project is an attempt to reshape that emerging role as a woman writer . . . *Salve Deus Rex* Judaeorum is a carefully-structured and organised attempt to put together the discourses of patronage, encomium, religious verse, defences of women, and the evocation of nature in a new way (Purkiss, *Renaissance* xxxiii–xxxiv)

In the poem, Lanier notes "That outward beauty which the world commends / Is not the subject I will write upon" (Lanyer ll.185–86), as

> 'Twas beauty bred in Troy the ten years' strife,
> And carried Helen from her lawful lord;
> 'Twas beauty made chaste Lucrece lose her life,
> For which proud Tarquin's act was so abhorred;
> Beauty the cause Antonius wronged his wife,
> Which could not be decided but by sword;
> Great Cleopatra's beauty and defects
> Did work Octavia's wrong, and his neglects. (Lanyer ll. 209–16)

This kind of direct engagement with the cultural history of constructing women, and her appropriation of a public, literary voice are actively effaced by *Shakespeare's Daughter* in favour of a Rowsian construction and objectification. It is this objectified Lanier who is established as a kind of role-model for Susanna, not Lanier the innovative poet.

As with the cultural containment of Emilia Lanier, Hassinger offers a romantic plot for Susanna which carries her around the margins of the theatre world, but never inside it. She falls, like *The Tempest*'s Miranda, in love-at-first-sight with Thomas Cole, a Catholic chorister. While a shared passion for music strengthens the bond between Susanna and Tom, he is unlike her in being able to move between the worlds of theatre and music. When he goes to Shakespeare's theatre looking for Susanna, he is co-opted to help during a rehearsal and performs well enough that Shakespeare makes him an offer that is never extended to Susanna, "[i]f your singing ever fails you, you might want to have a try at the theater" (Hassinger 213). Thomas also outstrips Susanna in his combination of skill as when he is able to apply his musical insight to Shakespeare's verse: "[t]he rhythm of the speech in tension with the meter . . . it's what gives such range of expression" (217). Where musicality is linked with sexuality for the feminine (Emilia and Susanna), it provides insight and cultural fluency to Tom Cole.

A case could be made, in fact, that Tom's mere interpersonal interaction with William Shakespeare marks him as special in the novel, as the playwright is almost irrelevant to the development of either the plot or the protagonist. The unknowing reader could be forgiven for coming away from the novel with almost no sense of Shakespeare's cultural significance. In and of itself this is not necessarily a problem, but when Hassinger's own dependence on (and appropriation of) Shakespearean capital is borne in mind, the author's withholding of such knowledge seems to be a political choice. So, for example, Susanna provides the inspiration for another of Shakespeare's great heroines, Miranda, but the reader is given little information about the play beyond basic plot points. Even where Shakespeare's model of writing is constructed as autobiographical, no real understanding of the play's plot is rewarded, and beyond the notion of falling in love with the first man she sees, the correspondences between the play and life are less about Susanna-Miranda, than Prospero-Shakespeare. Similarly little reader competence is rewarded regarding the significance of including characters such as Emilia Bassano or Lord Hunsdon. It seems that Shakespeare is present as a character almost entirely for marketability, as Hassinger ignores all historical evidence and imagines an idyllic future for Susanna singing in Italy with her beloved Catholic Tom by her side. There is no sense—even in the limited fashion of Tiffany's novel—that Susanna has experienced a vibrant, culturally valuable Shakespeare in London and then had to return to her domestic life in Stratford; she seems to have no sense of London at all. Rather, in a move that exemplifies the limited deployment of Shakespeare throughout the novel, Hassinger ignores completely the historical record of Susanna's marriage to the physician John Hall in Stratford, sending her to live 'happily ever after' in Italy instead. Hassinger therefore rejects the very historical context he appropriated in using Susanna Shakespeare as a character, but does not do so in order to critique ideologies of gender nor agency, but to mask (and thus, arguably, affirm) them via fantastic plot resolution.

Given that, unlike the other novels I am reading in this chapter, Hassinger uses a third-person narration focalised through Susanna, readers are encouraged to simultaneously identify with Susanna as a subject and also to participate in the patriarchal gaze that naturalises her subordination: the novel encourages feminine readers to participate in a vision of feminine reading as aberrant. The reader participates in, and is made the subject of, the reinscription of a limited and limiting model of femininity connected with Shakespeare and his work, as can be seen when Susanna exempts her father from paternal responsibility, in explaining to her sister:

> "Our misfortune is to have a poet for a father, Judith," Susanna said. "He doesn't see the world the way most men do, nor his children like most fathers. He is airy when he needs to be solid and sulphurous when he ought to be sweet. He is all tied up and backward when he should be straightforward. I deeply do not understand him. And yet I can only tell you that he loves us." (Hassinger 245)

Just as Susanna avoids the consequences of trying to be a professional female artist in England by travelling to Italy, Hassinger avoids the issue of constructing a feminine reader of Shakespeare by making the playwright and his work almost peripheral in a teenage romance plot thinly veiled as historical fiction. Hassinger has constructed a cultural model in which reading Shakespeare's plays is all well and good, but the central priority for young women is, and should be, finding a romantic partner who will render such reading irrelevant. Shakespeare's personal authority within the novel is limited, but his cultural authority is associated with this model of feminine subjectivity, indeed appears to originate it.

The novels I have read here offer a variety of gendered cultural formations, with examples of both male and female protagonists, written by both male and female authors. Given the variety of combinations, it is disappointing that in all cases, the feminine reading position both intra- and extra-textually offers at best a limited or temporary engagement with Shakespeare, both as a character and a significant literary figure. Perpetually bound up in patriarchal models of paternity (both literal and symbolic) and cultural inheritance, these novels perpetuate the privileging of a public, patrilineal model of Shakespearean cultural inheritance which was overtly deployed in the nineteenth-century appropriations considered in Chapter 1, but do so covertly and via their narrational strategies encourage the juvenile reader both to participate in and approve of the model.

Judith and Susanna Shakespeare are limited as figures of identification insofar as no twenty-first century girl can occupy their position, even via reading, in the ways that contemporary child readers might theoretically or symbolically occupy Widge's position. Nonetheless, their bearing of the Shakespeare name might seem to offer some legitimate participation in the discourse of "Shakespeare". In imagining Judith and Susanna as protagonists, however, Tiffany and Hassinger suggest that Shakespeare must literally or symbolically reject his domestic, Stratford life in order to lead a successful theatrical, London life. In other words, to be an author, Shakespeare cannot be a father. Even further, these authors disingenuously depict the girls themselves as the originators of this model, and encourage via narrational strategies the implied reader to identify with, internalise (even, in the extreme, to co-construct) this logic of cultural exclusion. In the Blackwood trilogy, readers would have to identify with Widge, and to thus accept or even endorse the exclusion of Judith and Julia, to participate in Shakespearean subjectivity. In Tiffany and Hassinger's novels, to identify with the protagonists is to be excluded from Shakespearean subjectivity.

While exclusion of the feminine from the stage can be seen as historically accurate, the cultural work such exclusion is made to do moves beyond authenticity into the realm of patriarchal propaganda. Authenticity does not seem to impinge on fantasies about masculine alignment or co-production with Shakespeare, but is quickly called up in order to explain, but not take responsibility for, a social vision that may have an historical aesthetic but is unavoidably speaking to and about its moment of production as much if not more so than its moment of representation. Thus, where masculine readers are encouraged to recognise and ultimately appropriate the cultural authority of Shakespeare, feminine readers are encouraged simultaneously to recognise both the cultural value of Shakespeare and his work, and the extent to which their own natural distance from it is authorised *by* that value. Shakespeare, as figurative and literary subject, is constructed in terms of gendered development; and behind all these lessons looms the cultural capital of "Shakespeare", pressed in to the service of patriarchally normative values, exemplifying and enacting the notion of author and authority. In these novels, Shakespeare can function as cultural but not biological father.

Chapter Three

"Be These Juggling Fiends No More Believed": *Macbeth*, Gender, and Subversion

> Linda Stevens, Year 5 student from Broke Public School, revelled in the opportunity that Shakespeare presented to her to deal with real life situations. "Inside you have these feelings, like anger, but you don't want to say them because if you did, people mightn't like you. But, being a witch (in *Macbeth*), you can say those feelings." (Lane 6)

Linda's response to Shakespeare's *Macbeth* raises two central points for this book: one is the relationship between reading/literary consumption and real life, the other is the question of what is speakable for young people (particularly girls) and how the authority to speak is created or maintained. *Macbeth* seems a highly unlikely narrative for children as the genre of Renaissance tragedy is counterintuitive to contemporary constructions of childhood innocence: the only figures within the play with whom a child can literally identify are either killed (Macduff's son) or witness their father's murder (Fleance) and the surrounding plot and themes (violence and the supernatural) appear unsuitable for children. Nonetheless, the play has been appropriated by a number of authors, most often in texts concerned with child protagonists engaged in some form of rebellion or subversion against their social surroundings. From this perspective, the play's concerns with socio-cultural hierarchies, gendered subjectivity, power and authority, and aberration subordinated to a sense of 'restored order' make it conceptually available to the ideological goals ascribed to children's literature. Indeed, given that "there is a sharper conflict between good and evil and a different mix of morality, politics and individualism in the tragedies than in the other plays" (Stephens, "Not" 29), *Macbeth* offers a range of tropes and plot-points useful for authors constructing a normative world-view. The play's gendered taxonomy of subversion and containment is transferred into contemporary children's texts as gendered models of reading:

feminine subjects are allowed a limited sense of cultural subversion, aligned with passive reading praxes; masculine subjects are offered a self-reflexive model of reading that enables long-term cultural power.

Contemporary children's authors take advantage of the normative closure inherent in *Macbeth*'s generic mode. As a tragedy (compared with the comedy and romance plays read in later chapters) its very genre produces a *temporary* point of identification for its viewer/reader. Williamson argues: "*Macbeth* concludes with a single ideological orientation through which the cultural problem of violence and other contradictions peep, to be sure, but the end seems to be a victory for natural, virtuous, legitimate sovereignty" (149). Further she believes the play suggests the "healthy state is one in which the patriarchal family may flourish; the patriarchal family becomes a site of nostalgic longing for a civil society" (164). Appropriations of the play combine these thematic concerns with its generic function of "effecting through pity and fear the purification [*katharsis*] of such emotions" (Aristotle 10) in its audience. Genre and gender come together in the appropriations I am reading, and serve to reify temporary identification and normative conclusions as reading praxes: the child protagonist (and reader) identifies with a character from *Macbeth,* but their development is predicated on rejecting or transcending that identification by the end of the novel. Where Isaac suggests that "[i]nstead of focusing on Macbeth and Lady Macbeth, most of these authors concentrate their literary revisions on the witches" (78), I am arguing that appropriative focuses depend on gender *and* genre for their shaping. Where a feminine protagonist/reader is constructed, it is certainly true that the witches are emphasised (as in Konigsburg, discussed below), but when a masculine protagonist/reader is produced, the Macbeths are just as likely to be constructed as central. Whether the witches and Lady Macbeth (always negative models of femininity) or Macbeth are produced as points of identification, it is the negative feminine that must be rejected. These trajectories will be explored through texts with either masculine or feminine protagonists, and will be finally tested by a novel that constructs *both* genders via alternating protagonists: Welwyn Katz's *Come Like Shadows* (1993).

Macbeth's thematisation of gendered identity has long been noted by critics: Lady Macbeth and the witches are marked as aberrant not only by their own challenges to normative femininity, but also by their subversive manipulations of Macbeth's understanding of his own masculinity (see, for example, Adelman; Callaghan; Schiffer; Stallybrass). If a reader identifies with Macbeth himself, the play can be seen as a cautionary tale about masculine subjectivity. Macbeth is introduced to the audience as an ideal who excels in the categories of masculinity prescribed by his culture:

Cap. For brave Macbeth (well he deserves that name),
Disdaining Fortune, with his brandish'd steel,
Which smok'd with bloody execution,

Like Valour's minion, carv'd out his passage,
Till he fac'd the slave;
Which ne'er shook hands, nor bade farewell to him,
Till he unseam'd him from the nave to th'chops,
And fix'd his head upon our battlements.
Duncan. O valiant cousin! worthy gentleman!
(Shakespeare, *Mac.* 1.2.16–24)

Indeed, Duncan's valuation of Macbeth is such that Ross reports "His wonders and his praises do contend / Which should be thine, or his" (1.3.92–93). Macbeth's valued position, however, although gained through the sanctioned violence and nationalism of his culture, is effectively negated when Duncan disrupts the existing homosocial order by instituting a patrilineal rather than tanist system of royal inheritance.[1] In naming Malcolm "Prince of Cumberland" (1.4.39), Duncan denies Macbeth's previously legitimate claim on the throne, and in extension, his privileged masculine status. More significantly, Macbeth himself further undermines his own gender in failing to sustain autonomy in the face of challenges, both linguistic and behavioural, from aberrant women, most obviously Lady Macbeth and the witches.[2]

The feminine characters are constructed by the play as marginal, dangerous, unstable and, perhaps ironically, as unfeminine. The witches,

> are dangerous because they refuse to obey the dictates of patriarchy—they are unreliable, like Fortune (their language is a bewildering mixture of interrogative formulations and slippery pronouncements that, once articulated, cancel themselves out) and they assemble on the heath, away from the household, the domus, and the seat of masculine authority. (Burnett, "Fiend" 9)

As the witches' aberrance is marked primarily by physical and linguistic ambiguity, Lady Macbeth's aberrance is marked by sexuality and language. She has, of course, become a kind of cultural shorthand for the dangerous woman, "the embodiment of the witch woman, a woman of tremendous appetite with a great hunger for power" (Holbrook 165) who wields 'unnatural' influence over a man. Her suicide is, like the witches' eventual disappearance from the play, a form of symbolic cultural containment of the aberrant feminine. Contemporary children's appropriations strip the play of ambiguity in favour of using the witches and Lady Macbeth as symbols of aberrant femininity which *need* to be controlled or contained. Most insidiously, the feminine reader is encouraged to become self-controlling and self-containing: fundamentally, self-policing.

Neil Arksey's *MacB* (1999) constructs an implied masculine reader encouraged to identify with Macbeth but who, rather than repudiate that identification, must repudiate the feminine influences 'responsible' for Macbeth's downfall. Arksey appropriates the plot of Shakespeare's play and modernises it as a football story. Hence, the novel opens with two young footballing friends, Banksie and MacB (Banquo and Macbeth), who each dislike the captain of their school football team, Duncan King. The parallels with Shakespeare's play are immediately obvious, and facilitate a gendered moral fable. *Macbeth* also informs understanding of character relationships, and helps to discern what is appropriate and what is inappropriate within these relationships. Within this context, gender codes of *Macbeth* are never interrogated, but are rather imported with the plot and re-articulated as the natural order. The title of Shakespeare's play is never named by the novel, and the only time "Shakespeare" is mentioned in the novel, it is to be rejected by Banksie. When the police remove him from class to interview him about youth violence, Banksie does not mind as the class are "doing Shakespeare" (Arksey 81); the reader may be encouraged to reject Shakespeare consciously while subconsciously absorbing the plot of *Macbeth.*[3]

The opening chapters of the novel show Banksie and MacB functioning as an effective football-playing pair involved in a "ragtag game on the heath" (Arksey 1). This opening, which observes "the two of them together tight as a drum" (3) emphasises the masculine focus of the novel (particularly in comparison with feminised opening of Shakespeare's play) and the homosocial relationship between MacB and Banksie. The production of sport as an expression of legitimate homosociality and codified violence is nothing new, and the football field simultaneously provides a substitute for the political field in Shakespeare's play and justifies the literal marginalisation of the feminine. As Messner notes,

> modern sport is a 'gendered institution.' That is, it is a social institution constructed by men, largely as a response to a crisis of gender relations in the late nineteenth and early twentieth centuries, . . . a homosocial world, with a male-dominant division of labour which excluded women [. . . and] has played a key role in the construction and stabilization of a male-dominant, heterosexist system of gender relations. (16)

This sidelining of the feminine extends to the narrative itself, as Arksey's novel tends to erase or efface the feminine and the supernatural as feminised; elements central to *Macbeth.* Arksey constructs a world in which masculine and feminine cultural identities are almost completely separate.

The feminine in the novel is divided between characters who represent the witches and Lady Macbeth. However, where the play symbolically aligns Lady Macbeth with the witches on a continuum of feminine power, Arksey renders the witches ineffective and exaggerates his Lady Macbeth character to monstrous proportions. Thus, where Callaghan suggests that "at the start of the play the tragic heroine is firmly aligned with the witches who lead her husband to perdition. In fact, by seventeenth-century standards, not to mention those of the statute of 1604, prior to her hysterical somnambulism, Lady Macbeth is a witch" (358–59), in Arksey's novel 'Lady Macbeth' is frankly evil, and the witches are powerless.

Banksie's elder sister Shanice is coded as the first witch, and her friends as her coven. Throughout the novel they bring news to Banksie and MacB, although this knowledge is gossip-based rather than supernatural in origin. For example, when they tell MacB that he has been selected "to play up front with Duncan King" (Arksey 31) they have simply heard the news before the boys; similarly when they 'warn' MacB about his impending defeat, they are actually reading from a magazine's horoscope column (101). Their serendipitous information performs a function more appropriate to a chorus than to seers; thus, although they are paralleled with the witches, Shanice and her friends have no actual power beyond the ability to outsmart and humiliate MacB. This mimics the relationship between MacB and his mother, as will be explored later, but it also quickly reveals Arksey's erasure of any supernatural elements present in Shakespeare's text.[4] The girls make no prophecies, but play on MacB's insecurities to control his behaviour: "Then go visit the fortune teller. Go on, if you're so fearless. I *dare* you" (11). Although the fortune-teller identifies herself as 'Hecate', and offers predictions about who will gain the captaincy of the football team, she is safely confined to a tent at the fair: as with the witches in *Macbeth*, her agency is dependent on the males' behaviour.

In comparison with the symbolic disempowerment of the witches, Arksey's Lady Macbeth figure, rendered here as the terrible mother, is clearly and consistently revealed as manipulative and dangerous. MacB's mother, Mrs MacBride, embodies the infamous anti-maternal claim made by Lady Macbeth:

> . . . I have given suck, and know
> How tender 'tis to love the babe that milks me:
> I would, while it was smiling in my face,
> Have pluck'd my nipple from his boneless gums,
> And dash'd the brains out, had I so sworn
> As you have done to this. (Shakespeare, *Mac.* 1.7.54–59)

The sustained characterisation of Mrs MacBride as a monstrous mother willing to sacrifice her son, reifies Lady Macbeth's rhetoric, and exempts MacB from responsibility for his actions. Where Shakespeare's Macbeth could be criticised as unmanly for not adhering to the general tenets of honourable masculinity prescribed by his society, here Mrs MacBride is shown to be wholly transgressive of her maternal role. In this sense, Mrs MacBride is inscribed as the true criminal of the piece and MacB as complicit victim.

The centrality of the relationship between MacB and his mother and the extent to which his development is codified through football reveal that the novel is concerned with the process of 'becoming a man', and uses

Shakespeare's *Macbeth* as a reverse-role model: MacB must avoid the pitfalls of aberrant feminine influence to which Macbeth fell prey.

As in Shakespeare's play, the relationship between the Macbeth figures is revealed via discussions of gendered identity. Readers experience most of these exchanges through the (moral) eyes of Banksie; the third-person descriptive language creates a space for the reader simultaneously to identify with MacB and maintain some moral distance from his actions. The first exchange reveals the extent to which Mrs MacBride has gained total control over her son by articulating his failure to fulfil the maturing process as she has defined it. In the following exchanges, masculine identity is linked explicitly to father-son competition, public physical achievement, and the feminine gaze as measure of approval:

> "What happened to 'I'm going to be captain'?"
>
> "I am. I am going to be."
>
> "Not if you don't score goals, you're not. Not if you don't get picked for a proper match."
>
> "Give me a chance! I told you . . ."
>
> "*No*!" Mrs MacBride's tone silenced her son.
>
> Banksie shivered.
>
> "*I* am telling *you*." Mrs MacBride's piercing dark eyes had Mac skewered to his seat. She advanced. "I want to be *proud* of my son. I want you to make something of yourself. And I know you have it in you to do so. You're *not* your father. I say those things about you, because I want to make sure you don't turn out like him."
>
> . . . Mac's head dropped. "I don't want to be a disappointment to you," he croaked.
>
> "Then *don't* be." Mrs MacBride touched the back of his neck. "Show me what you're made of, what you're *really* made of. Be a *man*." (44–45, original emphases)

As with Shakespeare's *Macbeth*, the major cultural weapon at the female's disposal is normative masculinity, and their interlocutor's failure to live up to its requirements. The extent to which these discussions are sexualised in Shakespeare's play is unsurprisingly erased in Arksey's novel. Rather, the power dynamic is refigured in psychological terms, enacted primarily via comparisons with the absent father. Mrs MacBride is here Lady Macbeth as single-mother, filtered through contemporary sensibilities of the Freudian family-romance.

Spurred on by his mother's denigration, MacB performs the transgressive acts of Macbeth, with the significant difference that death is transformed into serious injury. So, MacB organises for Duncan King to be injured, and in his place takes on the role of team captain. When it seems to MacB that Banksie is getting too skilled on the football field, he arranges for Banksie to be beaten up. While this correlates with Arksey's relocation of events to an adolescent environment, it also facilitates the erasure of the supernatural in the novel.

For example, Banksie's reappearance at a football match after he has been hospitalised by MacB's 'foot soldiers' (Arksey 128–29) reproduces the psychological impact of Banquo's ghost appearing to Macbeth (Shakespeare, *Mac.* 3.4.40–106) but removes the supernatural connotations. After causing injury to team mates, and using his mother's money to hire thugs, MacB eventually admits his transgressions. His confession defers responsibility to his mother, and consequently removes him from her control:

> Mac shrugged. Suddenly, he ducked and broke lose [sic] from his mother. "Guess!" He laughed. "Guess where the money came from!"
>
> "Don't listen to him!" shrieked Mrs MacBride. "He's sick! Don't listen to him!"
>
> "Mummy darling!" Mac grinned. "You look after me, don't you?"
>
> . . ."Shut *up*!" shrieked Mrs MacBride. "Everything I've done, I've done for you!"
>
> "Motherly love!" Laughed Mac. "All for me!"
>
> . . ."You are *stupid*!" Rivulets of mascara ran, like black tears, down Mrs MacBride's cheeks; her lank, bedraggled hair clung to her face. "But worse," she shrieked, struggling to make herself heard over the downpour's roar, "you're *gutless*. I didn't just give you the money, I gave you *fire . . . I gave you the strength to do the things you had to do.*"
>
> Banksie watched Mac's face twitch.
>
> Mrs MacBride pushed her son. "So when I say shut up, you DO IT." (132–33, original emphases)

The *denouement* of the novel is constructed as MacB's triumph over his domineering mother. He is ultimately led off the field by male police officers, thereby entering a masculine discourse of authority from which his mother is entirely excluded.

The ending reduces *Macbeth* by implication to a moral fable about the maintenance of "hegemonic masculinity" (Connell), in the face of aggressive and/or manipulative women. Where, in the Shakespearean text, the resolution of Macbeth's aberrant subjectivity comes in the form of his death, and the (albeit tenuous) restoration of acceptable social order, MacB is integrated into a normative patriarchal society having learned the lesson Macbeth failed to. Banksie may see the defeated MacB as "something pitiful, stumbling through the mud" (Arksey 137), but the reader can imagine a productive future for MacB now that he is independent of his mother.

As well as appropriating the plot of *Macbeth,* Arksey thus reinscribes, and naturalises, the discourses of gender which are present in Shakespeare's text, even exacerbating the disempowerment of the feminine. "Shakespeare" is used to authorise a model of subjectivity for the juvenile masculine reader that is dependent on rejection of the feminine, and a simultaneous acquisition of privileged knowledge.

Jackie French's Australian novel, *Macbeth and Son* (2006), is explicitly concerned with masculinity as a state of honourable actions and ideas. Unlike Arksey's text, *Macbeth and Son*, rather than a rejection of the feminine, enacts a transcendence of the feminine via masculine bearing of privileged knowledge. The novel alternates between chapters from the perspective of Lulach, the son of Gruoch who was not present in Shakespeare's play, and Luke, a young man growing up in rural New South Wales. The historical chapters are framed as truth, and are experienced by Luke as dreams. Historical events operate as a text in competition with Shakespeare's *Macbeth* for Luke to assess his own behaviour and context.

Each of the boys is dealing with a stepfather whose actions have the potential to influence and shape the boys' own codes of conduct. Lulach quickly learns that Macbeth is an honourable leader who complicates notions of war, and functions as a role-model of ideal masculinity: "But warriors didn't run. Or did they? There was more to the art of warfare, he realised, than holding a broadsword" (French 42). Lulach's development into an appropriate future leader of his clan in turn functions as a template for Luke's development into a mature male. Luke's moral crisis is not one of war, but is of honour nonetheless as he realises that his stepfather has turned him into an academic cheat, providing Luke access to an entrance and scholarship exam for a boarding school before taking it. Initially, Luke rationalises his participation in the cheating: "he hadn't really cheated, he told himself. Cheating was when you meant to do it. How was he to know that the exam paper would be one he'd seen before?" (27). One might suggest that the real problem Luke is facing is the lack of an appropriate masculine role-model after the death of his own father.

Luke is studying Shakespeare's *Macbeth* at school, and treats the play as an escape from his own life, "*Macbeth* was another world, four hundred years away from his problems of lies and cheats" (French 70). The play initially seems to expound a moral code relevant to Luke's problems, "Shakespeare seemed pretty sure about lies, at any rate. Evil people like witches lied, Macbeth lied. Good guys like King Duncan told the truth" (93). This dependence on literary text mirrors Lulach's increasing faith in written texts:

> Lulach had learned to read fluently these past few years. The laws that the people of Alba had brought over from Ireland were fascinating. Law was what protected the powerless, and made sure each person had equal access to land and care when they were sick. The law laid down how criminals should be punished. What other nations, Lulach sometimes thought with pride, had laws like these? (French 126)

The novel constructs these legal texts as both privileged and worth fighting for; in comparison, Shakespeare's play as moral text begins to fail as Luke realises that the historical events he has witnessed in his dreams are also about Macbeth. Luke's moral consideration of honesty and lies now shifts from the content of

Shakespeare's play, to the conditions of its production. Just as Lulach's reading is morally valuable, Luke wants his consumption of Shakespeare to be morally valuable: "The real Macbeth had been a hero, just like in his dream. Then Shakespeare had written a play, making him a villain" (112). Although his teacher states, "Luke, you keep using the word 'lie'. Fiction isn't a lie. A lie is when you deliberately change things" (117), this reasoning is obviously too close to Luke's own justifications for cheating, and thus do not suit his requirements.

Shakespeare's play is "brilliant", but is critiqued for not being "brilliant *and* true" (French 117). This is the core of the problematic cultural politics at the heart of the novel: Shakespeare is inherently valuable, particularly as a vehicle for keeping Macbeth's name in the cultural imaginary, but is devalued for being false. Luke's personal development is initially aided by reading Shakespeare's play, but is ultimately is indexed by telling the truth, both about his own cheating and Shakespeare's misrepresentation of the historical Macbeth. Although asked to give a class presentation about Macbeth's descent into villainy, Luke instead gives a speech about Shakespeare's misrepresentation of history, and concludes that: "Some things are important. Some things are worth fighting for. Truth matters. Because if we don't tell the truth we don't just cheat other people. We cheat ourselves. How will we live if we don't know what's true, or who to trust?" (198). This noble gesture, both on the part of Luke and the novel as a whole, is in and of itself not offensive, but the politics it is used to shore up might be. I suggest this, not because the novel constructs Shakespeare as playwright rather than historian, such a claim is patently obvious. Rather, the sub-plot of the novel, revolving around ownership of land is potentially dangerous in the Australian context.

The over-arching cultural agenda of questioning representation and trusting one's own experience is itself problematic given that Luke experiences Lulach's life in his dreams, but might be seen as valuable in the context of international politics (a context which is only briefly referred to) at the time of the novel's production. French stages a mini-debate between Luke's schoolmates:

> "Those Iraqis," said Jingo. "They're all terrorists, aren't they? Get rid of the lot of them."
>
> "Why? Aren't we supposed to be liberating them? How can you nuke someone and liberate them at the same time?"
>
> Luke grinned. He knew Megan really meant it. She wasn't just showing off back at Jingo.
>
> "It was all a lie, anyhow," said Megan, shoving her hair out of her eyes. "All that stuff about the weapons of mass destruction." (French 90)

This exchange is exemplary of the novel's attempts to link the broad questions of truth and lies to real-life events. However, Megan—who here is a truth-teller—later constructs a narrative about Australian history that the novel not only does not question, but implicitly identifies as true: "People talk about how Aboriginal people are close to their land,' said Megan vehemently. 'And they are. But we've been here for a hundred and seventy years. It'd kill Dad to have to stop farming here" (152). Just as, for Luke, there is no grey area in Shakespeare's use of history, the novel offers no grey area to think about non-Indigenous settlement of Australia. For all the novel's posturing about Luke's moral development, and the importance of truth and untruth, it nonetheless offers a range of simplistic moral positions which are endorsed as absolute truth. This is emphasised by the "Author's Note" which appears at the end of the text, where French writes:

> Historical fiction is a window to the past. But it has to be as true as you can make it—not a historical lie. When you write historical fiction you have a responsibility to slip your fiction into the cracks in the historical record, not change history for your own ends, unless you make it clear that this is what you're doing. (218)

Nonetheless, one might suggest that French has herself changed history for her own ends. Where Lulach's development is towards being as great a leader for his people as Macbeth, Luke's development is towards a romance plot (with Megan), the admission of cheating, and towards being an author: "I'm going to write a play about Macbeth one day. But a true play, not a lie" (208). And here, the reader is returned to questions of authorship and authenticity: Shakespeare is great but a liar, Luke may be good one day but is a truth-teller. Despite the novel's clear dependence on Shakespearean cultural capital for its structure and content, it seems vexed about Shakespeare's use in contemporary Australia. Perhaps just as Shakespeare has given Macbeth cultural longevity, but Luke has saved Macbeth's memory, Shakespeare also gives the novel cultural status, but the novel attempts to save Macbeth's memory. In any case, Luke's personal development depends on the acquisition and expansion of privileged knowledge. In the projected case of Luke writing his own play about Macbeth, he arguably takes up Shakespeare's position, and plans to morally (if not necessarily artistically) trump him. Luke's own legitimacy is affirmed by Lulach telling of a dream *he* has had:

> "I promised I'd tell the truth. And I did. I got up before my friends and I told the truth. It doesn't seem like much of a battle, does it? Not as glorious as fighting the English. But just as hard. Because there was only me to fight it. Just one boy. I didn't have an army on my side." (211)

One might suggest that this is indeed making personal use of history. The telling of truth is removed from the realm of Shakespeare (because truth in this novel is about literal events, for the most part) and awarded to two boys who are on the path to mature masculinity. Each of them must learn to respect but reject their mothers as inappropriate role-models, and embrace the ideal masculinity embodied by the historical Macbeth. Although their romantic interests identify each of them as heterosexual, the novel is barely concerned with the feminine, except as an intermittent counterpoint to the masculine. Megan may offer an interesting account of Shakespeare's Lady Macbeth, when she suggests to her class that:

> "Lady Macbeth wasn't evil, . . . She was trapped. It was her duty to help her husband, who was too much of a coward to do what he wanted without her pushing him into it. Like him, she was trapped by the witches. But most of all, she was trapped by the time she lived in." (193)

However, Megan's claim is immediately trumped by Luke's presentation, not only in terms of audience appeal but in the sense that Luke is committed to dismissing all Shakespearean representation: it really does not matter if Shakespeare's Lady Macbeth is evil or not, as she is a misrepresentation of, "the calm, the dutiful Queen Gruoch" (189). Luke's superior knowledge of Shakespeare as historically inaccurate renders Megan's critical insight irrelevant. Outside the classroom, although Megan has been a political agitator throughout the novel, she is contained as Luke's romantic partner by the novel's conclusion. Similarly, both Lulach's and Luke's mothers are increasingly marginalised until they are effectively absent. This novel is concerned first and foremost with the development of appropriate masculine maturity.

The strangeness of *Macbeth and Son*'s use of Shakespeare is best captured by one of the few moments at which Shakespeare's play is directly quoted. During Macbeth's penultimate battle, Lulach hears lines from Shakespeare's *Macbeth*:

> "*I will not yield, To kiss the ground before young Malcolm's feet* . . ."
> Who said that? thought Lulach vaguely. Was it the King?
> Clash, parry, clash . . .
> "*And damn'd be him that first cries, 'Hold enough!'*" (French 176)

Presumably the reader is expected to recognise these as Shakespearean lines, and is perhaps even invited to compare the desperate last stand of Shakespeare's Macbeth with the noble battle French depicts for the historical Macbeth. It is indicative, I think, that French here seems to rely on shared Shakespearean knowledge, but depicts it as both inaccurate and irrelevant to historical events. A generous reading might suggest that Luke's dreams are more fantasy than history, but the reader is made privy to scenes about Lulach which bracket the novel, and which are not perceived by Luke; but these scenes' consistency with the other representations of Lulach would not seem to invite the reader to question their accuracy. Perhaps the novel as a whole cannot evade Shakespeare's portrait of failed or challenged masculinity being as important as the idealised masculinity presented as historically true to the dominant understanding of Luke's developing maturity and masculinity. If so, masculinity is conceived as a dialectic between Shakespeare and history rather than as a term defined relationally with femininity. Where Shakespeare constructed a binary, French seems to efface the feminine almost entirely from her understanding of masculinity as an autonomous state of being.

In comparison with Arksey and French, Kate Gilmore's *Enter Three Witches* (1990) features a masculine protagonist who literally lives with witches, and who must—rather than reject the maternal/feminine—reconcile it as part of his identity. That said, the novel nonetheless figures such reconciliation as ascendency *over* the feminine, a taking-up of authority based on a superior gaze (knowledge) and physical strength. Where Arksey's novel featured pre-adolescent males, Gilmore's protagonist Bren is firmly adolescent, and the drive of the novel is its romance plot. The secondary plot (also romantic) is a staple of adolescent fiction: Bren's parents are separated, and he would like them to reunite. Unusually, the parents acknowledge continuing feelings for each other, making this dream of Bren's attainable. Each of these plots revolves around, and is resolved by, symbolic and real witchcraft. Although the text focalises through multiple characters throughout, the developmental focus is on Bren West and his ability to reconcile witches with his family life. Where romance plots for feminine readers revolving around *A Midsummer Night's Dream* operate as means of containing independent young women, in Gilmore's novel, the romance plot offers the masculine protagonist a measure for growing independence and maturity.

The novel is set in contemporary New York, and Bren lives in a feminised space with his mother, grandmother, and two elderly female lodgers. It is revealed early that his father left the home because of his inability to cope with a house full of magic: Bren's mother Miranda, grandmother Rose, and a lodger Louise LeReine, are witches, and the second lodger Madame Lavatky, is a retired opera singer. Immediately, then, Gilmore establishes a world in which fantasy is reality; here there is no need to make-over witchcraft as Arksey must, and witchcraft provides a contemporary register of femininity that is conflated with the theatrical and the carnivalesque throughout the novel. Bren's mastery of his mother is a form of mastering himself, and he is, as a result, able to enter a romantic relationship. Mastery is not rejection (as in Arksey), but control over and responsibility for.

Bren's school is putting on a production of *Macbeth*, and he has volunteered to work on lighting the show. The play is identified as a witch-play throughout Gilmore's novel, and when Bren tells his family about the production, the real witches he lives with establish the text's treatment of Shakespeare's play:

> "What play?" Miranda asked.
>
> Bren hesitated. "*Macbeth*," he said finally.
>
> "Oh, Lord, not old bubble, bubble, toil and trouble," Rose said. "What a bore. They'll get it all wrong." (Gilmore 13)

As this discussion continues, it is revealed that neither Bren nor his father have actually read the play, but the witches all have, and Miranda eventually pronounces that "Shakespeare was full of wonderful witch lore and witch language" (14). Throughout the novel, *Macbeth* is discussed so consistently in relation to witches that an unknowing reader would not be aware the witches only appear in three scenes. The play's production thus produces a site where Bren can symbolically control feminine elements in his life: his family's literal witchiness, and his prospective girlfriend's independence (she is aligned with his mother by playing a witch in the play).

That the site of this progress is "Shakespeare" *may* add symbolic weight for the reader to Bren's achievement, but the novel produces a vexed mode of Shakespearean consumption. Very little reader competence is provided of the play's content; the few scenes described either include the witches, or are inaccurate. So, for example, the "wife of Ross, hotly pursued by a murderer [catches] her foot on a strut projecting from the tower of her castle" (Gilmore 152); similarly, the drama teacher misquotes "I'll unseam you from the navel to the chops" (146) but is never questioned.

The production creates a shared public space where Bren, his mother, and Erika can negotiate their roles; but the availability of the play itself to juvenile readers is called into question by the focalised judgements of the director, the school's drama teacher, Mr Behrens. During rehearsals, the reader is told that "Edward Behrens spent the hours after school in the cafeteria trying to persuade his young cast that the words of Shakespeare expressed the passionate lives of people as real as themselves. It was uphill work" (Gilmore 91); and again, later, that he has come "from a disheartening rehearsal of his principal actors, who, it seemed, were simply too young to convey or even to understand the primitive evil that informed the black history of Macbeth" (119). Even as the novel privileges "Shakespeare", then, it constructs Shakespearean language and themes as inaccessible for young readers/actors. This symbolic space though, of the theatrical, the carnival, and the linguistic (the feminine), gives way in Gilmore's novel to the theatre as technical/scientific space, and in this masculinising of the theatre Bren is able to develop. Alongside Mr Behrens's concerns about his young cast not having the capacity to understand *Macbeth*, the novel also highlights technical concerns such as how "would the witches disappear into thin air or Banquo's ghost come and go in the crowded banquet hall?" (91).

Bren initially knows nothing about stage-lighting, but in his first experience with the equipment, he immediately learns the power of controlling people's gazes, and first sees the girl whom he will court throughout the novel. Bren and his friend are initially focussed on the technical equipment in the lighting booth, so that "[n]either of them bothered to glance out the long window that ran across the front of the booth, giving a view of the stage where a slim girl in a leotard was dancing in the cold, gray light" (Gilmore 21). Thus the young woman is made the object of the reader's gaze before she is seen by the boys; however, their attention *is* drawn by her "banshee howl of rage" (21) when they switch the stage lights off. Having noticed her, Bren states that he wants "to watch that skinny girl for the rest of my life" (22). Bren learns that her name is Erika, and she is playing the First Witch in the production. Even as he admires her, Bren is conscious of the extent to which witchcraft pervades his life: "It had to be witches, didn't it? And even the immense distance that separated the ladies of his house from Shakespeare's savage grotesques did not seem great enough" (25).

Having organised a date with Erika to attend a dance recital, Bren feels that he is having some success despite the witches who surround him. However, this date emphasises the extent to which the novel aligns the feminine (consistently supernatural power) and the theatrical. The dance concert is one of the two key sites of establishing the relationship between the gendered gaze and control over the theatrical/carnival. In his attendance, Bren is symbolically maturing and rejecting his mother. The abstract ballet invokes a kind of pre-linguistic understanding for Bren that marks this 'rebirth' and which is masculinised: "There was no story, or if there was, it was one his bones and blood had known before he was born—one his ancestors had known in the firelight that pushed back the dark at the mouth of the cave" (Gilmore 71). However, Erika is clearly the authority on the form as she produces an appreciative but critical reading of the performance that is in opposition to Bren's (feminised) emotional response: "If Erika said to herself, Perfection; every move is perfect, every tiny angle of wrist and toe, of neck and shoulder and knee, Bren thought, Magic. Enchantment" (71). Subconsciously then, Bren links the dancing to his witch family while Erika appreciates it on its own terms. Thus the space remains feminised, and Bren in fact eventually leaves because his mother is able to psychically call him away from the date. This reified version of maternally-induced guilt, the 'call', forestalls his date as Bren fakes a headache and abandons Erika. Clearly he has not matured away from his mother too far, as there is "one clear channel of his mind that was always open to her" (74).

Similarly, Bren fails as lover when he takes Erika to see the Halloween parade in New York; initially, this is a location of authority and superior knowledge for him as he has grown up in the city where Erika is a newcomer. He is able to explain the geography of the city, and 'guide' her through the parade which is overtly carnivalesque. Bren is marked as secure in his masculinity by his acknowledgement of the beauty of drag-queens (Gilmore 132), and experienced by his recognition of participants in the parade from earlier years. However, his authority is completely undermined by the presence of his mother *in* the parade. She is described as having an explicitly powerful gaze as she stares at the spectators:

> Miranda wore black from head to toe, the simple splendour of her robe broken only by a girdle of golden serpents. Her fair head was crowned

> with dark laurel leaves. In her right hand she carried a staff encircled by runes of power and in her left the shining, black-hilted athemé. No broom or pointed hat for Miranda, but hardly anyone in the crowd could have doubted that she was a genuine witch.
>
> It was clear, at least to Bren, that Miranda was having a lovely time. She cast stern, piercing glances from side to side; it would only be a matter of seconds before her eyes fell upon her only son and his unsuspecting date. (Gilmore 134)

In order to avoid his mother's gaze, Bren abandons Erika again. This time, however, his abandonment has dangerous connotations, as Erika is left wandering the night-time streets of an unfamiliar city. As she tries to find a train station, Erika encounters Bren's romantic rival, Jeremy. Although she does not like this boy and has a miserable time with him on Halloween, Erika nonetheless flirts with him during rehearsals in order to make Bren jealous. An actor tells Bren that Erika "sits in a corner with a book except when Jeremy wants her for something . . . to hand him props or whatever" (Gilmore 149). This information precisely coincides with Bren making numerous mistakes in his lighting of scenes and delaying a rehearsal. Crucially, this romantic competition takes place backstage rather than onstage, reflecting the novel's move from the artistic (feminine) to the technical (masculine) sphere as central. Bren's own technical abilities are indexed to his relationship with Erika. After they reunite, the reader is told that the "reconciliation with Erika had, he felt, transformed him utterly from a wretched, miserable incompetent into someone strong, brave, and confident in the exercise of his craft" (180). The language use here clearly identifies an appropriation of power and authority on the part of Bren, who even more explicitly realises, "I have my own witchcraft now, he thought with a wry smile, but mine is real. I've got calluses and a couple of burns to prove it" (184). This would appear to suggest that his mother's witchcraft is not 'real', and in orchestrating the audience's gaze towards the witches on stage, Bren symbolically appropriates control over the feminine (both his mother and girlfriend) and individuates himself.

His new maturity is further represented by his physical defeat of aberrant witchcraft that saves his mother. Alia, the new girlfriend of Bren's father, is "a woman scorned and a thwarted witch, [who is] furious [and] dangerous" (Gilmore 205). Throughout the novel she functions as the 'wicked stepmother' familiar throughout children's literature. Eventually, her rivalry with Miranda causes Alia to overtly challenge the more experienced witch. When she attempts to perform a spell to destroy Miranda, Bren stops Alia through physical intervention when he seizes her arm "twisting it behind her back" (207), and 'saves the day'. This enables the reunion of Bren's parents, and his own reconciliation with Erika (whose 'return' to patriarchal family structures is symbolised by her willingness to reconcile with her father). 'Real' masculine (technical/physical) craft is rendered superior to 'unreal' feminine witchcraft.

If Gilmore illustrates the transcendence of the feminine witch figure by the masculine subject, E. L. Konigsburg notionally offers the reader that same trajectory from the feminine perspective, but in this case, the reader is expected to identify *with* being controlled, rather than symbolically acquire authority. Konigsburg's *Jennifer, Hecate, Macbeth, William McKinley, and Me, Elizabeth* (1967) tells the story of a girl who must reconcile her difference in order to develop a confident and independent identity.[5] Elizabeth's quest culminates in the articulation of a subjectivity that recognises and accommodates the extremes of two role-models, without mindlessly mimicking or being entirely dependent on either. One girl, Cynthia, is an idealised figure, approved of by the adult culture's perception of childhood; and the other, Jennifer, whom Elizabeth admires as a rebellious and independent child, must be rejected due to her extended commitment of subversion, and her racial identity.

The moral subtext of the novel is clear: 'worthwhile' people are both confident in their own identity and capable of establishing and maintaining strong friendships *within* the context of their culture. The novel focuses on the relationship between Elizabeth and Jennifer, a relationship mediated by *Macbeth,* witchcraft and, crucially, race.

The novel's opening line, "I first met Jennifer on my way to school" (Konigsburg 3), establishes the first-person narration, Elizabeth's focus on her relationship with Jennifer, and the liminal space this friendship operates in, between school and home. Both Elizabeth and Jennifer are constructed as outsiders, but their difference originates in different ways. Elizabeth is attending a new school, and is the only child of hard-working parents with little money. Hence, Elizabeth is on her way to school on Halloween, wearing a costume that she inherited from a cousin and which "was only a little short, and only a little tight, and only a little scratchy where it was pinned, and it was only absolutely uncomfortable" (7). Though Elizabeth is alienated due to her economic status, she is not necessarily isolated as she notices that "after checking over [my classmates'] costumes and shoes, I decided that at least three of them had cousins who had been Pilgrims the year before" (9).

In comparison, Jennifer's alienation is a product of racial difference. As the only Black student in a White school, Jennifer is easily and permanently identifiable by her classmates as Other. Significantly, this fact is hidden from the reader until someway into the novel. Jennifer's race is only mentioned when Elizabeth recognises "Jennifer's mother because she was the only Black mother there. She looked as normal as mine" (Konigsburg 56). It would be easy for a White reader to be pleased by Elizabeth's seeming race-blindness; however, this blindness extends to Elizabeth's ignorance of the fact that where her own otherness is circumstantial, Jennifer's is permanent.

The idealised child against whom each of them is measured is Cynthia, who is held up both by teachers and Elizabeth's mother as a role model. However, as 'outsider' Elizabeth is privy to Cynthia's fundamentally flawed nature, and her wilful manipulation of adult perceptions.

> Every grown-up in the whole U.S. of A. thinks Cynthia is perfect. She is pretty and neat and smart. I guess that makes perfect to almost any grown-up . . . It didn't take me long to discover that what Cynthia was, was not perfect. The word for what Cynthia was, was mean. (Konigsburg 11–12)

When the ideal girl is White, wealthy, and well-behaved, it is unsurprising that Jennifer constructs an identity for herself that is marked by language rather than physicality as a way of appropriating cultural authority. Jennifer clearly subverts the 'Cynthia-model' when she identifies herself as a witch, rewrites American history, and informs Elizabeth at their first meeting that:

> Witches convince; they never argue. But I'll tell you this much. Real witches are Pilgrims, and just because I don't have on a silly black costume and carry a silly broom and wear a silly black hat, doesn't mean that I'm not a witch. I'm a witch all the time and not just on Halloween. (Konigsburg 6)

From this point on, Elizabeth views Jennifer as a repository of secret knowledge and power. She willingly agrees to become Jennifer's apprentice, and they establish at this point a clear (albeit temporary) hierarchy for their relationship. Elizabeth's admiration for, and interest in, Jennifer is not just informed by their secret meetings in woods and parklands, but by Jennifer's refusal to accept Cynthia's dominance.

As Elizabeth develops confidence, Jennifer becomes less authoritative, although she attempts to retain power by giving Elizabeth a promotion to "journeyman witch" (Konigsburg 76) in order to justify setting down complicated rules or 'taboos' for Elizabeth to live by. Nonetheless, Elizabeth accepts an invitation to Cynthia's birthday party, a social space that Jennifer is emphatically excluded from. Jennifer attempts to maintain some control over Elizabeth by instructing her via a note to "Give Heed!! While at the party / Be on awares / Do not eat cake / Or play musical chairs" (82). While Elizabeth would appear to be negotiating between her approved and disapproved friends, this party nonetheless marks a symbolic rejection of Jennifer as authority and an appropriation of explanatory authority on the part of Elizabeth herself:

> After I had told Cynthia "yes" and after I had received this permission from Jennifer, I was glad that I was going to the party. I enjoyed getting mad at Cynthia. I also thought that it would be fun to tell Jennifer all about how ordinary girls act at a party; (83)

Jennifer's authority is further undermined by her symbolic fatherlessness, and Elizabeth's recognition: "I somehow knew that she mentioned the potion just to stop me from thinking about her father. I enjoyed knowing without letting her know that I knew" (Konigsburg 93). This pleasure in 'knowing more' than the African-American subject demonstrates the covert racism that informs the text overall, and ameliorates Elizabeth's otherness.

Recognising that she is losing power, Jennifer attempts to inscribe authority permanently by invoking Shakespeare's *Macbeth* as a master-text of witchcraft. For her, the play functions as a discrete and authoritative discourse of power wielded by the disenfranchised; although she initially cites *Macbeth* as justification for including a toad in her potion, the citation quickly evolves into proof of her superiority over Elizabeth.

> "Witches always have toads," she answered. "Toads are the first ingredient." She paused a second, looked up toward the sky and said, "What's the matter, didn't you ever read Macbeth?"
>
> "Well, no," I said, "I've heard about Macbeth."
>
> "Every modern witch ought to read Macbeth," Jennifer said. "Those witches cooked up a wonderful brew. Not flying ointment brew. Trouble brew. And the first ingredient to go in was a toad. (Konigsburg 95)

When Elizabeth takes a simplistic view of the warnings the witches offer Macbeth as 'being nice', Jennifer takes offence and corrects her: "It wasn't nice," Jennifer insisted. "How can you be a witch and be good, too? The two just don't go together" (Konigsburg 96). Their different readings of the play demonstrate their differing dependence on being a witch: what is a game for Elizabeth is a serious attempt at retaining autonomy in the face of exclusion on the part of Jennifer. Ultimately, Jennifer's authority is as limited as her citation of the play. That she only ever uses 'witch scenes' and is unwilling to provide specific details may indicate a lack of specific knowledge:

> "They told [Macbeth] the truth in such a way that he got to feeling too sure of himself. He became careless and brought about his doom."
>
> "What did they tell him?" I asked.
>
> "I won't tell. You have to read Macbeth. Every modern witch should. Those witches were wonderful."
>
> "Give me an example," I begged. "Please?"
>
> "I'll give you an example of the kind of thing they did." (96–97)

This use of Shakespeare appears simultaneously to mark cultural capital while also limiting it on the part of the very character who introduces the playwright to the novel. In her inability to 'cite' Shakespeare extensively, Jennifer is made complicit in her own subordination as she is unable to maintain power over Elizabeth. Jennifer calls into being the very structures of marginalisation and disenfranchisement she originally sought to challenge via identification with the witches. In comparison, Elizabeth performs her independence when she articulates her dislike of Cynthia, the approved girl child:

> "Mother," I said, "if you really want to know, I'll tell you why. Cynthia is a phony. I've known for a long time that she's a phony. And worse than that, she doesn't know she's a phony. She believes in Cynthia. She's a serious phony. And the only way I can stand her is to absolutely ignore her." (Konigsburg 112–13)

In this rejection of adult expectations Elizabeth claims authority and exorcises the otherness which contributed to her alliance with Jennifer. The novel concludes with the lesson the girls have learned: In the final line, Elizabeth states that, "Neither of us pretends to be a witch any more. Now we mostly enjoy being what we really are . . . just Jennifer and just me . . . just good friends" (Konigsburg 117). The reader could be forgiven for forgetting by this point that these girls 'really are' raced *and* gendered subjects whose access to Shakespeare has been limited to the symbolic and transitional. The very contingency of the witches' lives in *Macbeth* offers a clear point of identification for two young girls who feel disenfranchised, but the novel makes clear that they must accept or reconcile this disenfranchisement, rather than embrace it as a means of power.

Even as Elizabeth must become self-regulating, she recognises the value of that self-regulation: Not only does she participate in a discourse of cultural authority, but this participation marks her superiority over one who does not understand authority as it should be. In Konigsburg's cultural hierarchy, White femininity is above Black femininity, and this hierarchy is ironically reinforced by the very discourse of knowledge and temporary subversion to which the Black feminine introduced the White feminine. The African-American child figure is, here, responsible for the tools of her own exclusion and oppression.[6] In concert with this, the fact that in regulating the other one is also regulating the self means that the novel possibly foregrounds the acceptable regulation of the other as a culturally efficacious and convenient mask for the broader cultural project of regulating the subversive feminine generally.

The figure of the self-policing feminine subject is also present in Catherine MacPhail's *Another Me* (2003), which tells the story of Fay, a young Scottish woman who discovers that her mother is committing adultery at the same time as she herself has been cast as Lady Macbeth in a school production of *Macbeth*. The novel is fundamentally concerned with a romance plot, but is elaborated through the trope of the "fetch" (MacPhail 118) or *doppelgänger*. Fay believes that she has a double invading her life and personal relationships.

The sense of the doubled female self is clearly a psychological response to Fay's belief that she has discovered another mother, one who is cheating on her husband and daughter and therefore leading two separate but linked lives. In turn, Fay reads her own burgeoning sexual identity through the lens both of her mother's adultery and Lady Macbeth's madness. Initially, Fay's response to the play is hatred (MacPhail 8), and frustration: "It was the 'beautiful words' I had the most trouble with. Why couldn't they just talk like real people?" (42). Soon, her dislike of the play focuses on the role she is to play: "I don't think I like this Lady Macbeth very much . . . She's a nag. She's horrible. She wants her husband to murder somebody" (57).

As Fay increasingly believes that her own double is taking over her life, she stops disliking the play, and even begins viewing Lady Macbeth as a sort of role-model. As her anxiety about her life and identity increases, she even engages in self-harm that references but does not replicate Lady Macbeth's hand-washing:

> I wouldn't listen to this anymore. The letter opener was on the desk in front of me and I grabbed it. "Well, from now on you will definitely know when it's me!"
>
> I dragged the sharp end right down my hand. Droplets of blood fell like rubies on to the desk. My blood. (MacPhail 106)

Fay's identity crisis is resolved via normative sexuality when Fay forms a romantic relationship with a school-friend, Drew, and Fay's mother abandons her adulterous relationship to ensure Fay's health. A school teacher informs Fay's mother that Fay is undergoing intense emotional stress as a result of family tensions. Fay's response to her mother's return to a normative family is one of both relief and denial: "She'd given him up for me. Forever. Because some daft teacher had made her believe that I was having delusions because of her affair, because I couldn't face her leaving. That was rubbish" (MacPhail 136). An insightful reader may not be convinced by Fay's claim of this development being 'rubbish', particularly as the return of her mother to the family home coincides with the novel's use of *Macbeth* being transferred to Fay's love interest, Drew. When Fay is returned to a normative family setting, she no longer needs nor desires engagement with Shakespeare: She no longer is Other to her setting.

Despite an early disavowal of Shakespeare, Drew has developed a liking for *Macbeth* and identifies the "Life's but a walking shadow" soliloquy as his favourite lines (MacPhail 125). Just as Shakespearean language and ideas are transferred to Drew, so too is the authoritative, interpretive gaze. It is Drew who offers the solution to the disappearance of Fay's double: "I think, you were meant to die in that lift . . . End of story. A portent of your own death. And yet, in a strange way, she actually saved your life" (173). Where Fay's involvement in *Macbeth* only feeds her emotional or psychological problems (makes her into a stereotypical Lady Macbeth), Drew's superior understanding of the play allows him understanding of Fay's life that is unavailable to her.

But perhaps it is unfair to examine too closely MacPhail's use of Shakespeare's play in her novel. Beyond a convenient plot device for facilitating the text's romance plot, it is unclear why *Macbeth* specifically is referenced, beyond its provision of a culturally authoritative lexicon for feminine aberrance and/or madness, or perhaps the fact that *Macbeth* is set in Scotland. Fay's own final perspective concerns romance rather than Shakespeare, as she notes: "The Christmas disco was before me, and a holiday in Majorca. And Mum and Dad together. Forever" (MacPhail 174). Just as her mother has been returned to an acceptable domestic/familial role, so too is Fay willingly entering a normative feminine position, one which is marked as much by romance as it is by distance from Shakespeare.

The symbolic connections with the witches and Lady Macbeth deployed by Konigsburg and MacPhail are rendered as actual interactions in Caroline B. Cooney's *Enter Three Witches: A Story of Macbeth* (2007). This historical novel is variously focalised through three young women whom Cooney imagines living in various homes of the Macbeths during the period recounted by Shakespeare's play. These three girls, Swin, Ildred, and Mary, all occupy differing social positions, and therefore offer a range of insights into the society of *Macbeth*'s Scotland. In addition, Fleance and Seyton occasionally function as focalisers, usually when the issue at hand is violence. The society is represented as violent, dangerous to women, and in need of order.

Mary is the novel's protagonist: she is the daughter of the traitor Cawdor, and has been made the ward of the Macbeths. Her most important lessons in the novel deal with the choosing of an appropriate husband, and to recognise Lady Macbeth as a poor role model. Although Mary admires Lady Macbeth, and is indeed "wearing a gown discarded by Lady Macbeth" (Cooney 4) when the novel opens, she shares qualities or experiences with characters familiar from Shakespeare's play. So, her thumbs are often "pricking" (13), which seems to act as an alarm when Mary is near dangerous men, and intriguingly: "Mary looked back at the chair. Banquo was still there. He had acquired color and form. But he did not breathe. Banquo, dead and drenched in blood, sat in the seat of the King" (176). While it may be possible to read these gestures as simply rewarding reader competence, the effects of refusing Lady Macbeth, the witches, or Macbeth, focalisation (and therefore reader identification) but rewarding their clothing, physical experience, and perception to Mary arguably confuses rather than clarifies meanings. This is made particularly clear when Mary seems to combine all three of these positions towards the end of the novel: "Mary's thumbs pricked. She lifted her thumbs to her eyes, to see what was happening to her poor hands, and it made her eyes prick as well, like brambles in the brain" (208). Of course, as figure of reader identification in a young adult romance plot, Mary cannot (apparently) actually occupy any of the arguably powerful positions of the Macbeths; instead, she is positioned as an observer (and occasionally, victim) of the events and characters of Shakespeare's play. By the end of the novel, Mary is married off to Fleance, and is therefore interpolated in Scotland's future monarchy, but does not acquire any autonomy. Throughout the novel, Mary is observer rather than agent; if she challenges the *status quo* it is only for the greater good. Even so, the novel forecloses both Mary's vision and limited agency by its conclusion.

The plot follows Shakespeare's, but although Mary is active in smuggling Fleance into Dunsinane so that he might instigate a rebellion amongst Macbeth's remaining soldiers, and disguises herself and her friend, it is Fleance who achieves a violent defeat of Seyton (who functions as a personal nemesis equivalent to Macbeth's oppression of Scotland): "he shoved the sword forward into Seyton's gut until Seyton, trying to get away, fell backward rather neatly into the coffin of Lady Macbeth" (Cooney 274). Not only is Fleance rewarded with physical victory, he acquires personal and cultural authority over Mary when, despite her determination to "watch the duel between a wicked king and a doomed thane" (273), Fleance "protects" her from seeing its conclusion. Just as Macbeth's decapitation takes place offstage in Shakespeare's play, Mary—notionally the protagonist of the novel, is denied the observation of this event even as it is offered to the reader: "He pulled her close to his heart so she would not see Macduff yank the sword out of Macbeth's heart, then chop off the man's head. The deed was done" (276). The newly-crowned Malcolm gives Fleance permission to marry Mary at the conclusion of the novel.

Cooney engages, in a note at the end of the text, in the familiar authorial enterprise of noting that "Shakespeare's *Macbeth* isn't history and isn't fact. It is drama, and it is tragedy" (279), in order to justify her own rewriting of the story. Nonetheless, she appropriates Shakespeare's cultural capital throughout the note (and indeed the novel), and although she denies her own protagonist any cultural authority or agency, she encourages readers to, "[n]ow read Shakespeare's *Macbeth*" (280). I am not convinced that this brief extratextual instruction is enough to counter the extended, thematised denial of feminine knowledge or agency (except romantic) that characterises the novel which preceded it. Given that the novel is historical fiction, it would be anachronistic to depict Mary as the bearer of twenty-first century feminist ideas, but as with the novels discussed in Chapter 1 , implicit commitment to so-called authenticity does not seem to disallow reimagining masculinity (Fleance here is bordering on being a Sensitive New-Age Guy), but apparently cannot enable reimagining femininity.

These gendered trajectories—the masculine to individuation, the feminine to subordination—merge in Welwyn Winton Katz's *Come Like Shadows* (1993). This Canadian novel for young adults is set in contemporary Stratford, Ontario, and revolves around two adolescents involved in a production of *Macbeth* for the Stratford Shakespeare festival. The novel engages metafictionally with *Macbeth* as a narrative of historical and literary meaning, offering the reader perspectives on the ways individuals engage with (Shakespearean) artefacts of meaning. The central teenagers, Lucas Cormier and Kincardine (Kinny) O'Neil, are involved in a production that appears to be plagued by the notorious *Macbeth* curse. In resolving this curse, each of them connects, literally and symbolically, with the figures of Macbeth and the witches who become problematically gendered role models. Kinny and Lucas alternate as focalisers of the story, rapidly demonstrating that the masculine view is perceptive and objective, while the feminine is associated with emotive subjectivity, and instinctive rather than rational thought.

There are two competing discourses of "Macbeth" present in this text, and associated with them are accompanying conceptions and characterisations of gender which appear to compete, but which actually collude to reinforce one another. The two discourses can most simply be described as 'Art' and 'History' (somewhat in the vein of French's novel) and are embodied by, and filtered through, the figures of Macbeth and the Witches whom the text engages with historically *and* textually. Their adolescent analogues, Lucas Cormier and Kincardine O'Neil, embody and enact the tensions between these discourses in the contemporary plot.

The Shakespearean artefact deployed has an obvious existence and identity as the well-known Scottish play, but the historical discourse is established when Katz opens the novel with an imagined encounter between the 'actual' Macbeth and the 'actual' witches. Under the guise of an imaginary past, Katz constructs her historical protagonists—the witches and Macbeth—as representative of opposing forces in eleventh-century Scotland, and imbues them with very specific characteristics and associations in order to establish a binary gendered discourse that is maintained throughout the novel. This initial encounter not only offers an alternative portrait of Macbeth to that offered by Shakespeare, but also establishes clear paradigms of gender identity and authority which are used throughout the text to test the legitimacy of Shakespeare's *Macbeth*, the strength of the contemporary characters, and the legitimacy of various appropriations of both Shakespeare and history.

Hence the novel opens with an event focalised through Macbeth as he seeks the witches. Reader identification and sympathy is created for Macbeth via his memory of being "fifteen years old and fleeing his father's murderers through the darkness" (Katz 2). Macbeth's view of the witches enforces reader sympathy and establishes the *novel's* view of the witches, one which rests on a gendered binary reinforced throughout the text:

> The three witches had often offered him help during the seventeen years of his reign. He had never accepted. He didn't trust them; their magic was old and dark, nothing to do with enlightened men and their laws and duties. (4)

Thus Macbeth and the witches are identified as representatives of their respective genders and the values those genders imply.

Macbeth is a patriot who is seeking the witches in a desperate attempt to save his country from English invaders. They refuse to help him as they are performing a spell to ensure their survival: they are not individuals, but identities that need to be embodied in order to exist. The three witches rotate through the roles of maiden, mother, and hag, until the last becomes too decrepit and must find a new young body to inhabit. The witches explain to a young woman that when the spell,

> *. . . is done I will be Maiden, and the other Maiden will become the Mother. And the Mother will be—*"
>
> "She will be me. She will be Hag."
>
> "And what will happen to you?"
>
> "*There are only three Sisters. Your body will contain one of them. It is what the ceremony achieves. A blending, more or less.*" (Katz 127)

This mode of existence sharply contrasts with Macbeth's determined individualism. Although he feels that Scotland is lost, Macbeth attempts to save the girl (whom he views as a symbol of his land) and is drawn into the spell himself. The result being that he and the hag are trapped within a mirror together.

The novel now transports the reader (and the mirror) to seventeenth-century England and refocalises the narrative from the Hag's perspective. She observes a working playwright who is using Holinshed's Chronicles as a resource for his new play, "TH* TRA**DIE *F MACB***. By W'L**M ****SPEAR" (Katz 18). The Hag immediately recognises that the drama is "about the man who shared her own mirror prison" (19). Shakespeare's use of earlier narratives is accepted as standard practice by scholars, but here it is constructed as problematic because it allows the Hag to affect Shakespeare's writing. The Hag knows that history has revered Macbeth as an ideal leader; out of revenge she alters the *Chronicles* so that Shakespeare will be working with her version of history as a source.

The actual process of Shakespearean creation creates a tension in the novel: the Shakespeare at work is an 'ordinary man'. However, the Hag perceives (or presumes) that he has had difficulty accepting Holinshed's idealised Macbeth as evidenced by his much amended draft. Presuming that her own understanding of events is the true understanding, the Hag (as the malevolent feminine) 'rewrites' history and inscribes Shakespeare as having 'extra-human' intuition and knowledge. Within the fictive world of the novel, then, the Hag has become the creative force behind both the myth of Shakespeare and Shakespeare's *Macbeth*, each of which is extratextually authoritative. Importantly, Shakespeare is carefully moved from the discourse of history into the discourse of art, and is thus simultaneously saved from accusations of 'betraying' Macbeth's history and made the subject of supernatural authorship. Once he consults the altered Holinshed, Shakespeare is transformed into the Romantically-inspired author of popular mythology:

> Then he opened up the leather-bound Holinshed, turning to the marked pages. He read, gave an exclamation, and read some more. Then almost feverishly, he pushed aside the Holinshed, picked up his quill and a fresh sheet of paper, and wrote.

> When shall we three meet again? In thunder, lightning, or in rain?
>
> "Whatever happens after this," he murmured happily as he scribbled, "my troth, but it begins well!" (Katz 22–23)

It is here that the book initiates its two visions of Shakespeare; one as great playwright, the other as bad historian. Katz has commented that, "[i]t fascinated me how an artist like Shakespeare could manipulate history to make something work better for him and how then it becomes true, insofar as what most people believe" (Jenkinson 65). Shakespeare is absolved of such manipulation in the novel, because the Hag has altered the Holinshed, and thus the competing discourses of Art and History are gendered as masculine and feminine respectively. This moment of inspiration also causes Shakespeare to write a mirror into the play. This is, of course, the mirror that the Hag and Macbeth have been trapped in; and its inclusion ensures that future productions of the play will require a prop-mirror. Creating a symbol of the connections between the historical and the artistic Macbeth, the mirror becomes the 'magical object' common to children's literature; Osborne notes that the "'truth' is anchored magically in a prop that is itself authenticated by its presence in a Shakespearean play" (L. E. Osborne, "Harlequin" 146).

Just as the opening vignettes offer masculine and feminine focalisation in the perspectives of Macbeth and the Hag, the rest of the novel alternates masculine and feminine views. Crucially, the novel also retains the gendered values of the historical figures in the later sections, so the feminine is aligned with false history, selfishness, manipulation and ignorance, while the masculine is aligned with art, altruism, honesty, authority, and knowledge.

These binary oppositions are embodied by two twentieth-century adolescents involved in a production of *Macbeth* for the Stratford (Ontario) Shakespeare Festival. Lucas and Kinny are the spiritual and symbolic inheritors of Macbeth and the witches, and although they initially share a quest (to solve the 'curse' on the production) each of them must accept their assigned gender roles in order to achieve success. The comparative experiences of the teenagers repeat the trajectories found in the novels discussed earlier in this chapter: Kinny has a temporary relationship with the witches which she must repudiate by accepting a patriarchal model of authority, while Lucas aligns himself with Macbeth and transcends the feminine. At its most basic point, the plot suggests that Kinny must move away from power where Lucas must embrace it. If the reader of this novel identifies with their gendered equivalent, the young masculine reader is encouraged to be questioning of accepted wisdoms and to have confidence in his ideas and perceptions, to appreciate Shakespeare but not to subordinate himself to his work; whereas the young feminine reader is encouraged to identify against her own potential for resistant reading—the novel models a self-undermining feminine focalisation, affirmed by Shakespeare—which could readily be adopted as normative by a reader.

Alternating focalisation encourages readers to identify with, and approve of, these explicitly gendered outcomes, even as it demonstrates the superior gaze of both Kinny and Lucas: They see more than those around them. Notably, however, Lucas is established as the superior observer from early in the novel. While he sees the whole of the "hunchbacked" (Katz 53) woman at the theatre who evades everyone else's perception; Kinny can see only "pair of eyes gleaming pale and cold" (60) reflecting her own gaze back at her: She is of the moment, where he is above it. In extension, the reader is encouraged to depend on Lucas's understanding as inherently reliable, while questioning Kinny's judgement, as she repeatedly does herself.

Even their functions in the theatre enforce these oppositions: Kinny is interned to a director, Jeneva Strachan, who disregards theatrical and real history, where Lucas is an actor with an instinctual understanding of Shakespeare's meaning and value. Comparing this with the privileged off-stage gaze of Bren in Gilmore's *Enter Three Witches*, one might be led to believe that the superior gaze is assigned first and foremost on the basis of gender in these children's texts.

The production is going to be "political dynamite" (Katz 36) because it is being designed to make a statement about British and French-Canadian history and politics: A statement of Strachan's personal, unpopular reading of local history.[7] Although the novel has already dismissed Shakespeare's play as historical *document* it still adheres to the acceptance of the play as historical *artefact*. Any sense of inaccuracy on the part of Shakespeare is here subordinated to the importance of fidelity *to* Shakespeare (exemplified by Katz's awarding of descriptive knowledge of Shakespeare's play, rather than direct citation; protagonists and readers learn language *about* the play, rather than *from* it). *Macbeth* is transmitted as a 'complete' artefact (which extratextually maintains and respects Shakespeare's cultural authority), but the 'space' around the text—origins, transmission, performance, superstition, interpretation—is open for contest and critique.

Jeneva functions very specifically as the transgressive or monstrous feminine embodying the values assigned to Lady Macbeth—"shadows swirled beneath her" (Katz 75)—and her transgression is enacted by her wilful refusal of fidelity to either of the two discourses of authority in the novel: history or Shakespeare.

> "I can cancel the play, if I choose; I can change it; I can drop scenes; I can make it say something about Canada when the playwright barely knew such a place existed. I'm not under the play's control, and neither are any of you. On the contrary, we control it." (78)

Kinny recognises Jeneva's arrogance, but her eagerness for theatrical experience quashes her doubts. Other people involved in the production also have suppressed doubts about Jeneva's interpretive strategy but do not articulate them until things start to go obviously wrong: The production appears to fall prey to the curse of 'the Scottish Play' when an actor is killed by exposed electrical wiring, Jeneva demonstrates her dictatorial nature, and reveals her true interest:

> "The Scottish play isn't just about a man who kills a king and takes his place," Jeneva went on. "It isn't even solely about his motivation—his ambition, his fascination with witchcraft, his dark love for the wife who persuades him to murder King Duncan. I think this is a play about power. Power. Who has it, who wants it, who takes it, who abuses it. And who is defeated by it." (Katz 75–76)

This thirst for power aligns Jeneva symbolically with Lady Macbeth (whose power Jeneva identifies as originating in sexuality (79). This is important because the novel's emphatic loading of masculine and feminine qualities as embodied by Macbeth and the Witches effectively dismisses Lady Macbeth from the play. Of course, Lady Macbeth's character with all its gendered complexity would destabilise the binary model of gendered identity in *Come Like Shadows*. Thus, Lady Macbeth is split between the figure of Strachan, who embodies boundless personal ambition, and Kinny, who endures feelings of guilt, and who is found "wondering if she would ever sleep without nightmares again" (222). In splitting the figure, Katz does not have to reconcile the challenge that Lady Macbeth's evolution poses for the novel's deployment of subjectivity as fixed and inherent, nor its demarcation between good feminine and bad feminine.

While Lady Macbeth may only be present in the text for readers familiar with Shakespeare's play, power is identified throughout as a destructive force when feminised. The witches have too much power, and their primary tool of seduction is the offer of power to the seemingly powerless. When Kinny eventually accepts one of the witches' offers, she unwittingly causes another death: In this case the actor playing Macbeth is virtually decapitated while rehearsing a sword fight.

Kinny is able to communicate with the Hag through the mirror that she has purchased to be used as a prop in the production. Of course, this is the mirror Macbeth and the Hag are trapped in and it throws art and history into sharp relief. Crucially, the mirror also reifies the gendered gaze: Kinny and Lucas not only see themselves but the historical events that opened the novel in the mirror. Their visions replicate the opening narration: the masculine is coded as perceptive and clear, whereas the feminine perspective is coded as unreliable and dangerous. Obviously, then, the mirror also reifies the 'inherent' connections between Lucas and Macbeth, and Kinny and the Witches.

Set against Kinny's unknowing gaze (so unreliable at times that she thinks herself mad) is the intelligent gaze of Lucas Cormier, the young actor who has come to Canada. Although he has minor roles, Lucas dreams of playing Macbeth, a character he reveres:

> there were things Lucas admired about Macbeth. Dullards can commit murder and not worry about it; but Macbeth knew what he was doing and knew what it would do to him, and he did it anyway. That took courage, Lucas thought, and he admired courage, especially when it came from a man as totally alone as Macbeth. He admired his imagination too. And though he didn't admire Macbeth's actions, he could understand what caused them. (Katz 46)

Of course in Katz's novel, Macbeth did not perform these disappointing actions, and Lucas's appreciation for Macbeth's nobility simultaneously confirms, and is confirmed by, the historical Macbeth whose voice opened the novel.

This operates in obvious juxtaposition with Jeneva's disregard for Shakespeare or history, and her actions are countered by Lucas's (I would argue authorially endorsed) understanding of 'acceptable' Shakespearean appropriation:

> A year ago [Lucas] himself had been in a terrific modern-dress *King Lear* set in the Southern US, and once on TV he'd seen a *Henry V* set during the First World War. Both of these had been exciting non-traditional productions that used the plays' truths to make statements about their unusual settings. But Jeneva was trying to do it the other way around. She had her own statement to make, and she was trying to mould the play to fit it. (Katz 93)

Leaving aside the notions of the plays's "truths", the novel makes clear that, like the historical Macbeth, Lucas is insightful and interested in the greater good. In comparison to Kinny, his perspective is characterised by analysis, while hers is characterised by observation, reinforcing the dynamic of masculine as active and feminine as passive.

Given the problematic shift in Macbeth's character in Shakespeare's play, Lucas decides to research the real Macbeth for himself, deciding that "as history, Shakespeare's *Macbeth* was apparently not much more than a pack of lies" (Katz 115). In his unquestioning acceptance of Berchan's account of Macbeth's life, Lucas embodies the novel's overall understanding of the real Macbeth. However, this does not lead him to reject Shakespeare; rather, he splits his understanding of *Macbeth* into the historical and the theatrical. In doing so, he replicates the approach of the novel, providing more evidence that Lucas's voice is privileged by authorial identification. This re-canonises Shakespeare as playwright if not historian, circumventing the Hag's interference and marking Lucas not just as privileged observer but *reader.*

Despite its problems, the production travels to Scotland, and all of the forces of history, art, knowledge, and agency are brought to a head. When their Edinburgh theatre burns down, the company takes a tour of historic sites related to Macbeth; Lucas's connection with Macbeth intensifies, and as Kinny physically approaches the town she was named for (Kincardine O'Neal), she mentally approaches a self-sacrifice to be performed *for* Lucas, one that she assumes will be unknown, and indeed that is deserved: "It wouldn't matter to him that it was something she had brought on herself, something that blood and honour and peace-of-mind and the terror of committing evil in the future all made necessary" (Katz 272). Here Kinny's madness approaches that of a sleep-walking Lady Macbeth. Crucially, Kinny's symbolic identification with Lady Macbeth operates on the spectrum of self-sacrifice rather than ambition: This connects Kinny's actions with Macbeth's self-sacrifice, constructing an approved element in her personality. This of course reinforces the public/private binary of gender relations: Macbeth's sacrifice is for his country and a young girl Kinny's is for a single boy. In other words, Kinny prepares to embrace destruction in an attempt to 'put right' what she sees as her own inherent evil. Such is her inability to analyse coherently at this point that she does not recognise—as Lucas does—that her self-sacrifice will only facilitate the Witches' power rather than contain it.

Lucas's identification with Macbeth also intensifies in Scotland. Katz draws heavily on traditional understanding of the power that place and names can wield, hence the climax of the book takes place at Macbeth's supposed death-site. Unsurprisingly, Kinny and Lucas replicate the circumstances of the opening scene of the novel. Lucas exactly repeats Macbeth's intentions, and attempts to sacrifice himself in order to save Kinny and Macbeth. He is stopped by Macbeth himself, and during this final engagement with the mirror, the reader has reinforced for them the essential natures of both the historical Macbeth and the Hag, in a final endorsement of the roles they have played in the novel, and the gendered lessons they offer:

> Macbeth said sadly, I can never accept your offer. I no longer know the truth of what I am, and I will not find it out in a world I can enter only by dishonour. But I thank you for what you would have done. I thank you mightily. (Katz 301)

> [Hag:] You are a fool, Lucas Cormier. Do you think anything you have done with this mirror has been of your will? It was I who made you see Macbeth and admire him and want to be him, I who had it in my mind all along that you would do what you have done here! (Katz 301–02)

Here the positive masculine and negative feminine are finally boiled down to two statements, in which the masculine is associated with honour and honesty, the feminine with manipulation and dishonesty. Kinny is excluded from the first, and warned against the latter. The conclusion of the novel makes clear that if the protagonist has been Kincardine, the *hero* is Lucas. Her struggle for independence and understanding has not been in vain, for she acquires truths about both life and acting,[8] and has incidentally learned—through experience and example—what constitutes positive femininity. I would argue that the most heavily endorsed trait of such femininity is passivity: both the Witches and Jeneva function as warnings of the dangers of determined assertiveness. In comparison, Lucas's perspective on and understanding of Jeneva's actions and intentions are legitimised by the novel as a whole, just as the historical Macbeth's perceptions of the witches is privileged and borne out by the text as a whole. Via their connections with Lady Macbeth and the Witches, Jeneva and Kinny become obstacles for Lucas's personal development: Jeneva in the theatre, and Kinny in the 'real' world. He cannot simply ignore them, as the protection of the feminine is constructed as an important aspect of masculinity. Jeneva is punished for her disregard for Shakespearean or historical integrity, when she is sacked and censured, and is literally destroyed by her own determination when she replaces Kinny as the sacrifice in the final confrontation between past and present. Jeneva's final speech enacts a classic undoing of a villain: "All I wanted to do was produce my own *Macbeth* in my own way. It would have worked, too, if only *they* would have let things alone. But they had their own agenda, and they didn't let anything get in their way" (Katz 308). Jeneva is ultimately absorbed by the archetypal monstrous femininity she has been participating in throughout the entire novel, and Kinny is saved.

While Kinny is instructed to embrace plurality—"there are always more truths than one" (Katz 318)—Lucas's achievement of maturity is marked through his ability to learn from Macbeth without replicating his fate or, in other words, to maintain the space *between* the 'truths' of the theatre, and the 'truths' of the real: "You will be a great actor one day, Lucas Cormier, but you will never play Macbeth" (316).

Where the Arksey novel offered the narrative of *Macbeth* and French's protagonist identified with Lulach, Lucas offers an example of self-reflexive reading of that narrative. As a result, the masculine reader is given, not just the cautionary tale, but methods for its integration into self-development. Lucas offers, through a process of thematised reading, a model of (limited) investigative reading that appears to lead to informed and autonomous decision making. That this is only really employed to 'save' Macbeth from imputations on his noble masculinity, I would suggest, is highly problematic, but it is worth noting that the juvenile masculine reader is a valorised figure here.

Macbeth fell victim to the Witches, and Shakespeare, in unproblematically accepting the textual authority of Holinshed, also fell victim to the Hag. Their failures are educational for Lucas; yet in splitting his understanding of them between the historical and the literary/theatrical, he is nonetheless able to maintain a broad cultural veneration of these male role-models while not necessarily accepting wholesale the play that symbolically was born of their errors: The play which itself illustrates the danger of listening to transgressive women.

This patrilineal model of cultural authority is precisely that which marks the reinstatement of order at the conclusion of Shakespeare's play and which is enacted by Arksey's novel. Such a model of self-reflexive reading is exclusively offered to the male reader; the female reader is encouraged unproblematically to accept the 'aberrant' portrayals of women in the play as culturally authoritative. Again, they are inscribed as passive objects of cultural formation, rather than active subjects in cultural production.

Kinny's final lesson comes from a wise old woman—Dana, newly liberated from dangerous witchcraft by the Hag's destruction, but nonetheless a questionable authority figure—and emphasises plurality:

> She turned to Kinny then. They surveyed one another, the elderly woman and the young. Neither of them said anything for a long moment. Then Dana gave an abrupt nod. "You are still water, Kincardine O'Neil. You can live on the surface and be safe, or dive deep and begin to discover the truth. But remember, there are always more truths than one." (Katz 317–318)

This didactic message displaces the very carefully constructed dichotomies the novel rests on. However, I would argue that this could be seen as a final protection of Shakespeare. Where the contemporary teenagers could be accused of ignorance and misunderstanding, certain sections of the novel indict Shakespeare's play as a blatant misrepresentation of history: effectively a crime in this world. At the same time, however, *Macbeth* has facilitated the resolution of a centuries-old conflict. Katz is virtually obligated, in order to legitimise her own deployment of Shakespeare as a tool rather than an object of enquiry, to emphasise the possibility of plurality, even as the rest of the novel undermines this concept in favour of essential natures and inherent values. This obtrusively tacked-on 'moral' only serves—through juxtaposition—to emphasise the novel's extremely conservative understanding of gender and culture. Thus, Katz is strangely apt in her claim that, "feminism has no place in my writing (I think that feminism is supposed to promote *equality* of the sexes, rather than *female superiority*)" (Micros 62, original emphasis), although her rationale strikes me as evasive at best: "I just write my characters to be what they have to be, given their initial problems and their need to sort these problems out" (63). This is not just because Katz constructs a world in which 'equality has been achieved', but because *Come Like Shadows* is not only characterised by Lucas knowing more than Kinny, but it appears to rest entirely on the very binary-model of gender relations that contemporary feminism seeks to question.

As is so often the case with "Shakespeare", the Bard proves adaptable both to confirming masculine cultural authority (even when his content is being questioned), and undermining feminine cultural subjectivity (when his content is rendered true and absolute). Appropriations of *Macbeth* for children clearly draw on the models of gendered identity and behaviour present in the play itself, but in simplifying these models contemporary authors (consciously or unconsciously) erase the ambiguities central to the play's construction *of* gender. That Lady Macbeth has become an unproblematic and uncomplicated embodiment of aberrant femininity within children's literature is readily demonstrated by these novels' occasional reiteration of the nineteenth-century model of Lady Macbeth as 'unwifely' or 'unmotherly'; but more insidious, in my opinion, is the deployment of the witches as *temporary* models of non-normative femininity that must be expunged. That young feminine readers are encouraged to be *self*-regulating on this issue, while masculine readers are encouraged to regulate otherness, indicates a deep investment in patriarchal visions of gendered identity.

Chapter Four
Puck vs. Hermia: *A Midsummer Night's Dream*, Gender, and Sexuality

> What happens when the fairy world and the mortal world collide? Disaster! Demetrius is in love with Hermia, who is in love with Lysander, who is in love with Helena, who is in love with Demetrius! Will they ever sort out this mess, or do they need a little help from the fairies? (Bevan blurb)

> . . . there's always something to learn, and if you let yourself get into its spirit, you may learn something new tonight. Remember, *Dream* is about love and theater and especially magic. So get out there and let yourselves be as bewitched as you are bewitching! (Singer 238)

Unlike *Macbeth*, *A Midsummer Night's Dream* does *not* seem counterintuitive as a pre-text for children's literature. Indeed, it appears so amenable to a juvenile audience that Peter Craven has commented, it is "a play that can delight people when they are young; it can be seen as almost a children's version of what Shakespearean comedy has to offer" (R8). Such a view of *A Midsummer Night's Dream* as a children's version of Shakespeare is at least attributable to its comedic, fantastic, and romantic elements. These three sub-plots, which I will be referring to as the actors', the fairies', and the lovers' plots, appear often in children's literature, often metonymically for the play's concern with maturing:

> *A Midsummer Night's Dream* focuses upon different crucial transitions in the male and female life cycles: the fairy plot, upon taking 'a little changeling boy' from childhood into youth, from the world of the mother into the world of the father; the Athenian plot, upon taking a maiden from youth into maturity, from the world of the father into the world of the husband. (Montrose 108)

It is logical then, that *Dream*'s sub-plots are frequently appropriated by children's literature. The exception ironically appears to be the play's framing, or primary plot, that of the Athenian court and the marriage of Theseus and Hippolyta, "the single occasion to which we have learned its four stories are moving" (Brooks xc). This storyline is effaced because it disrupts the idealised version of the play most often presented to child readers as a template for maturation and romantic love.[1] In appropriations of *Dream*, juvenile readers are exposed to the magic of Shakespeare's play, and the value of that magic in their own lives. This exposure is consistently inflected with heteronormative ideals of gender and sexuality.

Montrose's divisions between male and female plots of maturity in the play are useful in that they anticipate the gendered division which children's literature makes when appropriating *Dream*. I am arguing here that masculine readers are offered an active but limited reading position; pre-sexual feminine readers are also offered an active reading model, but for adolescent or potentially sexual feminine readers, the play is used to confine them strictly to conservative models of readership and subjectivity.

Craven's use of "children" clearly draws on Romantic/Rousseauian notions of the child as a receptacle, or the simple creature of nature: seeming simplicity equals childlike equals positive naturalism. Christine Edzard's *The Children's Midsummer Night's Dream* (2001) which, rather than being aimed at a juvenile audience, was performed entirely by a cast aged between eight and twelve years, offers a similar intersection between constructions of the play and children in popular culture. The production company, Sands Films, makes the following claims on its website dedicated to the film:

> Children will come to Shakespeare new, raw, fresh—and innocent. They will be baffled but amazed. To them it will all be new: the delirious inventiveness, the poetry, the "intoxication of words", the constant changes of perspective, the "untamed wildness" of this magical play. All the more so that the children were to come not from drama schools, but from ordinary local schools in Southwark, with their many different backgrounds and cultures, and above all, with no preconceptions about Shakespeare. ("Children's")

Taken with Craven, this film and its foundational notion of a romanticised child-figure, even ignoring the presumptions made about existing institutional education and its links to background and culture (presumptions that deal with cultural and social capital), demonstrate the extent to which visions of the child as object rather than subject are dominant in popular culture.

Mark Thornton Burnett argued of the film that, "because of the primary role of children, a renewed attention to the intricacies of Shakespearean language and situation is afforded" ("Fancy's" 168). Such a reading, although positive, is predicated on a model of childhood as an idealising mirror for adult culture; regardless of Burnett's rhapsodising, there is no space here for autonomous juvenile subjectivity. While it is true that children's literature constructs an ideal juvenile reader, it is nonetheless also true that a real child reader is presumed by the genre. Edzard's film however, like Burnett's reading of it, completely subordinates the child as a component of adult culture. The claim that "[c]hildren are reinstated in the imaginative process in a subversive capacity: an alternative generation of interpreters is given an urgent voice: and a new cinematic clarity and authenticity are celebrated" (Burnett, "Fancy's" 170), enacts adult-to-adult back-slapping, and fails to offer the juvenile subject voice or agency. 'The Child' is a projected image, whose stasis and objectification are justified through conflation with Shakespeare: *Dream* and the Child come each to signify the other.

Literary appropriations of *Dream* for a juvenile audience retain a symbolic link between the play and the child-figure, but presume an active and developing juvenile reading subject who is to be encouraged or controlled depending on the child's gender. Specific sub-plots of *Dream* are explicitly gendered, and offered to an implied reader as a point of identification. So the fairy plot, for instance, is (perhaps surprisingly) aimed at the masculine juvenile reader, where the lovers' plot is (less surprisingly) aimed primarily at the feminine juvenile reader. The play's own deployment of these stories is used to legitimise the production of patriarchal values within contemporary texts: the pre-adolescent masculine reader is constructed as necessarily (but temporarily) dependent on a paternal figure, in anticipation of wielding authority themselves; the adolescent feminine reader is constructed as only being able to liberate herself from a paternal gaze if transferring her dependency to a lover / husband. In one case, an appropriation of the actors' plot *appears* to challenge this binary system of cultural production, but in fact capitulates to the necessary dependence of feminine subjectivity on authority figures.

The court of Oberon and Titania, whose stories make up the fairy plot, is a fantasy realm that is significantly associated with nature and the natural, sexuality, emotion, and mutability. A conflict between the king and queen regarding the guardianship of an "Indian boy" (Shakespeare, *MND* 3.2.375), is affecting nature, and they attempt to resolve tensions created by competing parental and sexual desires. A reader familiar with the binary model of gendered behaviours might then expect this realm to be coded as feminine; however, in addition to the custody battle of the fairy monarchs, the fairy plot is also concerned with the relationship between Oberon and Puck as symbolic filial pair. These two fairies, lord and servant, are the only characters in the play to affect all subplots, in that they instigate the lovers' plot in the woods, and Bottom's transformation by the use of a potion; events which in turn affect the framing plot of Theseus and Hippolyta's wedding-feast. Within the world of the play, the fairy plot is the fantastic made real, and thus allows the exploration of filial and social obligation.

There are obvious ways in which Shakespeare's fairies offer points of identification for a child reader.[2] Fairies other than Oberon and Titania occupy a cultural position of doubled subjugation, in that they are other to the human society, and subordinate within their own fairy court (which mirrors the Athenian court). Physically, the fairies are smaller than the authority figures around them, mildly rebellious and disruptive, and perhaps most importantly in a post-Rousseau context, in and of nature. Socially and physically, Puck at once exemplifies the Shakespearean fairy and functions as an exception to the group: He appears to be more powerful than the other fairies, is central to the plot, and is the speaker of the epilogue. This speaking position attributes him with a position of theatrical power that negotiates the space between the theatrical and the real, just as Puck travels in the space between the human and the fairy in the play. Although he remains subordinate to an authority figure (Oberon), Puck also enjoys a 'first among equals' status among the fairies. This status is exemplified in an illustration by Dennis Nolan: Puck is larger than the other fairies but smaller than Oberon and thus functions as a figure of identification for the implied child reader (see Figure 4.1.). In this sense then, Puck can readily function as a symbol of pre-adolescent children's solipsistic view of themselves within a family (and society): subordinate to but cared for by parents; and lacking social status in the broader society but perceiving themselves as important to all they encounter.

Purkiss argues that despite a feminisation of fairies—a point emphasised by the word's etymology (Warner, *From* 14)—and despite the general perception of the fairy-tale as a feminised genre, Shakespeare's Puck has come to "swallow up all other English fairies, like some multinational fast-food outlet driving the idiosyncratic greasy spoons out of business" (*Troublesome* 173), and is predominantly gendered as masculine. In turn, Puck has become a commonly-used point of identification for masculine pre-adolescent readers in contemporary children's texts. What I am calling 'Puck Syndrome' describes a narrative that inducts implied masculine readers not only into a position of limited autonomy that is circumscribed by Oberon (the Shakespearean father), but also implicitly prefigures future authority for such readers when they become adults. The very qualities that render Puck attractive to a pre-adolescent reader, however, mean that in a standard model of child-to-adult development, the inner-Puck must be repudiated in order to wield authority. Failure to do so results in an end to development (quite literally in one case, as I will discuss below), but Pucks who abide by their Oberon's instruction have implied future success; similarly, the implied masculine reader who absorbs (and respects) the cultural capital and authority of "Shakespeare" can implicitly expect future success.

Figure 4.1 Illustration by Dennis Nolan, *A Midsummer Night's Dream.*

In 1906, Rudyard Kipling made Puck over into an embodiment of English culture and history. In a linked collection of short stories, *Puck of Pook's Hill*, siblings Dan and Una summon Puck accidentally when they perform *A Midsummer Night's Dream* three times over at Pook's (Puck's) Hill:

> The children were at the Theatre, acting to Three Cows as much as they could remember of *Midsummer Night's Dream*. Their father had

> made them a small play out of the big Shakespeare one, and they had rehearsed it with him and with their mother till they could say it by heart . . . Dan was Puck and Nick Bottom, as well as all three Fairies. He wore a pointy-eared cloth cap for Puck, and a paper donkey's head out of a Christmas Cracker—but it tore if you were not careful—for Bottom. Una was Titania, with a wreath of columbines and a foxglove wand. (Kipling 5)

The play is only mentioned in the opening scene, but this is enough to implicate Shakespearean text in a peculiarly English cultural continuity, as Puck is revealed to embody English history and narrative "as a kind of memory-trace; he contains all the stories of England which have to be understood, even internalized, in order for the Empire to flourish" (Purkiss, *Troublesome* 263). The question of cultural continuity through literature and story is emphasised repeatedly throughout Kipling's collection, finding its bluntest statement when Puck discusses "the sorcery of books . . . I warned thee they were wise children. All people can be wise by reading of books" (Kipling 100). The implied child reader is obviously flattered here, and such didacticism continues to plague *Dream* for children, although it is now performed through the privileging of a metareading function rather than such explicit commentary. In making the valorisation of reading covert, contemporary texts construct explicitly gendered versions of reading; where Kipling has both a male and a female protagonist, contemporary fiction constructs girls who learn to become self-regulating (not through playing Titania as Una does, but by identifying with Hermia or Helena), and boys who become Puck to Shakespeare's Oberon.

Rather than bring Puck forward in time, at least two contemporary timeslip novels send their child protagonist back in time to meet Shakespeare, and appropriate *Dream* at the same time as they appropriate the playwright himself: Susan Cooper's *King of Shadows* (1999) and Mary Pope Osborne's *Stage Fright on a Summer's Night* (2002). In these novels, the masculine time-traveller plays Puck in a Globe production, and in doing so forms a filial relationship with William Shakespeare.

Osborne's novel, part of her prolific "Magic Tree House" series for younger readers, is marketed to children and school teachers as being both educational and entertaining. In *Stage Fright on a Summer's Night,* the two regular characters Jack and Annie travel to Elizabethan London and meet William Shakespeare. As last-minute replacements they are conscripted to appear in a production of *A Midsummer Night's Dream* as fairies. Where Annie appears onstage with Titania (M. P. Osborne 46), Jack is pulled onstage by Puck (or at least the actor playing him), and successfully performs opposite him (41). The novel is focalised through Jack, and the reader is therefore encouraged to share his understanding of the play as romance plot-driven but fairy-focussed:

> Jack couldn't understand everything people said, but he could understand the story. It was about people in love. But none were able to marry the people they loved.
>
> The funniest part was about the fairy king and fairy queen. The king was mad at the queen. So he put magic juice on her eyelids to make her fall in love with the first person she saw. (M. P. Osborne 48)

Ultimately, Puck is constructed by Jack as the central protagonist of the play, and as a role model for contemporary boys. The children refuse Shakespeare's invitation to remain in Elizabethan London, and return to their own time to discover that their friend Will is a world-famous playwright. They have in instinctively attributed value to Shakespeare that is affirmed and affirming when they learn they were right.

Intended for older readers than Osborne's audience, Susan Cooper's *King of Shadows* features a young American boy, Nat Field, who travels back in time to Elizabethan London and joins Shakespeare's company. Cooper's title is of course drawn from *A Midsummer Night's Dream* (3.2.347), and offers a useful way of thinking about the novel in that this line is spoken *by* Puck but is *about* Oberon. The eponymous 'King of Shadows' here is William Shakespeare, and the novel is as much about Shakespeare and his cultural value as Nat's personal journey. This is in keeping with a cultural logic that describes Oberon as "the play's internal dramatist" (Montrose 107). The reader is offered a view of a patriarchal authority through the eyes of a subordinate boy-child figure. Indeed the two are inextricably intertwined. Joining the Chamberlain's Men, Nat is able to draw on his pre-existing knowledge of the play to consolidate the legitimacy of his place there. While this obviously validates knowledge of Shakespeare as socially useful, it also compounds Nat's place in a surrogate family: "I was as happy that moment as I think I'll ever be: standing there listening to [Shakespeare], knowing I was part—and a useful part, just now—of his company, safe in the small family world of the theatre. I wanted it never to end" (Cooper 92).[3]

As with the novels discussed in Chapter 2, Shakespeare becomes an idealised paternal figure, and the relationship with the playwright enables Nat to resolve the trauma associated with his own father's suicide in contemporary America. Shakespeare offers comfort that is not only immediate and physical, but also long-term and emotional insofar as the novel establishes literary text as a source of comfort:

> He sat down abruptly on the stage, pulling me down with him, and sat there with his back against the great wooden pillar while I sobbed into his shoulder. He didn't try to stop me, he just waited, patting me gently, saying very softly once in a while, like a mother to a very small child, "There. There now." (Cooper 70)

> "Listen to me," he said. "Do not say thou wast not enough for thy father. Never say that. Some things are beyond our command. A man so caught and held—men will destroy much for love, even the lives of their children, even their own lives. I have a poem that I shall copy for thee, that thou shalt read and remember. Remember." (72)

Thus a textual relationship develops simultaneously with Nat and Shakespeare's pseudo-filial relationship. Shakespeare presents him with a copy of the poem now known as Sonnet 116, "Let me not to the marriage of true minds admit impediments", telling him "[i]t is about love, and loving. I wrote it for a woman, but it could just as well be for thee and thy father. I give it to you to remind you that love does not vanish with death" (Cooper 101). Here, the Shakespearean text is established as holding universal and useful truths, and in reading the poem aloud to Nat, Shakespeare identifies his poetry as a legitimate substitute for himself.

This substitution is significant as it participates in a general cultural canonisation of Shakespearean text as a repository of truths and offers Nat a permanent connection with Shakespeare independent of physical or temporal proximity. This is particularly important as it lessens the pain of Nat's inevitable return to the twentieth century, while also explicitly offering the implied reader a personal connection with Shakespeare.

Cultural filiality is then reintegrated into *A Midsummer Night's Dream* and is symbolically enacted by Nat and Shakespeare's performance as Puck and Oberon in a royal command performance. Nat conflates the responses of his real and dramatic identities: "as Oberon [Shakespeare] had an eerie authority that made me, as Puck, totally his devoted servant" (Cooper 120). The performance provides a public, theatrical language for the personal relationship between Nat and Shakespeare, enacting a sense of Shakespeare's language as a useful tool of self-representation. Descriptions of the action onstage are easily applied to events offstage in Nat's life: "Puck and Oberon, Oberon and Puck: Together we watched and encouraged the lovers' jangling confusions, and Queen Titania's embarrassing love for an ass-headed clod, and then together, pulling the audience with us, we sorted everything out" (124). By implication, the contemporary child reader can also find in Shakespeare's texts a public, shared language for their personal experiences.

After his performance as Puck, Nat wakes up in contemporary London and must learn to integrate his 'Shakespearean' and 'ordinary' selves. Again, this adjustment takes place in both the filial and cultural sense. Nat's opportunity to engage with Shakespeare—and thereby resolve his emotional turmoil about the death of his father—is further justified as having literally saved Shakespeare's life:

> "It was 1599, Nat," Rachel said. "Shakespeare was only in his thirties, he wrote most of his greatest plays after that. If he'd acted with [the historical]

> Nat Field instead of with you, he'd have caught the plague and died . . . We'd have lost the best playwright that ever lived. You may feel you've lost him, Nat, but you saved him. If you hadn't gone back in time, William Shakespeare would have died." (Cooper 169)

Here then, Nat has been able to save the life of a father figure as he was unable to do with his own father, and in so doing, has ensured the production of Shakespeare's "greatest plays" and also saved the great father figure of Western culture.

Nat is somewhat satisfied by this knowledge, but it is really the contemporary director Arby's final piece of information that establishes a link between Shakespeare (as represented by his plays) and Nat that is truly satisfying:

> "Nat Field was made well, Will Shakespeare lived to give us his plays. But a part of you is still wounded, still angry, so there is one more thing I must tell you, to bring the healing full circle. I think Will missed you, Nat. He missed his Puck, his aerial sprite, when the sprite went to St Paul's and never came back . . . That play I gave you to read, *The Tempest*. It's about a great magician, called Prospero. Will Shakespeare played him, a few times—it was the last part he ever played. And in the play, Prospero has a servant, a spirit, a sort of ethereal Puck, whose name is Ariel. No doubt a good little actor played him, a pretty light-footed boy with a sweet voice, but Ariel was written for Will Shakespeare's vanished Nat, the boy in his memory. You . . . At the end of *The Tempest* Prospero lets Ariel go free. 'I shall miss thee,' he says, 'But still thou shalt have freedom'. Go free, Nat—free of grieving. And your two poets will go with you always." (Cooper 180–81)

Surviving as Puck (reconfigured as *The Tempest's* Ariel in yet another autobiographical model of Shakespearean authorship) because Oberon/Prospero/Shakespeare survive, Nat is implicated in the production of the Shakespearean cultural capital he has acquired. *King of Shadows*, like so many contemporary appropriations of Shakespeare for children, interpolates the child protagonist in the circular logic of the value of Shakespeare; in saving Shakespeare, Nat saves the legitimacy of his own development.

Puck Syndrome only appears to function for the pre-sexual masculine protagonist (and implied reader), perhaps because Puck himself can be read as a non-sexual figure. The limits of Puck identification for young masculine subjects is performed by the film *Dead Poets Society* (Weir). Set in a repressive boys' prep school in New England in 1959, the film charts the influence of a non-conformist (although nonetheless conservative) English teacher John Keating (Robin Williams). One of the central characters, Neil Perry (Robert Sean Leonard) is heavily influenced by this teacher (clearly a paternal figure), and rebels against his actual father to participate in a community production of *A Midsummer Night's Dream*. His father discovers the deceit, and removes Neil from both the production and the school. Neil's failure to find a 'middle-ground' between adolescent autonomy and paternal authority renders him powerless: What remains of his agency is spent in self-destruction. Wearing the 'crown of thorns' that was part of his Puck costume, Neil shoots himself in his father's study.

The film stages selected scenes from the play to highlight the facility and value of Neil's performance as Puck. The implied viewer watches an audience of the play as well as excerpts from the performance, and thus not only is exposed to "Shakespeare", but has acceptable responses to the play modelled for them. Within this framework, the viewer meets Puck, briefly sees Hermia and Lysander preparing for sleep, observes a tableau of fairies, and hears the entire epilogue (which is addressed to Neil's real father in the audience as an apologia). An unknowing viewer, who has already been convinced of the value of Shakespeare via an enthusiastic classroom scene, could be forgiven for thinking the entire play was about fairies, and that Neil, as he tells his father, has "the main part". The value of "Shakespeare" is never questioned by the film; indeed, Shakespearean language is constructed as inherently liberatory. Initially, Neil's 'Puck Syndrome' is successful, but his failure to accept agency and future authority (a failure to integrate the Shakespearean and the personal) renders his Shakespearean consumption unsuccessful. In other words, it does not seem that Neil would even be able to progress to a sexual independence; that which initially appears to perform separation from an overbearing father-figure actually affirms what Neil believes to be the impossibility of such separation.

The extent to which Puck remains a dominant figure for masculine development is demonstrated by a recent Australian novel for adolescents that has a female protagonist whose own development is subordinated to a Puck figure and an acceptable model of femininity as future sexuality rather than authority. Sophie Masson's *Cold Iron* (1998, published in the United States as *Malkin*) is the second in a loosely-linked trilogy, *Clementine, Cold Iron* and *Carabas,* that rewrites a variety of fairytale and mythical texts. *Cold Iron* performs a kind of bricolage rewriting, and although its two key intertexts are *A Midsummer Night's Dream* and the English fairytale "Tattercoats", neither of these provides a narrative of subjectivity for the focalised protagonist, Malkin.

The novel is fundamentally the story of Susanna/Tattercoats, who like the fairytale character, must overcome the denial of her existence by a grandfather mourning the loss of his daughter (her mother). On the advice of a gooseherd Pug, Susanna escapes from the castle she has been confined to in order to travel to a ball that is being held to find a wife for the Prince of the region.[4] In the fairy tale, Tattercoats meets a mysterious, handsome stranger on her way to the ball and falls in love with him. Of course, this stranger is the prince in disguise, and they live happily ever after. In Masson's novel, Susanna meets a stranger on the way to the ball (which is being hosted by Elizabeth I), but after meeting the wife-hunting Lord at the ball, Susanna realises that she truly loves the stranger she met on the road to the city. In this version, the stranger is not a prince, but a travelling musician. Malkin, ostensibly the protagonist of the novel, is a maid in the castle and is friends with Susanna and Pug. She agrees to travel with Susanna and Pug to London, and they are drawn into the court of the fairies, where Susanna must choose a husband over a father, and Malkin learns that she is the daughter of a changeling (and Susanna's half-sister). Although Malkin's gaze is notionally privileged within the novel, she is neither hero nor agent of the narrative.

Clearly, "Tattercoats" is used to structure *Cold Iron*'s narrative, but the setting and characters are informed primarily by Shakespeare's *Dream*. The primary connections between Masson's text and the play lie in the centrality of the gooseherd, Pug (a reconfiguration of Puck) and in her reification of the commonly noted symbolic correspondences between Titania's court and Elizabeth I's. When Malkin travels to Titania's court, she notes that "[t]his was a queendom, like England, and it was Titania who held the power . . . The odd thing was that this strange place felt like a dream version, a distorted mirror-image, of Elizabeth's court" (Masson, *Cold* 153–54). There is a seeming valorisation of feminine authority in the novel's interest in courts of queens, but the rather thinly characterised protagonist must forego her own power to ensure the happy marriage of Susanna and the survival of her friends. Thus, it is difficult to characterise this novel as a fairy plot or a lovers' plot, for it is far more interested in appropriating the English fairytale than Shakespeare's play. It is the progress and development of Susanna/Tattercoats that forms the bulk of the narrative, albeit through the eyes of Malkin.

Although the novel features Pug (Puck) as a central character, this naming move is only identified in the author's afterword (Masson, *Cold* 178), and given the limited and unnamed use of the play itself, it seems unlikely that a juvenile reader would recognise this as an appropriation of *Dream*, despite Masson's paratextual gestures towards rewarding reader competence:

> This novel draws its inspiration from many sources: the English fairytale Tattercoats, William Shakespeare's lovely play *A Midsummer Night's Dream*, Elizabethan history, and the traditions of fairies and fairyland, which occur all over Europe and which are a long way removed from our modern ideas of fairies as little things with wings. (177)

Nonetheless, there are arbitrary deployments of Shakespeare and his play in the novel. When the travellers arrive in London they visit the bookstalls in St Paul's. Although only a brief incident in the novel, it is heavily loaded in terms of the production of both juvenile literacy and Shakespeare as a literary figure:

> She picked up a book. *Holinshed Chronicles* she would have read on the cover if she had been able to read . . . before bumping into a shortish dark-haired man with sharp hazel eyes. He was obviously a known customer but not perhaps a rich or important one, for the pimpled clerk said, in a tone nicely familiar, "Good day to you Master Shakespeare! What would

> you like today?" Malkin hurried on, book under arm. It was the first she had ever possessed, and she felt its strange bulkiness keenly. She did not know what she would do with it, for what was a book if it was not read? (Masson, *Cold* 86–87)

This final rhetorical question is unfortunately never answered by *Cold Iron*. The *Chronicles* are never mentioned again and Malkin never learns to read. The focalised observer, presumably a point of identification for the juvenile reader, cannot read herself. Shakespeare is obviously a reader, but the novel never extrapolates a connection between reading and writing, consumption and creativity. Indeed, as they leave the bookstalls, Malkin observes Shakespeare "staring at Pug . . . [with] a smile of dawning—but surely mistaken—recognition" (88), a moment which implies that Shakespeare has met Pug/Puck before, and perhaps even got the material for *Dream* from the encounter, rather than from any autonomous creative impulse. This brief encounter is the extent of Shakespeare's presence in the novel, and seems gratuitous.

The play itself is referenced when the travellers enter Elizabeth's residence at Whitehall. Again, Masson participates in the conflation of Titania and Elizabeth, when she places direct references to the play (but not *as* a play) literally in Elizabeth's home:

> There were painted cloths on the walls, depicting famous scenes of classical fame: the doomed lovers Pyramus and Thisbe, whispering through their wall; the crowned Diana leaping through the forest with her hunters; the Amazon warrior queen Hippolyta, her arrow pointing at the heart of the selfish Theseus; and more, many more . . ."There's a man with a donkey's head, lying in that lovely woman's lap! What a silly smile he's got. No wonder! And look—little creatures flitting around him, bringing him . . . a drink, is it Pug? And look, in the shadows beyond them, a man who looks like a king, watching. And look! Someone with him, with pointy ears . . . someone who looks familiar." (Cold 93)

To a reader familiar with Shakespeare's *Dream* these cloths obviously contain tableaux from the play although Malkin never realises this. However, this undeveloped intertextual reference offers a useful metaphor for the novel's overall use of Shakespeare and his work: background detail that is decorative but non-critical.

On the return journey from London, the travellers are drawn into local woods, where they meet Titania and Oberon. Malkin must compete with Titania in order to rescue Susanna, who has been kidnapped by the fairies, and ensure the safe passage of herself and her friends to the human world. During conversation with the fairy monarchs, Oberon makes reference to events which Shakespeare portrays in *Dream* but which Malkin is clearly unfamiliar with despite her viewing the pictures at Elizabeth's palace:

> "This I have waited a long time to see: my Titania made uneasy! The queen of my heart embarrassed by her own wilful pride! Remember, my heart, the donkey's head, and be careful!" He could have been quacking like a duck, for all Malkin could understand what he was saying. (Masson, *Cold* 139)

This reference offers a brief reading of the play, in that it offers a motivation for Oberon's enchanting of Titania beyond the ownership of "[a] lovely boy, stol'n from an Indian king" (Shakespeare, *MND* 2.1.22), while also undermining the extent to which this is a court equivalent to Elizabeth I's. It also implies that the transformation of Bottom and the humiliation of Titania are history rather than myth in the fairy world. This again, in turn, implies that Shakespeare is a transcriber rather than a creator, and offers no reader competence in the play's content for an unknowing reader. Although the novel concludes with the final section of Puck's epilogue (5.1.415–22), this citation is only referenced *as* a citation in the afterword. As mentioned earlier, Masson uses this afterword to list a number of intertextual references, and even includes her own version of "Tattercoats" (*Cold* 181–85) for readers to familiarise themselves with. Again, the novel is shown to be a bricolage text which gestures towards a range of intertexts, but never fully appropriates them for the juvenile reader.

The journey taken into the woods, and its obvious resonances with the play, highlight Malkin's status as observer rather than actor. It is this journey, also, which links *Cold Iron* with the romantic texts read below. Where in *A Midsummer Night's Dream*, the journey into the forest can be read as a metaphor for an escape from parental rule, Mary Ellen Lamb notes that it also tropes a colloquial notion of illicit sexuality popular in the sixteenth century:

> The roles played by Oberon and by Puck, who refers to himself as Robin Goodfellow, in the lovers' wanderings make literal a popular figure of speech. Since going to "see the Fayries" refers to illicit sexual encounters, then the lovers are indeed going to 'see the fairies'. (M. E. Lamb 303)

However, Malkin enters and leaves the woods as a pre-sexual being. The female who undertakes the journey into sexual maturity (both via the woods and the novel's fairytale motifs) is Susanna. This observed relationship certainly rewrites the traditional narrative of "Tattercoats" in that it privileges merit and 'true love' for the male as well as the female partner (rather than meeting the prince on the road, for example, Susanna meets an itinerant musician), but is a transforming of narrative and subjectivity for Susanna rather than Malkin.

Malkin is neither of the fairies nor human: as a halfling she seems doomed to remain an observer of both cultures without fully participating in either. Pug has the same half-caste status, but he is able to move fluidly between the worlds, and have agency in each:

> "Me?" said Pug, taking his lips from the pipe for an instant. "Me? How can I go? I belong here. And there, too. I am of both, yet of neither. Guardian, and gooseherd." He grinned. "You can't get rid of me so easily, Malkin." . . . Like her, he was of both worlds. (Masson, *Cold* 172)

The novel crucially lacks a sense of feminine agency in a world informed by Shakespeare and his writing: The female subject is the illiterate observer, rather than an active producer or interrogator of meaning. Despite Masson's claim that she feels, "a strong sense of wanting to pass something important to readers, and particularly younger readers, of a world of tradition, potential, story, dream, romanticism, humour and melancholy" ("That" n.p.), *Cold Iron* appears only to offer an active participation in such a cultural tradition to the young woman who subordinates herself to a heteronormative narrative of romance and marriage (Susanna) rather than modelling an active feminine reader of Shakespeare, or indeed of anything.

In the world of Shakespeare's play, the actors' plot revels in a materiality seemingly absent from the fairy plot (indeed the actor, Bottom, introduces a concrete materiality to that plot). The actors' plot revolves around the casting, rehearsal, and performance of "The most lamentable comedy, / and most cruel death of Pyramus and Thisbe" (Shakespeare, *MND* 1.2.11–12) by some "rude mechanicals" (2.2.9). This performance is chosen by Theseus at his wedding celebration, and although the mechanicals offer above all else comedic relief, their success is a kind of triumph for the 'ordinary' people as opposed to fairy or royalty. Bottom, as the most individuated and developed of these mechanicals, has an almost autonomous storyline in which he is transformed into an ass and seduced by Titania. Although this transformation is one of the iconic touchstones of the play in visual and popular representations, the details of Titania's dalliance with an ass (with its implicit bestiality) do not fit easily with heteronormative readings of the play, and this storyline is rarely used extensively for children's appropriations.

The narrative origins of Pyramus and Thisbe (Ovid's *Metamorphoses*) identify it as tragedy, as can be seen in its influence on Shakespeare's *Romeo and Juliet*. The myth explains the origins of the mulberry's colour, and offers a cautionary tale of young love for both youths and parents. In *A Midsummer Night's Dream*, this is the tale the rude mechanicals seek to perform for Theseus's wedding celebration, but their execution of the story is rendered comedically to the exclusion of all else. The mechanicals' play does reflect the elopement of Hermia and Lysander, but given the happy ending of *Dream*, it is a farcical reflection. When choosing the performance for his wedding banquet, Theseus selects the mechanicals' play on the basis of the following description:

> 'A tedious brief scene of young Pyramus
> And his love Thisbe, very tragical mirth'?
> Merry and tragical? Tedious and brief?

That is hot ice, and wondrous strange snow!
How shall we find the concord of this discord? (Shakespeare, *MND* 5.1.56–60)

During the performance itself, forming in large part the substance of Act 5 the actors are infantilised by the literally patronising gaze directed at them by Theseus and Lysander (itself a reconfiguration of the homosocial bonds between Egeus and Demetrius), which in turn enacts their social status as inferior to the court. Hippolyta describes their prologue as the noise "a child / on a recorder" might make (5.1.122–3), and the audience of *A Midsummer Night's Dream* is encouraged to "identif[y] themselves with the onstage spectators through their unbelieving attitude to 'Pyramus and Thisbe'" (Nelson 14). The mechanicals then, as a group, both within and outside the play provide a ready point of identification for any child reader who has had to perform in public, or been constructed as culturally subordinate by the adult world. Nonetheless, as a stand-alone plot, the actors' story is used less often by children's literature than either the fairies' or the lovers' plots, possibly because the mechanicals, despite winning praise from the court, do not have a foreseeable trajectory of development. The very categories of rustic simplicity, lack of intelligence, and naturalised class-position, which contribute to the comedy of the mechanicals' scenes in *Dream*, simultaneously affirm their necessary stagnation.

A significant exception to the genre's non-deployment of the actors' plot is John Updike's *Bottom's Dream* (1969), a picture book that focuses on the experience of Bottom as an actor, and as bestial paramour of Titania. The Athenian lovers are excised from the story, and thus the actors are made as important to the play as the royal and fairy courts; indeed, Bottom is made over into the play's central figure. The book's sense of intertextual play is signalled by the cover, which deploys multiple notions of authorship, while also invoking a tradition of rewriting and appropriation with specific reference to *A Midsummer Night's Dream*. Throughout the text, Updike's narrative is combined with Warren Chappell's illustrations, and excerpted sheet music from Felix Mendelssohn's symphony. Updike also uses a substantial amount of Shakespeare's own verse, and emphasises the transformative and sexual nature of Bottom's experience: "Thus began for Bottom a strange and wonderful new existence. The fairies crowned him with flowers, and Titania cradled his heavy donkey head on her lap, and kissed his tremendous hairy ears" (Updike n.p.). On this page also appears a six-bar excerpt from Mendelssohn's *Nocturne*, linking peaceful sleep with maternal/sexual comfort. Though these elements are clearly present in Shakespeare's play, it is unusual to find them deployed so obviously in children's literature.[5]

That said, Ursula Dubosarsky's *How to Be a Great Detective* (2004) does focus on the narrative of Pyramus and Thisbe. The protagonist, Claudia, is in the tradition of Robin Klein's Penny Pollard: an opinionated and active young

Australian girl who determines to follow her own path regardless of adult advice or intentions. Like Penny, Claudia must eventually adhere to adult notions of acceptable behaviour, but it is the journey to this point, here figured through an engagement with Shakespeare, that provides the core of the novel. Part of Claudia's development is learning to privilege academic reading of Shakespeare above personal reading: In short, Claudia is encouraged to subordinate her own perceptions to those of approved adult figures.

Claudia is a reader, but she reads too much and non-critically. In this sense, she is the inheritor of a long tradition of female readers who, like Emma Bovary, are flawed *as* readers. Claudia's reading material of choice is detective fiction, which she unproblematically identifies as literary: "Literature means books and most of the books I've been reading lately are murder stories. The ones I like the best are written by someone called Agatha Christie who I'm pretty sure is dead, although I don't know if she was murdered" (Dubosarsky 14). The humour in Claudia's non-discriminatory (and implicitly incorrect) reading is reinforced by the novel's plot. The consumption of this genre means that Claudia has a pre-existing discourse to apply to her own experience when she discovers what she thinks are mysterious blood-stains on her school's playground. The narrative is structured so as to highlight the differences between Claudia's autonomous and active intellectual life outside the classroom (in the playground and at home), and her passive classroom existence where her class is learning about Shakespeare's *A Midsummer Night's Dream*. I do not mean to imply that the novel valorises this division; indeed, Claudia must learn to subordinate the former to the latter in order to develop.

The novel performs this split between approved and disapproved reading in its fictional paratext, and uses the Shakespearean text as a bridge between the two: a "Note to the Reader" written by Claudia herself prefaces the novel. It indicates that the ensuing novel will be a retrospectively written, first-person narration by Claudia, and that,

> The other unusual thing is that at the beginning of the chapters there are mysterious words in quotation marks. These are from a play called 'A Midsummer Night's Dream' by William Shakespeare, who is cold and in his grave. I put these in because I'm sending this book to a literary editor I met recently, and I thought he might like that sort of thing. (Dubosarsky 2)

The sense of play here is characteristic of the novel as a whole, and its self-conscious mediation of the perceived space between children's voices and high culture. Although the note is not worded as such, Claudia is exploiting the cultural capital of Shakespeare to make her tale marketable, and while each chapter indeed has an epigraph from the play, the novel also appropriates the play in a more extended manner to function as an index of Claudia's personal development. In more critical terms then, the paratextual devices frame and reinforce the intra- and intertextual functions of Shakespeare's play within the novel. Of course, the comedic foregrounding of self-interested use of "Shakespeare" does not exempt Dubosarsky from such gestures herself.

While Claudia is investigating the 'murder' of her teacher in the playground, in the classroom her class is studying *A Midsummer Night's Dream*. The students are expected to draw pictures of their favourite character in the play, and this act combines with Claudia's commentary to introduce the reader to her classmates, their gendered identity, and her own position in relation to the play and these children. While her nemesis Cinnamon, the very feminine girl whose hair is washed in "apple-scented shampoo" (Dubosarsky 60), draws a "spectacular" (38) picture of Titania, another child uses the play to articulate her own racial marginalisation: Anupam "was very involved with her drawing, which was of the Indian Boy. I did point out to her that the Indian Boy wasn't actually a character in the play (he is only mentioned in passing), but Anupam said she didn't care. She would draw his ABSENCE" (35). This seeming gesture towards a postcolonial culture is ultimately subsumed by the novel's concerns with normative gender roles.

Cinnamon is exceptional, as she is not only a girly-girl approved of by adult culture, but is also an attentive reader of Shakespeare's play, and is able to correct any factual errors about the narrative which her classmates might make. She is not particularly popular with her classmates, but is favoured by her teachers and offers a model of acceptable femininity towards which Claudia must work (much like Cynthia in Konigsburg's *Jennifer*). Claudia only reads closely those elements of the play (and the 'crime') which appeal directly to her. She recognises there are different plots within the play, but tells the reader, "most of the play is about fairies, which I'm not so interested in. But at the end there's an interesting extra story about these two people called Pyramus and Thisbe, and that's what my picture was of" (Dubosarsky 36). Thus, while for her classmates this drawing exercise illustrates identification with a specific character, even in the case where that identification is with an absence, Claudia's sense of connection is to a plot rather than a character within the play.

Her close interest in this aspect of the play leads to a recuperation of the story's mythic function, but also blinds Claudia to the broader concerns in the play and her school. Selective reading is demonstrated to be a flaw: literally in the case of Shakespeare, and metaphorically in the case of the missing teacher. The solution to both the 'crime' and the depth of "Pyramus and Thisbe" is provided by the approved female teacher who has been absent throughout the turmoil of Claudia's investigation, Miss Moody. When she identifies the 'blood' on Claudia's costume as mulberry juice (Dubosarsky 134) she negates all homicidal anxiety Claudia has been feeling, and later,

> Miss Moody told me something very interesting about mulberries, which wasn't even in 'A Midsummer Night's Dream'. She said that in those olden

> Babylonian days, when Pyramus and Thisbe roamed the land, mulberries were really white in colour, not crimson at all.
>
> But then, when P and T killed themselves under the tree in the graveyard, all their blood soaked into the roots. Ever after that, the fruit of mulberries all over the world have been the colour of blood.
>
> That is quite a disgusting story, and not at all scientific, and I think Shakespeare did the right thing leaving it out of his play. But it makes you think, I think it does anyway. (134)

This arguably resonates with Ovid's version of 'Pyramus and Thisbe' which has a framing narrative of homosocial storytelling by "the daughters of Minyas / [who] stayed indoors and marred the feast with their untoward housecraft, / drawing the wool into thread and twisting the strands with their thumbs" (Ovid 4:32–34). The familiar image here of the female spinning storyteller creates a cultural genealogy for stories between women:

> Or should she relate the tale of the mulberry tree, which used to produce white fruit
> but was stained with blood and came to burgeon with red berries?
> This was the story she chose, because it was less familiar;
> and thus she began, as the thread whirled round on the twisting spindle. (4:51–54)

Miss Moody's storytelling demonstrates to Claudia not only the (newly learned) value of self-reflexive reading, but models a methodology *for* it.

Shakespeare, of course, excludes the mulberry element from his version of 'Pyramus and Thisbe', for to keep it would mean retaining a mythic and tragic function which would mar the comedic use to which the play is put in *A Midsummer Night's Dream*. Nonetheless, the story retains a semblance of a cautionary function for both young lovers and their parents, and in Dubosarsky's novel exists alongside a general appreciation of both Shakespeare and his work. Miss Moody's story initiates Claudia's self-reflexivity and seems to challenge Shakespeare as authority on Pyramus and Thisbe. However, although this marks Miss Moody as the bearer of (non-Shakespearean) cultural capital, as she is explicitly linked to Claudia's classroom, the fact that Claudia is predetermined to leave her class as she progresses through school means that Miss Moody's influence is valuable but temporary.

The students' classroom performance of 'Pyramus and Thisbe' marks and limits the possibilities of contesting normative gender roles, and Claudia's recognition of them. Cinnamon, the girl idealised by the adults around her, nominates to play Titania (Dubosarsky 69), and takes the opportunity to publicly perform an approved hyper-feminine identity. In comparison, Claudia's friend Alaric, who, "has long fair hair and is round and cuddly, and people always think he's a girl, although not with that beard" (18), is "very over-sensitive"

(20), and "is keen on the dancing of many nations" (32), appears to represent a challenge to normative masculinity. I would note, however, that such a model necessarily informs Claudia's account of Alaric as differing from it. What begins as a descriptive account becomes judgment: when Alaric elects to play Thisbe in the class tableau, Claudia notes "it was a weird choice but I have told you about him already" (69). This weirdness presumably does not apply to Claudia's own preference for the performance: "'I don't care,' I said. 'I want to be Pyramus'" (69).

Logically, Claudia must progress through school into upper classes, out of the pre-sexual realm of Miss Moody, and into the sexual realm of adolescence. Arguably, Claudia's trajectory in the novel is the (beginning) acquisition of self-reflexivity and a willingness to negotiate between herself and her world (the hallmarks of liberal-humanist models of subjectivity). If so, then it is conceivable that as this trajectory continues, Claudia will learn to examine her own behavioural choices through the lens of gender, as she has begun to do with Alaric. Miss Moody might offer reading positions beyond the Shakespearean, but she nonetheless affirms a fundamental belief in the value of reading as educative:

> "Think hard," she continued, manfully, "about what lesson you might learn from the story of Pyramus and Thisbe. What it teaches you, what you can learn from it."
>
> She paused, desperate.
>
> "This is what literature is for," she said at last. "Isn't it?" (Dubosarsky 135)

I believe it is this notion of academic and educative Shakespeare and reading which will outweigh Claudia's current reading position. Shakespeare's cultural authority and value are implicitly linked with *gendered* reading positions which must, if they are to be acceptable, adhere to normative patterns of maturing. If I appear to be overstating the case, or pessimistic, it is because I turn now to books *for* adolescent female readers which without fail, offer a limited and heteronormative relationship to Shakespeare, reading and sexuality.

The move to an older readership appears to produce a shift in genre and gender. The texts for younger readers I have examined thus far have all been directed at a masculine audience, or at an ambiguously gendered (pre-sexual) audience. In comparison, appropriations of *Dream* for teen readers tend to participate in the feminine-directed romance genre. Given the generic focus of these texts, and accepting that "[t]he love story has been one of the most pervasive and effective—yet least deconstructed—of all ideological apparatuses: one of the most effective smokescreens available in the politics of cultural production" (Charnes, "What's" 1), it is not surprising that the lovers' plot of Shakespeare's play is the focus of their appropriations, and is used to produce constructions of feminine passivity as though authorised by Shakespeare.

The play's lovers' plot consists of the ongoing confusion between the two young Athenian women, Helena and Hermia, and their potential mates, Demetrius and Lysander. The plot thematises the competition between adolescent agency (sexual and romantic) and parental, particularly paternal, authority. Thus, as the play opens, Hermia's father appeals to Theseus for legal confirmation of his paternal authority:

> Full of vexation come I, with complaint
> Against my child, my daughter Hermia.
> Stand forth Demetrius. My noble lord,
> This man hath my consent to marry her.
> Stand forth Lysander. And, my gracious Duke,
> This hath bewitch'd the bosom of my child.
> Thou, thou, Lysander, . . .
> With cunning hast thou filch'd my daughter's heart,
> Turn'd her obedience (which is due to me)
> To stubborn harshness. And, my gracious Duke,
> Be it so she will not here, before your Grace,
> Consent to marry with Demetrius,
> I beg the ancient privilege of Athens:
> As she is mine, I may dispose of her;
> Which shall be either to this gentleman
> Or to her death, according to our law (Shakespeare, *MND* 1.1.22–28; 36–44)

As Theseus explains to Hermia, her culture circulates an understanding of paternal authority as absolute: "be advis'd, fair maid. / To you your father should be as a god" (Shakespeare, *MND* 1.1.46–47). The adolescents' plan to escape from this model is clearly comprehensible to a modern audience. However, despite the fact that the play concludes with the happy marriages of Hermia and Lysander, and Helena and Demetrius, these unions offer problematic models for contemporary young women: Hermia only ends happily because the paternally-approved Demetrius relents his 'rights' to her, and Helena's happy union appears to be primarily the result of an altered-state on the part of Demetrius. Further, Hermia's future happiness has been achieved through her suffering a symbolic isolation in the woods, and the necessary dissolution of the strong homosocial relationship between herself and Helena, in "a move from one sort of 'incorporation'—the idyllic union about which Helena reminisces bitterly—to another: the union of husband and wife as one flesh that Helena believes to be prefigured in Hermia's emotional estrangement and antagonistic mockery" (Boehrer 103). Thus the romantic pairings are not the mark of developing agency, but a convenient masking of the retention of a patriarchal model of social relations. The children of the play learn to exorcise rebellion via a fantastic journey, and to cohere within their society; the 'first' type of "the return-to-reality closural frame" that "completes a history of psychic growth and interprets the fantasy narrative as a salutary exposure of forbidden wishes and emotions [. . . and] neutralizes antisocial impulses" (Gilead 278).[6]

Where young masculine readers are offered a somewhat active and autonomous cultural role, connected with but always subordinate to William Shakespeare via *A Midsummer Night's Dream*, adolescent feminine readers are consistently offered a far more limited model for cultural subjectivity when the lovers' plot is deployed. Predominantly, feminised appropriations of the play focus on the discourse of romance and the feminine position within such a discourse: focalised female protagonists are constructed according to Shakespeare's lovers' plot within their own romance plot. The tangled relationships of the four young Athenians should be problematic as source-material for contemporary narratives, but in fact their experiences can be fitted into the cultural fantasy of adolescence. Lesko identifies: "four 'confident characterizations' of adolescents: they 'come of age' into adulthood; they are controlled by raging hormones; they are peer-oriented; and they are represented by age" (2). These characterisations certainly seem to inform the construction of both the protagonists and implied readers of adolescent fiction, and when combined with the cultural anxiety about "teenage pregnancy" (6), it is unsurprising that teenage girls/women, with their potentially mutable and excessive adolescent bodies and subjectivities, become the target of normative romance fiction. Shakespearean playtexts are useful for such fiction because their, "narrative structure, with some extensions, can suit the generic requirements of romance [in that] he offers both the obstacles to union and potential mechanisms for alliance" (L. E. Osborne, "Romancing" 62). If romantic "alliance" can be used to limit adolescent femininity, and "Shakespeare" to authorise any such limitation, it is not surprising that *Dream's* lovers' plot has been used as the template for contemporary adolescent romance fiction. In such cases, "Shakespeare" functions as authority on, and for, patriarchy-friendly models of feminine subjectivity and sexuality as voluntarily self-policing.[7]

Where Osborne has argued of Shakespearean romance novels written for adult readers that "Shakespearean allusions are undoubtedly of secondary concern to the creators of these commodities" ("Harlequin" 144), I would suggest that Shakespearean romance novels for adolescent readers *rely* on their allusions to authorise the text as a whole. Indeed, in adolescent romance fiction, the individual romance of girl-meets-boy becomes inextricably intertwined with the cultural romance of Shakespearean value: their happy endings are mutually legitimising. The implied feminine reader is implicated in a model of cultural consumption that links Shakespeare cultural capital to heteronormative romance, and necessary feminine passivity in relation to each.

Shakespeare's *Dream* does thematise youthful sexuality, but popular appropriations tend to efface the extent to which this sexuality is not universally heterosexual. As with a recent film adaptation, children's literature participates in: "[t]he sentimental romanticization of certain relationships in the play, particularly the Theseus-Hippolyta and Titania-Bottom relationships, and the exaggerated emphasis on the theme of romantic love [suggesting that] Shakespeare represents the paradigmatic heterosexual romantic narrative" (Mayo 299). Nothing throws such trajectories into relief like romance novels for young female readers which deploy the play as a model. So, for example, Meacham's *A Mid-Semester Night's Dream* (2004) clearly invokes Shakespeare's play via its title, but also uses the play as a medium for its protagonist, teenaged Morgan Yates, to consider questions of romance generally, and her own relationship with her beau, Ben:

> Morgan thought about the play they were reading in English. *A Midsummer Night's Dream*, by William Shakespeare. She sighed. It was so romantic. For a minute she imagined that she was Hermia and Ben was Lysander. They would give up everything for love and leave their homes to be together, just as Hermia and Lysander planned to do. (Meacham 5)

While discussing the play during an English class, Ben demonstrates his own interest in the play's discourse of romance when he announces that "[i]f people really love each other, they should be allowed to get married, and Hermia's father shouldn't be able to tell them they can't" (Meacham 15). Ben is thus identified as a suitable partner and a proto-feminist of sorts. The play in Meacham's novel is therefore constructed as a love story, focussed firmly on the romance plot of Hermia and Lysander as the one true-love story of the play. Although Meacham has a fairy helping her protagonist, and the play itself is constructed as an archetypal romance plot, her use of the play is so limited that I do not believe it qualifies as an appropriation. Nonetheless her intertextual citation of *A Midsummer Night's Dream* exemplifies the ends to which children's literature deploys the play in the service of heteronormative patriarchy.

The Course of True Love Never Did Run Smooth by Marilyn Singer (1983) signals via its title both its use of Shakespeare's play, and its interest in the discourse of romantic love. The protagonist is a Jewish girl, Rebecca (Becky) Weiss, who while rehearsing as Helena for a school performance of the play is trying to resolve her own love life. As the novel progresses, she learns that physical attractiveness, the hallmark of her first love, Blake, does not ensure romantic compatibility and that friendship is a more valuable basis for a romantic relationship.

Becky's high-school is mounting a production of *Dream* and in that sense Shakespeare is deployed here institutionally. However, as it is offered to students as an extracurricular activity this production is explicitly opposed to classroom English where Becky is bored by "studying Thornton Wilder" (Singer 4), and spends her time gazing at handsome classmates. In comparison, she willingly reads and re-reads *Dream* to prepare for auditions and, before she has even won a part, appropriates Shakespeare's language to articulate her own anxieties:

> "'O, teach me how you look, and with what art/You sway the motion of Demetrius' heart,'" I muttered.
>
> "Well, what a surprise! And here I thought love made one at a loss for words."
>
> "Not in Shakespeare's plays," I said, wishing Shakespeare could supply me with the right words to capture Blake Harris' heart. (7)

Becky's best friend Nehemiah (Nemi) also reads the play repeatedly, and the two share a passion for "Shakespeare", but their differing abilities to perform Shakespeare introduce a clearly gendered discourse of cultural authority to the novel. Shakespeare is circulated as both literary and dramatic text within the novel, with reading coded as feminine and thus inferior to masculine performance. Becky notes that "I'd already read *A Midsummer Night's Dream* three times and I thought I understood it pretty well, but performing it was another matter" (Singer 15). In comparison, Nemi as hero of the text plays Puck effectively, and his Shakespearean proficiency identifies him as a suitable partner for Becky. The women who perform are shown as struggling to understand their characters, whereas the male actors are constructed as naturally talented. Becky notes that "something happened to [Nemi] up there onstage" (40) and she feels a "link with the past, the present and the future that theater is all about for me" (38), rather than having her own public proficiency.

Rebecca's personal engagement with the play nonetheless functions as an index of her developing self-reflexivity and, as she moves away from the play and focuses on other projects, her personal life is increasingly marked by disappointment and error. Shakespeare's play is identified early on as difficult but worthwhile, and the development of Becky's romantic feelings towards her best friend Nemi is linked to the rehearsal and performance of *Dream*, and is also 'difficult but worthwhile'. Their drama teacher takes the value of Shakespeare for granted, and tells them, "I chose [*Dream*] because not only is it one of the—if not *the*—most enjoyable and understandable of Shakespeare's comedies, but also because it has twenty-one speaking parts—good ones" (Singer 37). This mix of cultural capital and pragmatism informs the novel's overall approach to appropriation of Shakespeare.

Performance and the personal blend in Becky's developing understanding of and identification with Helena. Despite her familiarity with the play, Becky depends on the interpretive frameworks of her drama teacher when analysing the part she is to play. Initially, he tells her that "Helena is really about your age, and she's jealous, has a low opinion of herself and is obsessed with this guy Demetrius" (Singer 15), and she accepts it, applying this model to Helena and herself. When she repeats a similar reading of the character to the teacher later, he dismisses it saying, "Helena is one of the only two characters in the play to have a soliloquy. When Shakespeare gives someone a soliloquy it usually means she or he is a thinking, feeling person. Helena has plenty of depth. And so do you" (192). Becky just as readily accepts this reading, and given this approval, realises her true love for Nemi and polishes her performance as Helena. In a chain of instruction, the drama teacher functions as a pseudo-paternal voice of and for Shakespeare's own symbolic paternity, and as comparison with the range of missing or ineffective fathers in the novel. Becky's intellectual passivity is privileged via juxtaposition with the independent intellectual activity of her rival Leila. Not only has Leila "read a lot of criticism about the play" (68), but also ably performs a sexualised interpretation of Titania. Just as Becky's passivity is rewarded, Leila's agency is punished as by the end of the novel she is disliked by staff and students and is socially isolated.

The close and long-standing friendship between Becky and Nemi would appear to work against the homosocial relationship inscribed by the play between Hermia and Helena as a pre-sexual phase; however, Nemi is very much a feminised male when the novel opens. He is small, tends to friendships with females, and is viewed as asexual by Becky. Rather than rejecting a homosocial friendship with another woman, then, Becky must learn to recognise Nemi's masculinity and reject the symbolically homosocial aspect of *their* relationship in favour of the heterosexual. A major part of this recognition is facilitated by their shared discussions and rehearsals of the play, where they consider issues like character motivation and realism.

Nemi's early feminisation is marked for the knowing reader via a symbolic identification with Helena. It is clear to the reader, despite the third-person narration being focalised through Becky, that Nemi has strong feelings for her that she does not herself recognise. This (somewhat) unrequited love places Nemi in a similar position to Helena and Becky herself. As he engages in a relationship with the sexually-sophisticated Leila, Nemi demonstrates his heterosexual masculinity to both Becky and the reader. As she begins to perceive him as such, Becky also begins to develop conscious sexual attraction towards him as illustrated by a series of erotic dreams straightforward enough to render Freudian theory redundant. Later, this performance of heterosexual masculinity is revealed to be just that, a performance. Nemi confesses he has been unable to sustain an erection with Leila, telling Becky he is "a stupid little wimp who can't even get a hard-on" (Singer 234), a problem he does not seem to suffer with Becky (237). This physical marker of heterosexual masculinity also signifies the end of Nemi's homophobic jokes and attitudes towards two gay friends (whose relationship is discussed below), implicitly suggesting that any sexual confusion Nemi may have been experiencing has been resolved.

Despite the construction of adolescents as being "controlled by raging hormones" (Lesko 2), the novel circumvents this model by having its central couple engage in sexualised activity with unsuitable partners that is halted by their lack of physical response: Just as Nemi cannot sustain an erection with Leila, Becky notes of a make-out session with Blake that, "while I should've been feeling hot as hell after half an hour of kissing, I was feeling nothing at all, except for tired and slightly depressed" (Singer 184). The novel has a sustained interest in teenage sexuality, but depicts it as functioning in concert with interpersonal compatibility. The consummation of Becky and Nemi's relationship is marked as much by successful performance of Shakespeare as it is by sexual performance.

Becky has an existing sense of the value of Shakespeare, and so in order to attribute Nemi with cultural authority, the novel shows him educating her about alternative forms of Shakespeare. Although Becky and Nemi have always shared a passion for the theatre, they initially enjoy different types of film. Nemi is established early as "the world's greatest movie freak" (Singer 4) with a love of *auteur* cinema, particularly the work of Ingmar Bergman and François Truffaut. He takes Becky to see a film version of *A Midsummer Night's Dream*:

> then I realized it was an old, old film version of the play, starring such unlikely people as Mickey Rooney as Puck and James Cagney as Bottom. "This is going to be ridiculous," I said.
>
> But surprisingly enough, it wasn't. Instead, it was really lovely—the magic of cinema and the magic of the play blended together, and I found myself spellbound by the cellophane-covered fairies and the tinselly sets. (Singer 103)

Max Reinhardt's 1935 film adaptation of the play here becomes a metaphor for an idealised blending of forms and interests, a precursor for the idealised blending between Nemi's filmic and Becky's theatrical interests. It also enables the maintenance of a discourse of "Shakespeare" within the novel's alternate index of personal development: While the characters are involved in preparing for the school production throughout the novel, they are also involved in an amateur film project.

Nemi and Becky decide to make a short film in order to get closer to their respective love-interests, siblings Leila and Blake. The narrative of this film which is concerned with eroticised fantasies reflects, perhaps unconsciously, their true feelings about these objects of affection:

> "Well," I could hear Nemi explaining, "the film is about fantasy and reality. There is no dialogue. A boy and a girl, played by me and Becky, are walking on the beach when we see this other boy and gir-uh-couple also strolling along. Then the fantasies begin . . . after the fantasies, we show you two going off and then cut to the next morning—Monday—and show what you're really like." (Singer 110–12)

Eventually, Nemi does form a relationship with Leila, and Becky with Blake, but neither of these relationships seems comfortable, and when the group of classmates go camping to film the final scene of their project each relationship ends. This literal journey into the woods marks the failure of both the film and these (inappropriate) relationships, while initiating Becky and Nemi's romantic relationship. Thereafter, the novel's and their attention is refocused on Shakespeare. The reifying of finding the true self in an alien environment that *Dream*'s lovers' plot thematises is also metaphorically reinforced within the novel by constructing the Shakespearean text as an alien environment.

A sub-plot of the novel revolves around a gay couple, Richie and Craig, who are going through the process of coming-out to their friends and families. Throughout the novel, Becky is gay-friendly and specifically happy for her friends: "now that Richie had 'come out' to Marisa and me (and I felt flattered by that confidence), I suddenly felt happy that these two had found each other" (Singer 97). However, this position of acceptance and empathy is only established as the majority view in the novel once Nemi has accepted the boys' relationship. This is ironically an inversion of the central romance: Richie and Craig are embracing their feelings and ideas, regardless of the fact that this will marginalise them within a heteronormative culture. In comparison, Becky and Nemi's progress as a couple is marked by their repudiation of aspects of their identity: Nemi must perform an embodied masculinity, and Becky must limit her identification with the Shakespearean text to the onstage space—her subjectivity is carefully delimited.

The final confirmation, both of the value of Shakespeare, and Becky and Nemi's romance, comes via the opening night of their school production of *Dream*. Significantly, Becky as focalised protagonist cannot report on the performance, as her subjectivity has been so completely displaced by Helena:

> So many things in this play were bewitching, were magical. Spirits. Theater. And most of all, love. And then I realized that somehow all of those things were connected by a single magical thread. To act you had to let the spirits enter you, and you had to love them and yourself and your audience. Suddenly, I got goosebumps, and I reached out and touched an invisible hand. It was Helena's. I felt us blend, melt into one. (Singer 242)

Later, offstage, Nemi and Becky remain dependent on "Shakespeare" to communicate and confirm their relationship: Their happy ending is constructed as Robin Goodfellow's 'amends' (246) and their union is Shakespearean rather than one of friendship, shared ethnic identity, experience, or ideas.

Charlotte Calder's *Cupid Painted Blind* (2002) is set in Sydney and tells the story of Persephone Harkness (Sefi) and her attempts to find romance as a high-school student. The novel uses *A Midsummer Night's Dream* as both a motif and a structuring narrative. Rather than constructing a fantasy discourse, Calder establishes the Internet as an alternative world for the teenagers; a model which simultaneously makes over the magic of Shakespeare's play as technology and creates an analogy for the Athenian woods. Similarly, adolescent emotional turmoil stands in for the effects of Oberon and Puck's potion in an extension of the novel's commitment to realism over fantasy.

As with the experiences of the young Athenians in Shakespeare's play, tracking the interpersonal relationships between the teenagers in *Cupid Painted Blind* can be confusing. The novel centres on Sefi (a kind of Helena figure) and her best friend Pia. Unlike the play, which has not only two male suitors, Calder's novel is populated by a series of men who function as irritants or objects of affection for these two women, whose homosocial relationship suffers because of their relationships with men. Perhaps as confusing as the lovers' plot in *Dream*, Pia is dealing with her absent father, has unwanted attention from a boy named Wez, is attracted to Tom and also to her friend Pia's boyfriend Simon, while also developing an attraction to a new boy, Zac.

Sefi is studying *A Midsummer Night's Dream* at school, and is trying to resolve her love-life outside of school. The play provides a way of thinking and speaking about the divisions and links between Sefi's school and home lives, and the Internet and reality. The novel opens with a section which visually and linguistically seeks to replicate an online discussion between teenage friends; the register is casual, grammatically horrifying, and intimate, rapidly establishing the alternative world for both the protagonists and the reader. Immediately following this exchange, the reader travels with Sefi back to her 'real life' where "her battered school copy of Shakespeare's *A Midsummer Night's Dream* sat beside the monitor, unopened and accusing" (Calder 3). Academic reading of Shakespeare is not beneficial in Calder's novel until it is combined with personal experience.

As Sefi starts to read the play, she discovers useful aspects of Shakespeare's text. Implied readers have modelled for them, yet again, an idealised reading relationship with the Shakespearean text, but this relationship is emotive rather than intellectual, feeling rather than thinking. Sefi's experience of a personal Shakespeare is resolutely constructed as romantic experience, and her initial confusion about the *plot* of the play is replaced by an appreciation of the play's *language*. This change is in keeping with the broader cultural veneration of Shakespeare's language rather than plots, but unfortunately, Calder's first direct citation of the play, which becomes a touchstone for Sefi, is a misquotation:

> All those woods and silvery moons and weird names (how on earth could you imagine a hero called Lysander—it sounded like a toilet cleaner), and she'd had to keep going back to the beginning just to find out who was falling in and out of love with who. It was totally confusing . . . And lots of quotes, including the oh-so-famous one about 'the course of true love never did run smoothly'. Gave her a bit of a shock to see it right there in the first act—fancy old Bill Shakespeare being the first to think that one up. A total cliché nowadays, but still true. (Calder 6–7)

This non-pentametric version of the line may well give a knowing reader quite a shock as well, but other attempts to reward reader competence are more successful, although obvious, so that when a gremlin appears in the teenagers' online chat-room, and appears to know all their secrets (Calder 47), the next day in class, Sefi learns about Puck (53), readily providing a link for the reader between the gremlin and the sprite. Eventually, this gremlin is debunked as being Sefi's younger sister playing pranks, erasing any sense of the supernatural. As the novel progresses, the correlations between Sefi's school-time reading of the play, and her extracurricular personal life become stronger, until the two intersect when the students are assigned to perform a scene for their classmates, necessitating after-school rehearsals. The students select the performance of 'Pyramus and Thisbe' and cast themselves in roles which reflect their offstage positions and emotions.

As the group of friends start rehearsing their version of the play within the play, the Shakespearean text provides an acceptable language of performance for the developing interpersonal relationships. Most significantly, Sefi is cast as Thisbe to Tom's Pyramus/Bottom. The scene is performed as farce, but also offers serious resonances with the offstage action. The centrality of this production to the novel's plot might seem to mark the novel as an 'actors' plot' text, but in fact, the mounting of the play serves ultimately to further the romance plot of *Cupid Painted Blind*. The performance provides Sefi with her first physical contact with Tom, and gives them opportunities, albeit comedically, to exchange linguistic signs of love.

The performance of the play provides a concrete example of Sefi's newfound links between school and reality, and the capacity of Shakespeare's language to bridge the two. This scene arguably performs a self-discovery function within the novel, but if so, this is useful primarily for the development of romantic interpersonal relationships.

Sefi does form a couple with Tom, seemingly providing the happy closure of a romance plot; however, this relationship comes at the (temporary) expense of her homosocial friendship with Pia, who believes Sefi and Pia's boyfriend Simon are having a covert relationship: "'No, seriously,' said Pia. Her voice was suddenly shaking with anger and jealousy. 'Why don't we just get it out in the open? Why don't you two admit—'" (Calder 209). This friendship is only repaired once it is established that the girls have different love-objects. There is certainly no challenge to the privileging of heterosexual over homosocial relationships.

Not only does the novel naturalise a link between Shakespeare and romance for the female reader, but it also explicitly opposes romance to academic achievement:

> Brains didn't need boys; they just sailed on through in a cloud of brilliance and when they graduated with perfect scores and had unis all around the country begging them to enrol in astrophysics or cosmology,

> then all the Toms of the world would be shaking their heads and sighing, "God, she's stunning. Missed our chance—guess she's lost to us forever now . . ." (Calder 18)

Ultimately then, Sefi's beneficial reading of Shakespeare is for personal/emotional values, certainly not for public/academic value. The Shakespearean discourse is also implicitly attached to a notion of maturing, as Sefi moves from a feminised space (at home and school) into a heterosexual space. This new maturity, which establishes regulated sexuality as a key indicator of feminine growth, is marked linguistically in the novel by Sefi's name changing to Seph, a nickname which bears a greater morphological relationship to her full name, Persephone (although she avoids her namesake's mythical fate).

There is a sense, however, that the novel challenges pat endings to the standard romance plot in that after getting together with Tom, Sefi discovers that her early fantasies of perfect union are not realistic:

> Seph moved closer to Tom; they laced their fingers together, their feet stamping along the pavement. But she couldn't quite keep time with him; their strides didn't seem to match. Sometimes, she'd come to realise, it was a bit like that with their conversations, too. They didn't really think the same about a lot of things . . . She pushed the thought from her mind. (Calder 218–19)

This brief moment demonstrates Sefi's conditioned response in constructing Tom's behaviour or stride as the dominant norm with which *she* must keep time; further, when she realises that their opinions differ, she suppresses such thoughts. This is an example of self-policing within patriarchal heteronormative culture: Seph apparently feels that her own feelings, behaviours, and ideas are subordinate to Tom's. The romance-ending is complicated further when Sefi realises she is attracted to males other than Tom, specifically a young actor/waiter she has met called Zac, who seems to return her attraction. When she finds herself having a conversation with both Tom and Zac, the reader is encouraged to identify with her pleasure at their sexual competition: "Seph suddenly wanted to giggle; they reminded her of those two dogs that night at Pia's, just before they'd hurled themselves at one another's throats" (Calder 223). Within what I see as a stereotypical model of feminine adolescent sexuality/romance, Sefi nonetheless self-reflexively rereads the conclusion of Shakespeare's play for her final school assignment on *Dream*. In this reading, she comes close to interrogating the Shakespearean happy-ending, although she does so in a way that reveals her conditioning on femininity: "Seph tried to imagine Helena five or ten years hence. Would she be starting to get fat? Would she and Demetrius be taking one another for granted? Would they have produced at least one truly obnoxious kid? Maybe they might even have ended up getting divorced" (224).

Nonetheless, what might have challenged the standard romance plot, rereading Shakespeare and Sefi's interest in more than one male, is subordinated to the kind of father-daughter-lover formation that begins Hermia's troubles in *Dream*. As the novel opened, Sefi had an adversarial relationship with her father, Nick, whom she saw as responsible for her parents' divorce, particularly as he has started a new relationship with a younger woman. Part of the maturing process Sefi goes through in the novel is forming a relationship with this stepmother figure, and respecting her father. A key bonding scene between father and daughter revolves around Shakespeare's *A Midsummer Night's Dream*. While ordering lunch in a café Sefi tells her father, Nick, she is studying the play:

> Nick smiled. "A Midsummer Night's Dream, eh?"
> "Once I sat upon a promontory . . ." he suddenly declaimed, in what Seph called his barrister's voice:
> "And heard a mermaid on a dolphin's back
> Uttering such dulcet and harmonious breath
> That the rude sea grew civil at her song . . ."
> But Seph had become painfully aware of the waiter standing there at his elbow.
> "Dad!" Her face colouring, she cast an apologetic glance at the waiter. Who, she registered with a sinking heart, had spiky hair and looked cool.
> But the waiter was grinning at Nick.
> "And certain stars shot madly from their spheres," he continued, "To hear the sea-maid's music." . . .
> "Oberon," said the waiter, making a little bow . . . and whipping a pen from behind his ear. "Some dude, eh?"
> "You certainly seem to be familiar with him," said Nick, smiling his bemused, raised-eyebrow smile. (Calder 86–87)

In Shakespeare's play, these lines are spoken as a shared remembrance by Oberon to Puck, demonstrating the pseudo-filial relationship they share (Shakespeare, *MND* 2.1.149–54). Osborne suggests of romance fiction that appropriates Shakespeare, "using Shakespeare as a shared language often signals the intellectual compatibility between hero and heroine" ("Romancing" 50), but in this case the shared Shakespeare signals compatibility between the hero and the heroine's father. As the novel progresses, Sefi meets Zac again, and finds him even more attractive. As the novel closes, she is imagining a relationship with him rather than with Tom, and their final meeting again revolves around Zac and her father's shared knowledge of Shakespeare:

> "Your dad still spouting Shakespeare?"
> Seph rolled her eyes, warmth spreading through her in a rush.
> "Yeah," she said, "so embarrassing . . ."

> Or maybe it was just Nick who had stuck in his mind.
>
> "You're lucky," he said. "My old man would know precisely zilch about Shakespeare. Or anything else for that matter," he added with a shrug. (Calder 222)

Whether it is conscious or not, Sefi's projected choice of a romantic partner is associated with her father, and as the shared knowledge of Shakespeare demonstrates, is likely to be approved by him. In this sense, the implied conclusion of the novel is less a challenge to the standard romance plot, than to Tom as the hero of that plot. Knowledge of Shakespeare becomes an index of valued masculinity, shared between Sefi's father and Zac, replicating the mutual endorsement of Egeus and Demetrius at the beginning of *Dream*. This pattern can also be seen in appropriations of *The Tempest*, as discussed in the next chapter.

Thus, while *A Midsummer Night's Dream* is foregrounded as a romantic intertext for Calder's novel, it is covertly used as a discourse of patriarchal authority and measure of masculinity. The limited interrogation of first-love as true-love never challenges the broader cultural romance of heteronormativity. The Shakespeare function in *Cupid Painted Blind* reinforces the very patriarchal model the challenge to the romance plot *seems* to be producing.

The generic developments legible between Singer and Calder's novels reveal what I read as progressively insidious appropriations of Shakespeare in the service of patriarchal norms. Given that in the time between the publication of these texts feminism/s have caused significant social and cultural change, it seems that a patriarchal Shakespeare has gone underground. Female protagonists and implied readers who are adolescent—embodying a burgeoning sexuality and possible excess—are effectively conditioned towards heteronormative monogamy, which in turn is constructed as inherent *to* Shakespeare's *Dream*, and therefore authorised *by* Shakespeare. Cultural capital in these romance novels is linked with circumscribed sexuality: admirable subjectivity equals knowledge of Shakespeare equals chastity or a Shakespeare/paternally-approved monogamous relationship. Similarly to children's literature that deploys *Macbeth*, such a model requires implicitly reading the play conservatively: emphasising gendered elements which fit a patriarchal model, but ignoring the linguistic subtleties or ambiguities inherent in the Shakespearean text.

Puck may operate as a carnivalesque figure of limited autonomy for pre-adolescent masculine readers, but when children's literature appropriates *A Midsummer Night's Dream* for adolescent feminine readers, no space is made for autonomous development. As with the play itself then, young men are often assessed on the basis of socio-cultural status (in itself a problematic model) but young women are *always* assessed through categories of sexuality. Much like the rupture which Hermia's assertion of control over her own (sexual) body causes at the outset of *Dream*, the sexually autonomous feminine figure is implicitly excessive in this texts. Young men are directed towards a life of the mind, young women towards a life of the body. In response, the journey into adolescence is metaphorically produced as the play's journey into the woods (and indeed extratextually as the development of a *reading* subjectivity); a journey which, if negotiated correctly, will result in heteronormative marital coupling.

Chapter Five

"This Island's Mine": *The Tempest*, Gender, and Authority/Autonomy

> Prospero used to be Duke of Milan, but got chucked out and marooned on a distant island by his naughty brother. Since getting stuck on the island old Prospero has spent the years studying and is now a powerful magician. When his naughty brother sails near the island, Prospero plays weatherman and sends a big storm to shipwreck him. Now that naughty bro is also trapped on the same island as Prospero, will the magician take his revenge on his dirty Dukedom-nicking brother or will he forgive him? (Donkin 154)

This vernacular retelling of *The Tempest*'s exemplifies recent adaptations of the play for children in that it focuses almost exclusively on Prospero, his past, his intentions, and his methods, and mentions no other inhabitant of the island. *Adaptations* of the play for young readers (Lamb, Nesbit etc.) tend to focus on Prospero as protagonist, perhaps unsurprisingly, as he is arguably the creator of the play's events, and thus can be rendered analogously with Shakespeare himself. *Appropriations* of the play for older readers tend to focus more on child figures within the text, offering them as figures of identification for the implied reader; thus the texts I am reading in this chapter deploy Miranda *or* Caliban as model for their protagonists. Such appropriative focus on the child characters seems to entail effacing Prospero, who becomes the spoken-about rather than the speaking. Like Shakespeare, Prospero is figured as an origin at once venerated and oppositional. In his place the child figures of the play either find Shakespeare (cultural authority) without or despite a Prospero (father figure) and in doing so either become 'Prosperos' themselves or accept cultural subordination.

Shakespeare's 'final' play *The Tempest* (1611) has long been an object of rewriting and appropriation as critical texts like Alden and Virginia Vaughan's *Shakespeare's Caliban: A Cultural History* (1991) and Chantal Zabus's *Tempests*

After Shakespeare (2002) attest. *The Tempest* offers a convenient symbol of the cultural fantasy of Shakespeare as Romantic author. If Shakespeare sets aside his pen when Prospero sets aside the tools of his craft, the playwright has offered his audience a considered farewell, and a meditation on what it means to be an artist. Critics invested in this fantasy conveniently ignore plays like *All is True/ Henry VIII* (1613), *Two Noble Kinsmen* (1613–14), and the lost *Cardenio*. Historically there has been a "repeated use of *The Tempest* as a site around which the age-old conflicts between colonizer and colonized continue to be played out and rehearsed" (Cartelli 89). It is thus surprising that appropriations of the play for juvenile audiences have not been objects of critical scrutiny, particularly given the arguably analogous cultural position of children and subjects of colonisation. Slemon and Wallace suggest that, like the 'primitive', the child is often treated "as a subject-in-formation, an individual who often does not have full legal status and who therefore acts or who *is acted against* in ways that are not perceived to be fully consequential" (20, original emphasis). From this perspective, *The Tempest* offers several points of identification for the reading child subject: the 'good' Miranda, the 'bad' Caliban, or even the problematic Ariel.[1]

The Tempest's central father-figure is of course Prospero: The deposed duke whose powers of language and magic can now only be exercised within the limited, pseudo-domestic space of an island home populated only by himself, his daughter Miranda, his "slave" Caliban, and a range of spirits metonymically represented by Ariel. The long history of symbolically equating Prospero with Shakespeare offers a convenient discursive connection between the thematising of paternity *within* the play and its appropriations, and the implied extratextual identification of Shakespeare as the father-figure of Western culture. As child readers are exposed to a specifically constructed filial relationship with Prospero in these texts, they are simultaneously interpellated into a filial relationship with Shakespeare in the real world. Unsurprisingly, this process is gendered, as subjectivity is linked with acceptable access to and uses of authority. The masculine/feminine juvenile subjects of the appropriations under consideration in this chapter are linked explicitly either to Caliban or Miranda as embodiments of gendered youth in the play itself.

This paternalistic Prospero-Shakespeare model is not new to children's literature. In nineteenth-century adaptations of Shakespeare for children, "Prospero, of course, was an ideally wise and protective father, and from him it was no very distant step to representing Shakespeare himself as the ultimate good father who understands" (Bottoms, "Read" 10). A nineteenth-century paradigm within which Shakespeare, the Father, and Prospero, are all idealised paternal figures, makes this conflation relatively clear (if problematic). However, when Prospero's paternalism is critiqued as culturally hegemonic dictatorship, patriarchal repression, and colonisation, the equation becomes harder to maintain. The undermining of any aspect might render the model difficult, but the undermining of all three should leave contemporary authors with a tough-sell on Shakespeare-Prospero as the ultimate father-figure, literally or symbolically. The discussion in Chapter 2 considered the ways in which contemporary texts literally construct William Shakespeare as a father figure for the young reader; here I read texts which construct Shakespeare as cultural father figure via an often vexed equation of Prospero with Shakespeare.

It is not exclusively the play's thematic interest in filiality which makes it useful for the genre of children's literature; White suggests that the play may be so available to appropriation because its "story is as tight and straightforward as one can imagine" (6), and further argues that "*The Tempest* obeys the literary rules set down by Aristotle, since it is unified in time, place and action" (7). White's optimistic reading of the play as unified fails to take into account the very elements I see as useful to children's authors: The heightened reality (or fantasy) world of the play offers a stage on which to play out similarly heightened versions of subjectivity and relationships. There is a touch of fairy- or folk-tale discourse invoked by the allegorical possibilities of 'the island', the fantastic, and the representative functions of the characters. Moreover, Brook challenges the play's 'straightforwardness':

> we see how nothing in the play is what it seems, how it takes place on an island and not an island, during a day and not during a day, with a tempest that sets off a series of events that are still within a tempest even when the storm is done, that the charming pastoral for children naturally encompasses rape, murder, conspiracy and violence. (94–95)

Treated as a narrative template for the fantasy island, *The Tempest* has been used in ways that seem to mark the invocation of Shakespearean cultural capital as an end in itself. For example, Sophie Masson's *The Tempestuous Voyage of Hopewell Shakespeare* (2003), establishes a fantasy world with multiple Shakespearean citations—indeed it even features William Shakespeare himself in a brief and meaningless appearance—and stages a journey to a mysterious "Lost Island" in 1600. The protagonist Hopewell Shakespeare is, as the reader is constantly reminded, "a distant relative" (Masson, *Tempestuous* 6) of the playwright. Hopewell joins a privateer on a sea-voyage in an archetypal quest to find this island,

> "ruled by a man they call the Lord of Alchemists," Wolfe said, abruptly pushing away the chair and standing up, "and he is the greatest magician that has ever been. It would be nothing for him to make the island disappear like mist, for ever. But that is not what he does. Every so often, the island appears out of the western sea, and he who finds the path to it will be given the greatest fortune that has ever been seen in all the days of the world." (Masson, *Tempestuous* 56)

When Hopewell arrives at the island, he meets a Dr Prosper Bonaventure, who never really fulfils a Prospero-function beyond dressing the part:

> Dressed all in rich black velvet robes, with a black velvet skullcap whence escaped strands of pure white hair reaching to the collar of the robes, the figure seemed to be a man a little below the average in height, if not in weight [. . . he had an] enormous floor-to-ceiling bookcase, stuffed full of books in deep colours of worked leather [. . . and introduced himself,] "I am Doctor Prosper Bonaventure, master in philosophy, astrology, alchemy, fortune telling and clerking, late of Paris, Prague, Venice, and many other places. And now of the Lost Island, or *Perdita*, as I have called it in my research, from the Latin and the French and no doubt the Spanish, is that not so?" (Masson, *Tempestuous* 124–26)

Masson also conflates Ariel and Miranda into a single character Flora, who is initially described as being the daughter of the Lord of Alchemists, but in a belaboured plot device is revealed to be the Lord of Alchemists herself. Flora neither functions entirely as a daughter nor a servant, and her narrative function is as a *dea ex machina*. Hopewell's lesson has been to love a girl for more than her appearance, and the Shakespearean elements have provided little more than a fantastic background despite Masson's claim that the novel was "inspired directly, of course, by two of William Shakespeare's plays, *The Tempest* and *Twelfth Night*" (*Tempestuous* 290); indeed, Ovid's *Metamorphoses* actually provides a more consistently used intertext for the novel than any of the many Shakespearean plays briefly cited. Masson's novel is effectively a pastiche text of empty citation. Perhaps most significantly for my purposes, the novel never fully imagines nor considers the issue of filiality or cultural authority, for while it is revealed that there is no *male* or patriarchal Lord of Alchemists, no account is taken of the broader repercussions of this.

The history of criticism and appropriation of *The Tempest* is filled with romanticised views of both the play and Prospero, but "[r]eacting, in part, to such characterisations of Prospero's autocratic rule as essentially benign, much recent criticism has sought means to critique what it reads as glorification of *The Tempest*'s exploitative colonialism" (Slights 360). Thus, the Prospero-Caliban relationship has been appropriated critically and creatively as a topos of both colonial subjugation and paternal authority in an intersection between the personal and the political.[2] Skura's influential critique of the dominance of colonialism in *Tempest* criticism links such tendencies with paternalism:

> To a man like Prospero, whose life has been spent learning a self-discipline in which he is not yet totally adept, Caliban can seem like a child who must be controlled, and who, like a child is murderously enraged at being controlled. Prospero treats Caliban as he would treat the willful child in himself. (78)

If indeed "sympathy with Caliban is a Romantic creation of Schlegel, Coleridge and Hazlitt, and it has proved tenacious" (White 7), it is not surprising that the interest in Caliban beginning with the Romantics has affected the genre of Shakespeare for children which this literary movement also established. This sympathy is, I think, a sympathy of identification—not of displaced indigene, but of embattled inheritor—an offshoot of what Harold Bloom describes as the 'anxiety of influence', or the ways in which "strong poets make [poetic] history by misreading one another, so as to clear imaginative space" (5) for themselves.[3] Oedipal models certainly inform contemporary appropriations of *The Tempest* for boys: Caliban becomes a model for a lived experience of Shakespeare which allows personal growth and ascendancy over dominant culture (expressed through the control of narrative).[4] The young masculine reader is encouraged simultaneously to recognise and *appropriate* the cultural authority of Shakespeare via *The Tempest*.

Dennis Covington's *Lizard* (1991) tells the story of a physically deformed boy, Lucius Sims, who recounts six months of his thirteenth year. He tells of being placed in the Leesville State School for retarded boys (Covington 2) despite the fact that he is not retarded, but has physical differences from most people: "My eyes are more on the sides of my head than most people's, but they're a real nice color . . . My nose lays down on its side . . . my shoulders are humped and . . . I still limp a little" (3). Lucius has been placed there by Miss Cooley, a woman who has taken him in after the death and/or disappearance of his parents. She has also told him a *story* about "how my daddy died. She didn't say much, only that it was 1963" (1). The novel's prologue, which establishes these elements, thus identifies the two traumas that Lucius must reconcile in order to find agency and autonomy: physical difference and fatherlessness.[5]

Lizard appropriates *The Tempest* as a text in performance, a lived experience, and a structuring narrative. Given the picaresque nature of the narrative, it would seem that the island motif of Shakespeare's play is effaced. However, I would argue that Lizard indeed occupies an island—one of othered isolation—that is a location of narrative. An index of Lucius's development is his ability first to consume, then critique, then produce, narratives (particularly those of paternity). The epigraph, "when I waked, / I cried to dream again" (Shakespeare, *Tmp.* 3.2.142–43), signals the novel's interest in waking or enlightenment but the text moves beyond this wish of Caliban's to dream again, as its protagonist gains power over his own fate rather than remaining enslaved to a negative father figure.

It is at the school that Lucius is renamed Lizard by a peer, and this name becomes a totem of his burgeoning independence. This insular environment is ruptured by the arrival of a group of actors performing *Treasure Island*; when Lizard goes backstage to "make sure Jim Hawkins was all right" (Covington 23), he is introduced to the gap between theatrical performance and reality when he discovers that "Jim Hawkins was a girl" (25). This recognition comes when Lizard overhears the actors rehearsing lines from *The Tempest* (24): Callahan (the leader) and Sallie ('the girl') are speaking dialogue of Prospero and Ariel, the symbolic roles they are to take on for Lucius's Caliban.

When Callahan, calling himself Simonetti (Covington 28) poses as Lizard's natural father, he 'kidnaps' Lizard, a voluntary victim, with the express purpose of having him play Caliban in a production of *The Tempest.* It is not Callahan who tells him this, though, but Sallie: "Didn't Callahan tell you? We're going to Alabama to do a play. It's about a shipwreck, and there's a part for you" (45). This beginning establishes the terms of the developing relationship between Lizard and Callahan, who does eventually become a useful father-figure, but they must first determine the boundaries and expectations of their narrative relationship (primarily honesty) and their mutual obligations (or lack thereof). By the end of the novel, Lizard will be able to claim that "he was not my real father, but he might as well have been" (197), and this progress will be indexed by *The Tempest.*

Simonetti is only the first paternal incarnation that Callahan performs for Lizard, and is indeed only one of the temporary fathers Lizard encounters during his journeys with the actors. This array of father-figures each fulfils an aspect of Shakespeare's Prospero, so Callahan is (initially) an exploiter, Bill (a sculptor) is an artist, Mr Howell (a museum curator) is a sage, and Waldo (a theatre manager) is a provider. In Birmingham, where the production is being mounted, Lizard has contact with all these men through the theatre and the local museum, and from each of them he learns about their special area of cultural production and then moves on. Taken as a group these men form a kind of amalgam father for Lizard, and the necessity of paternity is emphasised by the fatherlessness of other children Lizard meets on his travels.

Most significant of these are Sammy and Rain, an African-American brother and sister who live by themselves in a shack that Lizard happens across. When they meet, Sammy demands "You think the whole country belongs to you, don't you?" (Covington 59), and continues to berate Lizard until corrected by his older sister Rain: "Mama told us to always say our prayers and never refuse strangers something to eat" (60). This brief exchange establishes the different futures (and cultural statuses) of these children: an African-American matriarchy set against a European-American patriarchy.

> "I didn't think you could do that—not have a mama," Rain said.
> "Do you have a daddy?"
> "No," Rain said.
> "Well, see, that's not supposed to be possible either." (65)

The matriarchal model linked with the Black children is emphasised by their own idealising narratives of family history, "now this is the story of our great-great-grandmother" (Covington 70), and the violent reality of their substitute father, "The Preacher":

> "He's not really a preacher. He just claims to be. He was Mama's boyfriend a long time ago, and he says he's got the papers to show that we belong to

> him. Even though he lives in town, he's what they call a guardian. That means he can come out here drunk every so often, beat Sammy, and have his way with me." (72)

The symbolic Black father has been revealed as a failure, just as the various White fathers in the novel, although I would argue that this is a necessary failure given the feminising of African-American culture the novel also constructs. Although Sammy's dialogue invokes the Civil Rights movement throughout the novel, and Rain represents the (sexually) exploited Black feminine, these children are subordinated to the hegemonic authority of the legal system and an adoptive Black mother (their maternal aunt) who is clearly marked as a future civiliser, telling Rain to "put back on your clothes and follow me to the house" (Covington 177). Given the patriarchal logic that structures the narrative, this is an inferior development to the protagonist's. Thus, very real examples of exploitation are sacrificed to the development of a Caliban who may be "deformed", but is certainly not "savage" (Shakespeare, *Tmp.* List of Roles) or racially other to the dominant norm.

The stories of Rain and Sammy become part of Lizard's narrative as he retells their experiences alongside his own to another boy he meets at a hotel, Harrison. This boy is travelling with his father, and they appear to be an ideal father-son unit. However, it becomes apparent to Lizard that appearance does not denote actual meaning when Harrison, in response to the story of Sammy and Rain, confesses his own troubles:

> "That preacher who's their guardian and beats them?"
> "What about him?"
> "My dad's like that". (Covington 89)

The question of cultural fatherlessness is thus also refracted through a series of failed, absent or violent fathers. These children's experiences demonstrate the theatricality of the 'natural' legitimacy of masculinity, but do not do so in order to challenge patriarchy: These challenges are to inappropriate fathers, not fathers *per se.* Lizard becomes a connection-point between symbolic orphans who between them attempt to form narrative and textual links: Rain writes a note for Lizard to carry; and Harrison gives his address to Lizard asking that he "write and tell me what happened to Rain" (Covington 91). At this point Lizard is effectively a cipher. He realises that he has no idea of his own identity: "how can you miss yourself?" (102).

It is the physical, cultural, and (often unspoken) historical, setting of this novel which informs the broader model of father-son relationships, where Lucius becomes a Caliban embodying the national anxieties of 1970s America. That is not to say that this novel offers anything other than a nostalgic mainstream model of national identity—indeed it works hard to naturalise White masculine heterosexuality as a position of privilege—but it does gesture to the possible difficulties of realising this identity in a post-1963 American south. *Narrative* is marked as a corrective to this fatherlessness; and what more authoritative model of narrative than Shakespeare?

Beyond the specific invocation of the racially-motivated church bombings in Birmingham, Alabama, *Lizard* implicitly invokes both the assassination of President John F. Kennedy in Dallas (another vexed southern city) on November 22, 1963, and the various mythologies which have sprung from that event. Significantly, assassination-discourse has long been 'Shakespeared': in 1966, Leslie Fiedler used "the assassination of President Kennedy" to initiate his discussion of what he called the "Caliban-Hamlet Paradox . . . at the heart of American Literature" (401). This paradox is the attraction to competing American self-representation as Hamlet-like "wronged sons . . . psychologically and in the context of the family" (Fiedler 408), and Caliban-like constructions of 'the American' as "a deformed slave, rebelling against legitimate authority at the instigation of certain European turncoats" (410). This paradox was, Fiedler argues, crystallised in the Kennedy assassination and its discursive aftermath. In an intriguing synchronicity, in 1991 (the year of *Lizard*'s publication) "Oliver Stone cast the Kennedy assassination through the lens of *Hamlet*" (Boose and Burt 9) in his film-narrative of this same historical moment and its aftermath, *JFK*. Like Covington's novel, the film is set in a post-1963 American south, where District Attorney Jim Garrison (Kevin Costner) asserts to a jury: "We've all become Hamlets in our own country, children of a slain father-leader whose killers still possess the throne. The ghost of John F. Kennedy confronts us with the secret murder at the heart of the American dream" (Stone).[6] Here, clearly, is Fiedler's Hamlet model; however, I would suggest that this model is explicitly available to the *adult* male. Covington's novel implicitly evokes this model, but reserves the Caliban-role for the juvenile subject. Here, the adult male is constructed as the historical knower and analyser, while Lizard naively expresses a personal understanding of "1963" during a discussion of a sculpture representing child-victims of racial violence:

> "They're about your age," the black man said. "They were killed in the bombing of a church here in Birmingham in 1963. You remember that?"
>
> "No. That was the year I was born. The year my daddy died too."
>
> He nodded. "That's the kind of year it was, all right." (Covington 129)[7]

The novel functions as an indictment of a fatherless United States, embodied by Lizard, and figured not as Hamlet—the 'wronged son' of a unique father—but as Caliban, the natural son of no father: profoundly and absolutely fatherless. The dead Black children invoked here are only temporarily present, displaced perhaps as Sammy and Rain; objects rather than subjects of the novel's discourse which also displaces them *and* the political history of Birmingham in favour of a production of Shakespeare's *Tempest*.

This context thus produces a web of intertextual references which reaches beyond the genre of children's Shakespeare and engages with a peculiarly American use of "Shakespeare" as a discourse through which national anxieties about paternity and authority are expressed. However this is primarily true for the privileged individual, and is most clearly indicated by Lizard's own developing 'reading practice' and its potential modelling-function for the juvenile reader of the novel.

Initially, Lizard only knows that he is to appear in a play about 'a shipwreck' but as the novel progresses, and he comes closer (geographically and temporally) to appearing in the play, he also moves through a variety of reading praxes in learning about the play. The 'mentor'/teacher-figure throughout this progression is Sallie, and just as she plays Ariel as obedient servant to Prospero in the production, she functions as a mediator here between Callahan as the patriarch and Lizard as the son. In this sense, she communicates knowledge but poses no sustained threat to a patriarchal model of cultural authority, and leaves Lizard free to find his own understandings of, and authorities over, this knowledge.

Sallie begins by telling Lizard a version of the play's plot: "[i]t's a story about a magician and his daughter. They live on this island with a spirit named Ariel and the magician's slave" (Covington 54). It is presumably no accident that the only character specifically named in this retelling is the character she is going to play in the production, but this bid for centrality is soon displaced when she moves to reading the play aloud to Lizard. I am quoting extensively here to show the shifts in Lizard's reception between passive and active modes:

> Then Sallie began reading the play to me. It was called *The Tempest*, by William Shakespeare. I could hardly understand a single word she said. But some of it I understood without even knowing the words. Maybe it was the way she read the parts, or the sound of the strange words themselves. It started with a shipwreck. All the passengers had to jump overboard and swim to an island. The island was nearly deserted. But there was a man who lived there named Prospero and his daughter Miranda. Prospero was some kind of magician or king. He had a slave named Caliban. Sallie said that I'd be playing the part of Caliban. I didn't have a lot of lines, she said, but was very important to the play. It was my island before Prospero and Miranda got there. My mother, a witch, had left it to me before she died. My mother had also locked up a fairy named Ariel in a tree. When Prospero came to the island, he set Ariel free. From then on Ariel worked his magic for him. Callahan would be playing Prospero, and Sallie herself was Ariel. It was Ariel who had caused the storm that wrecked the ship, but Sallie stopped reading before I found out why. (Covington 105)

It is clear from this exposition that Sallie is not only reading the play aloud, but also providing explanatory comments primarily to do with the play's plot.

From a purely textual point of view, it would seem that in this session, Sallie has at least reached 1.2.332, "This island's mine by Sycorax, my mother", but either she is reading an abridged form (in that Lizard has not understood Prospero's narrative of his and Miranda's past), or he has only understood the literal narrative without understanding the implied motivation of revenge for 'causing the storm'. Lizard is constructed as having an instinctive, rather than a linguistic, understanding of the play's content. What Sallie's reading and commentary apparently do emphasise is a level of empathy between Ariel and Caliban as servants/victims of Prospero. The resonance here with the novel's plot is obvious; but it is worth noting these early strategies for encouraging Lizard emotionally to identify with Caliban, which in turn creates a sense of anticipation on the part of Lizard (and the implied reader) to know more about the play's plot.

Shortly after Lizard learns that "Callahan was a liar and a drunk" (Covington 111), Sallie begins explaining to him what individual lines from the play mean. In doing so, she necessarily constructs an interpretive reading of the play, and here, she furthers the emotional connection between Caliban and Lizard, but does not appear to move any further with the plot than the first tutorial did:

> At night Sallie read to me and explained what my lines meant in plain English. Then she helped me memorize them . . . I never did understand what the individual words meant. Sallie had given me the gist of it, and that's what I thought about as I learned the words.
>
> I was Caliban. I lived alone on the island my mother had given me until this magician Prospero and his daughter Miranda washed up on the beach one day. They taught me how to read. In return I showed them where to find fresh water and all the good things on the island to eat. I fell in love with Miranda, and when I tried to get her to sleep with me, Prospero set loose a fairy named Ariel on me and turned me into his slave. That was the situation at the beginning of the play. I was supposed to be mad at Prospero, mad enough to kill him. The words came out the way they were in the script because I memorized them exactly that way, but the meaning was something else, something in my head. (Covington 118–19)

Lizard needs to know the exact words of his lines because by this time the production is in rehearsal. However, it is made clear that it is not Shakespeare's specific language affecting him, but rather, more broadly, the chance of playing Caliban: Shakespearean language is displaced by personal, emotional experience and response. When he notes that "I repeated the words that I'd memorized, but this is what I meant" (Covington 120) and proceeds to translate his experience, Lizard offers the reader a plain English version of the play, as Sallie has to him. In this sense, the novel idealises a model of juvenile

Shakespearean consumption and identification. Lizard's recounting of Caliban's complaints against Prospero (Shakespeare, *Tmp.* 1.2.331–45) is similar to a contemporary English 'translation' such as that found in the "Shakespeare Made Easy" series and is thus explicitly educational, but is intertwined with his personal anxieties about Callahan/Prospero as a father-figure:

"Shakespeare Made Easy": 'When you first came, you stroked me and made much of me . . . I loved you then and showed you all the features of the island: the fresh springs and the salt pits; . . . curse me for doing so!' (Durband 53)

Lizard: 'I was king of [the island] then, and I knew every tree and marsh, where to find blackberries in the summer and where to watch out for wild pigs. There was nothing I couldn't do if I'd wanted to, until you came along and ruined it. I thought you were going to be my teacher. You said you'd teach me how to talk, how to count the shells I found on the beach. But you only taught me enough to know that I was nothing but dirt to you.' (Covington 12)

As rehearsals continue, Callahan fails as a father-figure both on and offstage: He has already disappointed Lizard, but also consistently arrives at rehearsals late and drunk. When Waldo (the director) announces that "I'll find another Prospero" (Covington 119) he is effectively speaking Lizard's position: he has psychologically rejected Callahan as a role-model.

Lizard continues to absorb Caliban's lines by rote, to the point when on opening night Callahan loses his line, Lizard is able to substitute his own understanding of the play to cover the error, and "words just pour[] out of [his] mouth" (Covington 139) until Callahan recovers as Prospero. At this point, Lizard and Caliban merge, together claiming ascendancy over Callahan/Prospero. Crucially, Lizard still does not use Shakespeare's language, even as he appropriates Shakespeare's authority: "[t]hey were what the lines meant deep in the back of my head, and they tumbled out the way I thought Caliban would have said them" (141). By the end of the play, Lizard feels as though Prospero's epilogue and Callahan as performer of it, were "addressing it to Caliban more than anybody else" (143). The play provides a site for Callahan and Lizard to resolve their symbolic filial role, and more broadly, for Lizard to take up a position of cultural knowledge and authority. That his performance is ultimately for himself is signalled by a reviewer's misrecognition of Lizard's face as a "beautifully grotesque mask" (153) and the closure of the production due to a lack of public interest.[8] Despite this closure, Lizard notes that "at the center of me there was a hard spot that hadn't been there before. I was proud of it" (123); effectively then, the performance has marked Lizard's entry into adult masculinity.

From here on Callahan and Lizard work together to try to find Lizard's biological father, and reverse their early journey to revisit Rain and Sammy, and take Lizard home. This leads to an unusual plot twist as they discover that the "Preacher" has been arrested for the murder of "one black female" (Covington 161). Lizard (and the reader) believes this crime to have been committed against Rain, but it is revealed that the crime is long past and it was Sammy and Rain's mother who had been killed. It is the Preacher's trial which causes their aunt to take custody of the children and 'return them to society', and in their attendance at it, Callahan and Lizard cement their own bonds. The White patriarchal model finally triumphs over the Black matriarchal, and "Shakespeare" has been exclusively associated with the former.

When they return to Lizard's home, Callahan learns from Miss Cooley (Lizard's guardian) that she is in fact his biological mother but she is unable to identify a biological father:

> "The truth is, I don't know who his father was."
>
> "What do you mean?"
>
> "I mean, I was seeing two men at the time. The one I was in love with was married. The other one was his friend." (Covington 194)

However, this does not really matter, as Lizard no longer needs a father in the way he did when the novel opened. He realises that Callahan is enough of a father-figure now, as he himself has become an autonomous being. The articulation of this autonomy comes with a claim of cultural capital when Lizard looks around his home town and realises that it is not as big or frightening as it initially appeared:

> I'd stay with [Miss Cooley] for a little while longer, at least till I turned sixteen. After that I'd be keeping my options open. In ways, I was already on my own . . . I look a lot different, my voice has changed, and I'm also more experienced. For one thing, I've been to Birmingham and acted in a Shakespeare play. (Covington 196–97)

Lucius/Lizard literally performs the role of Caliban in a low-budget production of *The Tempest*, but the novel depends on Shakespeare's play to provide a metaphoric model of his broader journey as he comes to accept and move beyond the fatherlessness that has plagued him since his birth, and which equally affects his nation. Lizard becomes a specifically *American* Caliban who finds through the culturally-authoritative voice of Shakespeare, a language to speak the trauma of self and nation crystallised by the extreme political history of 1963. Despite this specific historical context, however, the novel's ultimate refusal to engage in the relationship *between* self and history may mark a 'limit' of appropriation. A positivist reading of the novel might suggest that Lizard's "unambiguous moral goodness separates him from Caliban [. . . and his] redemption is not from a personal moral darkness, but from society's abusive darkness in its failure to appreciate him" (Perantoni

160), but I would suggest that Lizard is as flawed an individual as Caliban ever was. Certainly, where Caliban's profit on learning a language of power was to "know how to curse" (Shakespeare, *Tmp.* 1.2.365), this Caliban appropriates language *as* power, he becomes his own Prospero; but in allowing Lizard to tell new stories about himself but not his country, this novel's use of Shakespeare privileges the White masculine subject as individual rather than social subject, and identifies maturity as the ability to participate in privileged cultural production.

Tad Williams's *Caliban's Hour* (1994) also offers an appropriation which focuses on a Caliban figure for the juvenile reader; however, Williams's is an "extrapolated" and "revisionary" narrative (Lanier, *Shakespeare* 83) that imagines Caliban travelling from the island to Naples twenty years after the events of the play conclude, in order to find Miranda and make her an audience to *his* understanding of events. The novel's very content, then, presumes a level of reader competence in *The Tempest* that Covington's novel seeks to provide. Williams's appropriation is overtly postcolonial in ideological orientation, and takes as its central motif Caliban's acquisition of language, and his ensuing struggle for control over narrative in and through that language. Caliban's 'catharsis' and appropriation of linguistic and narrative authority come at the expense of a feminine voice, participating in:

> a tendency among the anti-colonial appropriations of *The Tempest* to reverse the roles of oppressor and oppressed. And more importantly, in doing so, they view the identities of the women—of Miranda and of the missing 'native' woman, Sycorax—simply as an aspect of the Prospero / Caliban opposition rather than in terms of the complex *sexual ideologies* underpinning colonialism. (J. G. Singh 209, original emphasis)

As in the texts discussed by Singh, Williams reinforces while simplifying the gendered and colonial ideologies detectable in Shakespeare's play: less a critique of colonialism than of a *type* of colonialism, the novel "ends up as a confirmation of the colonial premise" (Zabus 219). Williams recasts events of the play through Caliban's eyes, but never challenges the gender relations produced by those events.

Like Covington's *Lizard*, the majority of Williams's novel is given over to a first-person narration of Caliban's adolescence, the events of which are fundamentally the Oedipal complex writ large. The tripartite structure of the novel involves Caliban entering Miranda's bedroom, holding her hostage and forcing her to be an audience to his narrative; the middle section is that narrative; and the final section involves Miranda's daughter Giulietta agreeing to return with Caliban to the island in exchange for her mother's life. These framing sections borrow heavily from the fairy tale tradition of "Beauty and the Beast", and in terms of appropriating *The Tempest*, serve primarily to reinforce the dynamics and psychologies of authority established on the island.

In his narration of their origins, Shakespeare's Prospero displays a lack of faith in Miranda's capability as audience, and uses her as a sounding-board rather than an interlocutor: "The very minute bids thee ope thine ear. / Obey and be attentive" (Shakespeare, *Tmp.* 1.2.36–37), "I pray thee mark me" (1.2.67), "Dos thou attend me?" (1.2.78), "Thou attend'st not!" (1.2.87), "I pray thee mark me" (1.2.87), "Dost thou hear?" (1.2.106), "Hear a little further," (1.2.135), "Well demanded, wench: / My tale provokes that question" (1.2.139–49). Similarly, Williams's Caliban, when he discovers that Prospero has died, makes Miranda the audience to *his* narrative of origins: "You will listen now, Miranda. You will hear the sound of my secret heart before I destroy you. And before you travel into darkness, you will know just what you have done. *You will listen . . .*" (T. Williams 21). The very structure of the novel thus performs the reversal of roles between Prospero and Caliban that Singh critiques, while Miranda retains her position as passive audience. At regular intervals, Caliban simultaneously interpellates Miranda as an interlocutor, and denies her a voice: "Do not speak! At this moment I cannot bear to hear your lying voice. What would you tell me? That you begged your father on my behalf?" (150).

The early section of Caliban's narrative, pertaining to his time on the island before the arrival of Prospero and Miranda, is a kind of prelapsarian idyll. This time is explicitly matriarchal, with Caliban literally worshipping his mother Sycorax, and enjoying a pre-linguistic (and pre-sexual) communion with nature.

> I worshipped her, I feared her, I hated her. I loved her until it burned me inside. And she in turn was the only living creature who has ever loved me . . . To a child, his mother must always be a creature of power, a possessor of arcane knowledge, of healing arts and painful curses, but it was not only her son who saw her thusly. (T. Williams 30–31)

Caliban's Hour never challenges the notion that Sycorax is a witch, even as Caliban recounts how his mother came under suspicion in Algiers and implicitly critiques what a witch might be. Although he has never known Sycorax with a voice, Caliban accepts her narrative because it has been transferred via 'mind-pictures' rather than by language. He learns that "[s]o frightened were [the Algerians] of her magical words, her curses, that they scorched out her tongue with a fire-heated iron" (T. Williams 32); and thus he has never learned language himself. Sycorax is maternal *and* punishing, and Caliban learns to read her moods as he reads the island and its weather. This conflation of both Sycorax and Caliban with 'The Natural' is never challenged by the novel, and is retained as a mark of femininity with reference to Miranda later. The frightening authority of the sexualised feminine voice is linked with danger; a model which Caliban perpetuates in his denial of Miranda's voice in the present time.

In this section of the novel Williams constructs a monstrous feminine that finds its most obvious delineation in a kind of parable Caliban tells about a sow. This parable marks a change, both in Caliban's life and his retrospective narration of it: At this point the tone and register of the text shift to an Edenic model with the metaphoric identification of "serpents on the island" (T. Williams 49) disrupting the pastoral ideal. The sow, protecting her young, gores Caliban's leg and he is trapped up a tree for an entire day before he is able to return to his own mother to have his injuries tended. His fear during this event initiates a thirst for vengeance: "I began to concentrate instead on the injury done me, and the fear turned to black hatred" (55). Caliban digs a pit, traps the sow, and rolls a boulder into it to kill her (63), despite his recognition that "the sow [had] been protecting her own children as my mother would have protected me" (61). Here, then, Caliban's individuation, his journey into "manhood" (42), comes in both the recognition of the monstrous maternal and his defeat of it. In killing a sow who injured him while protecting her young, Caliban finds a masculine authority which is compounded by the death of his mother: Sycorax chokes on a fishbone after denying her own son food. In an obviously concentrated Oedipal progression, Caliban exchanges the female god for the male, the mother for the father, when he remembers his first sight of, "Prospero. Could ever your God have appeared to His followers with any greater effect?" (29) Prospero is explicitly marked as a father-god figure for Caliban even further when he remembers his maturity as both gendered and filial: "Becoming a man, I thought. Becoming a son, I sometimes dared to hope" (105). Clearly, Caliban seeks a mutually recognised filial relationship with Prospero; as in the play, Miranda becomes a potential marker of such a relationship, rather than an individuated subject, for "[t]hough Miranda has a position of cultural superiority over Caliban, she nonetheless has a marginal role within a *kinship* system in which all three males [Prospero, Caliban, and Ferdinand] are bonded through their competing claims on her" (J. G. Singh 213). As with Disney's version of *The Tempest*, *The Little Mermaid* (1989) Williams arguably deploys a "Shakespeare" that "authorizes essentialist, puritan models of development that tie growth to the acquisition of discipline and the taming of rebellious, simplistically defined Oedipal impulses" (Finkelstein 183).

With Prospero as the all-seeing God, Caliban and Miranda become a pseudo-Adam and Eve in this island-garden. The Edenic discourse runs alongside the Shakespearean in the novel as Miranda and Caliban grow into adolescence together; this is particularly significant as Miranda crucially performs an Eve function which is ultimately constructed as more detrimental to Caliban's developing subjectivity than any of the sustained methods of subjugation and colonisation that his tale outlines Prospero performing. Once they have reached adolescence, Caliban sees Miranda swimming naked in a pool, and describes her physicality in such a way that reintroduces the devouring or monstrous feminine to the novel but here it is inflected through sexuality:

"there was nothing else where your legs joined, a lack that was to me both pitiful and frightening" (T. Williams 123).

As in Shakespeare's play a key breaking point between Caliban and Prospero is a near-sexual encounter between Miranda and Caliban. In the play, Prospero claims that "I have used thee / (Filth as thou art) with human care and lodged thee / In mine own cell, till thou didst seek to violate / The honour of my child" (*Tmp.* 1.2.346–49). Shakespeare's Miranda makes no specific comment about an attempted rape, or indeed any form of sexual encounter between herself and Caliban, and the event occurs prior to the play's opening. In Williams's novel, the reader is made privy to the sexual encounter (through Caliban's eyes): He narrates *to Miranda* this event which is at once Edenically and psychoanalytically transforming. Caliban takes Miranda to a valley which he has previously kept hidden; readily legible as a scape of the psyche, this valley has at its centre a tree that Caliban uses as a "confessor" (93). Unsurprisingly, this is revealed to be the tree in which Ariel is imprisoned. As they enter the valley, Miranda catches her hand on a thorn:

> "*Merciful Lord! Something has stung me!*
>
> You held the finger up so I could see the shining bead of blood. I was ashamed and somehow terribly excited." (T. Williams 132)

After this obvious symbol of lost innocence, it matters little what takes place afterward. At the base of 'The Tree' Caliban and Miranda engage in (seemingly voluntary) petting, until interrupted by a voice from the tree hissing "*CHILLLLDRENNNN ... OF ... ADAMMMM*" (T. Williams 137). This voice is revealed to be Ariel pleading for freedom, but it effectively stops any sexual experimentation; functioning as a symbolic supplement of Prospero's parental voice, it frightens Miranda, who flees. The reader is not privy to her story to Prospero about these events, but certainly witnesses the sustained beating issued to Caliban as punishment:

> Whatever drove you, you did what you should not have done: you made me your scapegoat ... He proceeded then to beat me almost to death, smashing at my head and limbs and ribs as I lay curled on the floor ... Perhaps I was never beautiful, but as Nature or your God first made me, I was not crooked! (T. Williams 139–40)

Miranda, who has effectively been made the unknowing instigator of Caliban's sexuality, is here made responsible for the (inevitable) paternal punishment for this sexuality. Significantly for a psychoanalytic reading, this beating makes Caliban the 'monster' he is, in a reified version of psychological scarring from sexual guilt related to the father's authority.

This scene, and its accompanying illustration, provides a condensed example of the novel's overall project of appropriation: using the iconography and language of the postcolonial as a mask for a narrative of sexual competition within an Oedipal framework. Both the image and the scene—and indeed the novel overall—deny Miranda a subjectivity or a voice. Not only does this event deny any possibility of filial bonding between Caliban and Prospero (and further deny Caliban any path of maturity or ascension over the father figure), but it reveals the hidden valley and Ariel to Prospero. Caliban's failed masculinity provides the assurance of Prospero's success. Having heard about the tree, "Prospero marched through the wrack of the burning like a conqueror" (T. Williams 141), and releases Ariel:

> "*I name you and bind you, Ariel the Fallen!*
> *Beneath Solomon's Seal, your fealty belongs to me!*" (142)
> "*Ariel I am. You have freed me from my prison, Child of Adam. I will do your bidding*" (143)

Prospero's control over Ariel provides him with the power to exact revenge on his enemies as per the events in Shakespeare's play. Caliban recognises Ariel as the ideal son he could never be to Prospero, because Ariel is asexual: "He, she—whatever it was—sat on a slender branch which bowed only slightly beneath its weight. It wore the shape of a slender child, but the pale body was curiously featureless, un-nippled, un-naveled" (T. Williams 145).

Once he moves to narrating the events familiar from Shakespeare's *Tempest*, Caliban briefly allows that Miranda may have been "as much [Prospero's] slave as I" (T. Williams 154), and discovers that Prospero has arranged her marriage to Ferdinand in order to exact political revenge. As in the play, Miranda's virginity becomes a synecdochic representation of her value: "*pure, every inch,* answered your father. *Fit bride for a prince*" (159). However, this sympathy does not last long, and Caliban, having told his story, returns to his plan to kill Miranda. At this point Miranda's daughter, Giulietta, reveals that she has been hiding in the room, listening to Caliban's story, and offers herself in exchange for her mother's life: "I think you are no monster, but a man.' She spread her hands, imploring. '*I have listened.* I will go with you" (174). This agreement leads Zabus to suggest that "*Caliban's Hour* represents that middle ground in grappling with fantasy, between the emancipation from the former dominant discourse of which Prospero is the originator and the perpetuator, and the reconstruction of a dynamic and multicultural dialogue Giulietta could partake of" (220).[9] However, I would suggest that, given the novel's preoccupations with language and/as sexuality and knowledge, the framing story could indeed be read as a sustained 'rape' of the adult Miranda. As this dominator, only successful because Prospero is dead, Caliban is rewarded for this rape with the voluntary victimhood of Guilietta, Miranda's daughter. At the end of the novel, Caliban's happiness is literally dependent on Miranda not having a voice:

> "So now we come to the test. If I am the monster you and your father made me out, then you should run and throw open the doors and shout for help this very instant. For if I am that brute, surely no promise of mine can be trusted, and you would be abandoning your beloved child to ravishment and murder . . . If not, then give us until the candle burns down to escape." (T. Williams 178–79)

Caliban's journey to masculine maturity fails in his adolescence: neither language, sexuality, or colonisation provide him with authority. However, once the father is dead, he appropriates all three of these, and having done so, Miranda silently acknowledges that he is "a man" by not raising any alarm at Caliban's departure with her daughter, and thus may also be affirming the legitimacy of Caliban's testimony. Nonetheless, the feminine is reduced to the sexual, and that sexuality remains a commodity of exchange in the colonial project that *Caliban's Hour* ultimately affirms rather than challenges.

Extrapolating a reading relationship from this novel, the young masculine reader is encouraged to supersede the father (Prospero/Shakespeare), but not the paternal discourses of authority. The juvenile masculine subject is offered a model of cultural authority which is simultaneously predicated on the sexual subordination of the feminine (intratextual) and cultural authority (extratextual). In both *Lizard* and *Caliban's Hour* such cultural authority is yoked to a determinedly Eurocentric and patriarchal model of subjectivity and consumption. In the novels I have read thus far, the paternal function of Prospero has been maintained in what are essentially Oedipal narratives of masculine juvenile subjects appropriating cultural authority. Extending the identification of Prospero with Shakespeare himself, the masculine reader is encouraged to engage with texts of cultural authority in a similar manner: reading becomes a form of ownership and control, naturalised as part of the maturing process. Indeed, Caliban's lack of literal filial relationship with Prospero may paradoxically ensure the broader applicability of this notion for the masculine reader. For example, a young male reader need not feel that he cannot access and appropriate the authority of "Shakespeare": cultural capital is there for the taking by any willing and able subject (of course these willing and able subjects are White males). The social and individual circumstances which enable the acquisition of such capital, of course, seem to operate only within patriarchal or male homosocial contexts, and indeed, privileged knowledge or cultural production serves to affirm the legitimacy of such contexts.

As the father of a single daughter, Prospero can only act as symbolic father to young masculine subjects. To ask questions about Miranda's access to cultural capital or cultural agency is to intervene in a cultural image of Prospero as father *or* magician. When figured as a magician or wise man, symbolic sons can engage in an Oedipal struggle with him; when figured as a literal father, however, it seems that Prospero is distanced from his cultural power. It is perhaps for this reason that Miranda has become an important figure for female authors writing about power in postcolonial contexts (see Zabus; Vaughan and Vaughan). Certainly Miranda can function as a feminine subaltern (to a degree). However, when deployed in children's literature, Miranda often serves to affirm the politics of feminine subordination which can be traced in the play, and which underpin the male-focussed texts I have already discussed in this chapter.

Reading the familial relationship between Miranda and Prospero, *The Tempest* could be read as an allegory of the emergence of the female child into the adult world separated from parental dominance. To read the play so positively, one would have to be convinced of the legitimacy of patriarchy and read

> *The Tempest* [as] Miranda's coming of age ritual. It begins with the revelation of her true identity and ends with her betrothal. Every stage in this initiation process is overseen by her magician-father. Prospero is one of the earliest examples in literature of father as single parent. He protects Miranda, both from knowledge that would make her unhappy and from physical and emotional danger. He lavishes affection on her, never hesitating to say how and why he prizes her. At the same time, he respects her individuality. (Hamilton 24)

I cannot agree with Hamilton's enthusiastic reading of Miranda's experiences, as to do so would be to ignore the linking of feminine happiness with ignorance and matrimony, and the passing from one authoritative masculine gaze into another. It is precisely these elements which have made Miranda a useful figure for feminist and postcolonial discourse: "Miranda, the Anglo-European daughter, offers us a feminine trope of colonialism, for her lack of selfhood in *The Tempest* exposes the subjection of daughters to their biological or cultural Fathers before they come of age" (Zabus 105). Unfortunately, novels that appropriate *The Tempest* for implied female adolescent readers tend to focus on romance plots and issues of sexuality, and thus confirm Miranda's status as commodified object-of-exchange for the negotiation/confirmation of "relations between men" (Sedgwick 3).[10] *The Tempest*'s marriage plot offers a convenient template for contemporary romance fiction. However, in unproblematically transferring the father-daughter relationship of the play into contemporary texts, authors simultaneously inscribe and naturalise a female reading-relationship with "Shakespeare", or more properly, a female non-reading-relationship with "Shakespeare" and the Shakespearean text. Paternal authority figures, literal and symbolic, remain separate from but mostly in control of young women in texts where cultural capital is thematised, but is never the province of the feminine protagonist.

A prime example of this approach is the canonised children's text, *A Wrinkle in Time* (1962) by Madeleine L'Engle. Since winning the 1963 Newbery Medal, both the novel and its author have been the object of sustained critical interest. Megan Isaac implicitly claims it appropriates *The Tempest* in a subversive manner: "[w]hereas Shakespeare's play most often invites interpretations that maintain the patriarchal status quo, L'Engle's novel invites readers to challenge tyranny and value self-determination" (99–100). However, while the novel intertextually cites the play, I do not believe it *appropriates* it; further, L'Engle's citations in fact reinforce a 'patriarchal status quo' with specific reference to Shakespeare. Readings like Isaac's are conflating certain cultural moments/productions and overstating the play's place within L'Engle's novel in an attempt to link the contemporary canon of children's literature with Shakespeare, and Shakespeare in popular culture.[11] L'Engle naturalises the exchange or commodity element of Miranda's story under the guise of rewriting the coming-of-age plot. Therefore, while it is not strictly an appropriation, *A Wrinkle in Time* is a perfect example of the ways in which young female readers are encouraged to identify with a protagonist who disavows cultural capital: By identifying with such characters, readers are also encouraged to naturalise (and perhaps even reproduce) feminine disavowals of cultural capital.

The novel constructs a science-fiction world where Meg Murry must travel to another planet to rescue her father from a totalitarian ruler, IT, and return home safely in order to restore her family life. Isaac treats *Wrinkle* as a *Tempest*-text due to her focus on plot: "L'Engle's novel concentrates on Miranda and explores the consequences a modern young woman might face were she to invest her father with absolute power and unquestioned obedience like Shakespeare's heroine" (97). Even as I disagree with Isaac's simplistic reading of *The Tempest*, I would agree that the primary psychological quest Meg undergoes is individuation from the father. However, to view the novel's use of Shakespeare as limited to facilitating this quest in order to challenge "Meg, and the novel's readers to consider the limitations of authority, even parental authority" (99), crucially effaces the full functioning of "Shakespeare" within *A Wrinkle in Time*.

Thus, although I do not believe L'Engle appropriates *The Tempest*, tracking Shakespeare through the text nonetheless is useful as "Shakespeare", along with other canonical writings, provides an index of hierarchised knowledge which in turn marks the value of characters. If, as Isaac does, the novel is read as a resolution of the father-daughter relationship figuring Meg as a Miranda-figure, *The Tempest* would appear to offer a useful point of intertextual reference. However, although Meg is focalised, I want to suggest that she is not the 'hero' of this text, and that in fact, the novel works hard to empty her character while constructing a hero-plot for her love-interest, Calvin.

I am certainly not the first to question the positive centrality of Meg. Blackburn went so far as to suggest that the novel is more allegory than quest-narrative, arguing that "Camazotz is not so much a planet as a bogeyman—an early sixties American image of life in a Communist state . . . The novel makes it altogether too easy to identify the cosmic struggle of good against evil as the struggle of American libertarianism against Russian tyranny" (128). I will be returning to this question of competition in the novel, but recasting it as a struggle of types of knowledge, rather than political ideologies. Focussing on the gendered development of Meg in *A Wrinkle in Time*, Schneebaum suggests that, "[t]he criterion by which Meg and the others choose her as the savior is gender. Meg's strong emotions, misguided until now into masculine behavior will be the most effective in their intended mode: powerful, redeeming love" (36). I want to combine these notions of allegory and gender, and consider them through the lens of Shakespearean intertextual citation.

Firstly, I am arguing that there are specifically constructed and opposed modes of knowing in this novel, most readily described as the cultural and the scientific, or the emotional and the rational. Unsurprisingly, these knowledges are gendered, marking the cultural/emotional as feminine and the scientific/rational as masculine. While seeming simultaneously to privilege the former within the generic conventions of science fiction, this inversion does not result in any challenge to a dualistic model, but rather, uses one to justify the symbolic erasure of Meg as a rational, thinking subject.

The novel's deployment of science as a discourse of subjectivity is not surprising given L'Engle's participation in the genre of science fiction. Indeed, this aspect of the novel is constructed as central to the book's narrative by L'Engle: "I think one of the reasons that *Wrinkle* was rejected so often [by publishers] was, who's ever heard of a *tesseract?* Well, it's a real concept. It's an honest-to-goodness scientific word, which you'll find in the footnotes of large dictionaries. I think it's terrible to limit vocabulary" (Rausen 203). In her afterword to the 1995 'Puffin Modern Classics' edition, Elaine Moss addresses an explicitly juvenile audience:

> As you read you were probably so absorbed in the plot—Would Mr Murry be rescued? How would Charles Wallace escape? Was Meg going to understand that only the power of love could defeat evil—that you swallowed the mathematics and physics of the tesseract and the theory of the movement of atoms at a gulp. (215)

Each of these comments highlights the scientific discourse of the novel—indeed Moss attributes to it an overt educational function—at the expense of the moral critique the text performs of this discourse. Certainly, the concept of a 'tesseract' is central to the plot, and is deployed in such a way as to educate readers about its theoretical existence, arguing that "the fifth dimension's a tesseract. You add that to the other four dimensions and you can travel through space without having to go the long way round" (L'Engle, *Wrinkle* 77). This notion provides the text with the verb 'to tesser' which means to use tesseracts to travel through space and time, and this central conceit enables the symbolic journeys of the novel.

Ultimately, however, science as used by humans, is constructed as dangerous and egocentric. A key moment of Meg's interrogation of her father comes in the form of questioning his arrogant use of science, when he confesses to

Meg, "I know so little about anything that I can't be sure" (L'Engle, *Wrinkle* 171). Her response, later blamed on the influence of evil rather than a legitimate critique, is to tell him that, "'You shouldn't have tried to tesser, then.' She had never spoken to her father in this way before. The words seemed hardly to be hers" (171). It is this very *human* use of science that comes under critique as L'Engle constructs an 'ideal' science more accurately described as mysticism or spirituality. Throughout the novel, ideals and spiritualities are conflated in a Christian Platonist discourse in keeping with categories that L'Engle has elsewhere conflated and privileged as "scientists or adults or theologians" ("Childlike" 102). This conflation leads to a linking of Jesus (L'Engle, *Wrinkle* 88) and Shakespeare (89) as "Messengers of God" (192).

The anti-rational morality of the novel is most obviously inscribed via Camazotz itself, a world where everyone lives according to strict regimentation as dictated by IT, the non-human entity who controls the planet. IT 'embodies' or at least signifies absolute rationality:

> IT was a brain.
>
> A disembodied brain. An oversized brain, just enough larger than normal to be completely revolting and terrifying. A living brain. A brain that pulsed and quivered, that seized and commanded. No wonder the brain was called IT. IT was the most horrible, the most repellent thing she had ever seen. (L'Engle, Wrinkle 158)

Meg's embodiment of absolute love as a weapon is thus perfectly suited for challenging this opponent, later figured as abject, "lying pulsing and quivering on the dais, soft and exposed and nauseating" (L'Engle, *Wrinkle* 207). This IT is parasitic, depending on other lifeforms (humans) to carry out its wishes and ideals. Meg is able to resist IT's attempts at mind-control by embracing "Love" (209) and therefore rescuing Charles Wallace from IT.

Although 'it' is, of course, a neuter term, the novel's masculinising of rationality places IT at the opposite end of a spectrum from Mrs Who, Mrs Which and Mrs Whatsit, who appear most commonly in feminine form, and who represent the cultural/emotional knowledge which Meg must draw upon to defeat the brain. These three women 'originate' Shakespearean quotation within the novel (even though the Murrys's dog is named Fortinbras (L'Engle, *Wrinkle* 4)) when Mrs Who self-consciously cites *Macbeth* to initiate a private joke amongst the women:

> "*When shall we three meet again,*
> *In thunder, lightning, or in rain?*"
>
> . . . Mrs Whatsit and Mrs Who began to giggle, and they giggled until it seemed that, whatever their private joke was, they would fall down with the wild fun of it. The shimmer seemed to be laughing, too. It became

> vaguely darker and more solid; and then there appeared a figure in a black robe and a black peaked hat, beady eyes, a beaked nose, and long grey hair; one bony claw clutched a broomstick.
>
> "Wwell, jusstt ttoo kkeepp yyou girrlls happy," the strange voice said, and Mrs Whatsit and Mrs Who fell into each other's arms in gales of laughter. (L'Engle, *Wrinkle* 59)

Meg is the unknowing focaliser here, as she remains through most of the novel.

Shakespeare is only one of a series of canonical literary figures cited by Mrs Who, including Seneca (L'Engle, *Wrinkle* 35), Perez and Dante (54), Goethe (98), although it is Shakespeare who gets the lengthiest citation when she offers the following quotation to Calvin as "a hint" (97):

> . . . *For that thou wast a spirit too delicate*
> *To act their earthy and abhorr'd commands,*
> *Refusing their grand hests, they did confine thee*
> *By help of their more potent ministers,*
> *And in their most unmitigable rage,*
> *Into a cloven pine; within which rift*
> *Imprisoned, thou didst painfully remain . . .* (97–98)

This narrative of Ariel's history is translated into a narrative of Mr Murry's experience, implying that he has heroically refused to do evil, and has thus been punished. Significantly, L'Engle silently rewrites Shakespeare in this 'quotation' changing all the pronouns from 'her' to 'their'. When Prospero speaks these lines to Ariel (Shakespeare, *Tmp.* 1.2.272–78) he is reminding the sprite of Sycorax's ill-treatment, and implicitly, of the gratitude Ariel owes Prospero for rescue from the pine. This erasure of autonomous feminine power in favour of moral social commentary is emblematic of L'Engle's broader deployment of Shakespeare.

Meg, although exposed to "Shakespeare" along with Charles Wallace and Calvin, cannot retain or recognise this discourse of authority. When Calvin repeats the speech from *The Tempest* in an attempt to reach and rescue Charles Wallace from the influence of IT, "Meg recognized Mrs Who's words to him" (L'Engle, *Wrinkle* 146) rather than recognising them as Shakespeare's (albeit in edited form). Similarly, while Meg can suggest that her father is like Ariel trapped in a cloven pine, she refers to this idea as "your cloven pine thing" (147) again attributing its origins to Calvin. Thus, although *The Tempest* becomes a key cultural signifier in the battle against IT, it also functions as a marker of hierarchised knowledge *within* the group battling IT.

Meg is established throughout the novel as intellectually inferior or limited in that she can retain scientific (L'Engle, *Wrinkle* 161) or mathematical (191) formulae, but cannot think critically about subjects which could be labelled as 'humanities'. She apparently unknowingly 'cites' *Hamlet* when she thinks that "[t]here is definitely something rotten in the state of Camazotz" (126). From both her own and others' perspective, Meg is consistently marked as limited, as is demonstrated by the following patronising exchange:

> "Who wrote Boswell's *Life of Johnson*?"
> "Oh, Calvin. I'm not any good at English."
> Calvin groaned and turned to Mrs Murry. "I see what you mean. Her I wouldn't want to teach." (43)

This brief encounter encapsulates the commentary Meg is subjected to throughout, until it culminates in her becoming an anatomised body literally incapable of verbal exchange with her father and 'lover':

> "And then we could feel her heart, very faintly, the beats very far apart. And then it got stronger. So all we have to do is wait." Her father's words sounded brittle in her ears, as though they were being chipped out of ice.
> Calvin: "Yes. You're right, sir."
> She wanted to call out to them. "I'm alive! I'm very much alive! Only I've been turned to stone."
> But she could not call out any more than she could move. (164)

So sustained is this denial of Meg's intellectual subjectivity that she herself accepts and reinforces it: "She knew that her own puny little brain was no match" (L'Engle, *Wrinkle* 160) for IT. The novel ultimately constructs her acceptance of these limitations as Meg's most valuable asset and mark of development. Shakespeare is used simultaneously, then, to confirm that feminine knowledge is and should be emotional rather than rational, while also making such knowledge subordinate to masculinity.

Having accepted her function—to embody love—to a degree where she does not even question Calvin's assertion that "she's backward" (L'Engle, *Wrinkle* 198), Meg returns to Camazotz and does indeed save Charles Wallace. Before her departure though, the novel performs its most succinct appropriation of (Shakespearean) cultural capital for didactic moral purposes in the following pseudo-Socratic exchange between Mrs Whatsit and Calvin:

> "How can I explain it to you? Oh, I know. In your language you have a form of poetry called the sonnet . . . It is a very strict form of poetry, is it not?"
> "Yes."
> "There are fourteen lines, I believe, all in iambic pentameter. That's a very strict rhythm or metre, yes?"
> "Yes." Calvin nodded.
> "And each line has to end with a rigid rhyme pattern. And if the poet does not do it exactly this way, it is not a sonnet is it?"
> "No."

> "But within this strict form the poet has complete freedom to say whatever he wants, doesn't he?" . . .
>
> "You mean you're comparing our lives to a sonnet? A strict form, but freedom within it?"
>
> "Yes," Mrs Whatsit said. "You're given the form, but you have to write the sonnet yourself. What you say is completely up to you." (199–200)

Removed from an active role in the rescue, Calvin asserts a personal authority over Meg by appropriating a 'lover' role: "Calvin came to her and took her hand, then drew her roughly to him and kissed her. He didn't say anything, and he turned away before he had a chance to see the surprised happiness that brightened Meg's eyes" (L'Engle, *Wrinkle* 201). Again, it is crucial that Meg's own reaction to this event is unseen by (and implicitly unimportant to) Calvin.

Upon their return to Earth, it is clear that the nuclear family structure is reinstated, now incorporating Calvin as an 'adopted' son, thus completing his quest:

> there was a tremendous happy jumble of arms and legs and hugging, the older Murrys and Meg and Charles Wallace and the twins, and Calvin grinning by them until Meg reached out and pulled him in and Mrs Murry gave him a special hug all of his own. (L'Engle 212)

Within the framework of a dystopic narrative, L'Engle constructs an obvious value system of love versus hate and emotion versus reason which is carefully gendered seemingly to construct Meg as hero, but which actually reduces her to a sign of masculine achievements. Through all this, the cultural capital of Shakespeare as secular saviour is used to reinforce the novel's value system and make Meg a cipher who is rewarded for her vacancy by the return of a father, and the acquisition of a lover. Thus the novel retains Miranda's marriage plot from Shakespeare's play.

Zibby Oneal's *In Summer Light* (1985) tells the story of a seventeen-year-old girl, Kate Brewer, who is confined to her family home for a summer due to illness linked to incipient sexuality (mononucleosis/glandular fever which is known colloquially as "kissing disease"). This family home, literally situated on an island, is ruled over by her father Marcus Brewer, a famous painter who spends little time actually *with* his family, preferring his cell-like studio. The arrival of an outsider—a graduate student named Ian Jackson who is cataloguing Brewer's work—quickly emphasises the plot parallels with Shakespeare's play, and also initiates a key period of self-reflexivity and change on the part of the protagonist.

Insofar as it centralises the Miranda-figure, *In Summer Light* is one of the few appropriations of *The Tempest* to interrogate constructions of the feminine in the play itself. This interrogation is implicit, and is activated through the rewarding of a focalised narration to Kate, thereby privileging her perspectives, emotions, and experiences, although not providing her with full narrational authority. However Kate's success is marked not by a 'rewriting' of Miranda, but via the appropriation of 'Prospero'. Art, gender, and authority are intertwined in the novel, which uses "Shakespeare" simultaneously to structure and authorise its discursive constructions of subjectivity.

There is a layered binary logic at work in the novel of, art/literature, personal/professional, and natural/learned. I believe that these oppositions also extend to masculine/feminine, suggesting that Kate's success is constructed as symbolic masculinity as she becomes an artist using natural talent in the realm of her father. The novel works through these oppositions via *The Tempest* which is used both as a structuring narrative and as a text being read by the protagonist. There is a dual notion of reading in the novel, as Kate 'reads' her family, while also literally reading Shakespeare for a school assignment. This 'paper' recurs periodically throughout the novel, usually alternated with Kate's painting/artistry, and provides an important index of her development. Kate's responses to *The Tempest* follow the same progression as her responses to her own artistic ability: anger, denial and acceptance, while shifting agency from a father-figure to herself. As her 'professional' interest in Shakespeare declines, her professionalised interest in painting increases; thus, I will follow Kate's progression from Art to Shakespeare (and back again), and the final coalescences of these competing discourses.

The novel actually opens with a description of a painting, rather than Kate's 'reality', in an obvious inscription of the central authority art wields in her life history. The painting, which becomes a symbol of her adversarial view of her father, is read by visitors to the house as a portrait of Kate herself, but is described by her father as "only colors occupying space" (Oneal 21) rendering Kate as an object rather than a subject. When Kate discusses *The Tempest* with her schoolfriend Leah, links between Kate's own objectification and Miranda's are stated clearly:

> "He's good to Miranda."
>
> "Is that right? 'I have done nothing but in care of thee, my daughter'? If you believe that, Leah, you're crazy. Think about it awhile." (Oneal 26)

This connection, which is not made consciously by Kate, offers a model of artist and subject drawn directly from Act 1 , Scene 2 of the play. The line cited by Kate (Shakespeare, *Tmp.* 1.2.16–17) comes at the beginning of Prospero's narration to Miranda of their personal histories (as discussed above). This model, of supplicant daughter to all-knowing and creating father, is implicitly that which Marcus Brewer seeks. However, while Kate views him as a Prospero—"Down there he was painting, he and his canvas making an island together on this larger island where the rest of them lived" (Oneal 8)—she has refused the script, distancing herself from the painting which constitutes her father's magical creativity. Nonetheless, she has not 'rewritten' the script for herself beyond the rejection of visual art for the planned study of English. While she understands her father as Prospero, Kate does not consciously understand herself as Miranda, for even as she rejects the model of adoring daughter, she remains subject to the 'great artist':

> It was only after they moved to the island that his pictures had begun to change. The real world had stopped mattering, and bit by bit it had disappeared from his canvases, replaced by shape and color alone. Self-portraits, Kate thought. That's what they had become—painting of the contents of his mind. (22)

This construction of her father's work at once critiques the 'other' world he inhabits artistically, and his family inhabits physically, while also effectively endorsing the denial of her subjectivity in the portrait which hangs in the kitchen.

Her own self-portrait early in the novel is the construction of a Shakespearean reader, a role which Kate performs for her mother, drawing a distinction between "Shakespeare" and *The Tempest*:

> "The thing is, I don't like *The Tempest*."
>
> "You like Shakespeare," her mother said, saying it as if she were speaking of a slightly exotic taste.
>
> "That's beside the point, Mother. It's not Shakespeare, it's this play. Naturally I like Shakespeare. *Everyone* likes Shakespeare. Even Amanda likes him. I read her a couple of Ariel's songs. She thinks they're 'cool'."
>
> "Do you suppose she'll want to be an English major, too?" (Oneal 6)

This exchange rapidly forces Kate self-reflexively to realise, "[i]t's because of Prospero. He reminds me of Father" (Oneal 7). Significantly, her identification with the play is not as an actor, but an observer. Rather than identify *with* Miranda against Prospero, she takes up a Miranda-role, in recognising and centralising her 'Father' as key-signifier. This reflects his role as painter/artist in her life to date: As a pre-sexual child, Kate was able to function as an acolyte to her father, and working side-by-side in his studio, she learnt the basic tasks of painting. As Kate developed as a painter, she began to work on projects 'outside' the island, independently at school: "[s]he remembered how hard she'd tried, wanting so much to please him" (45). Once she recognised her father's antipathy to her growing skill, expressed through his complete rejection of her victory in an art competition, Kate decided to stop painting altogether. There is a space opened up by the discourse of "Shakespeare" here, a culturally authoritative space not ruled-over by Kate's father, which may offer an (albeit patriarchal) alternative to Art. While gestured to, however, this Shakespearean discourse is never fully appropriated by Kate, and the novel subordinates itself to masculinised art, while using Shakespeare implicitly to authorise this move.

The stagnation of creativity at this point—Kate can neither paint, nor write about Shakespeare—is experienced bodily as well as mentally by her. Suffering from mononucleosis, she knows "the heavy pull of fatigue, dragging her back into lethargy" (Oneal 5), and embraces the psychological lethargy which stems from it, thinking it "pleasant to feel slightly disconnected" (16). This alienating lethargy is broken by the weather, the novel's own tempest, which ushers in turn the arrival of a lover-figure, Ian Jackson, who arrives at the house "wet as the survivor of a shipwreck" (9). As with Ferdinand, the draw of the island has been the father-figure, but in this case it is consciously so, as Ian has come to catalogue Marcus Brewer's work.

Just as Ferdinand enables Prospero to take up the mantle of ruler, Ian enables Marcus to play the great artist. In each case, of course, this is a limited performance: Prospero will cede all power, and Marcus is reaching the end of his career (Ian is there preparing for a retrospective). In turn, Ian forces Kate to be self-reflexive about her own painting, and her understanding of her father as an *artist*: "'Your father *is* a great painter,' Ian said. 'That's the thing. And if you're as great a painter as your father, all kinds of people want things from you. He's right not to let them eat him up'" (Oneal 74). Thus, in accepting a 'lover' figure, this Miranda is forced simultaneously to accept her father as authority as well. Indeed, this seems to be Ian's primary function as lover: "[l]ittle by little, some of Ian's respect for her father's work infected her. He was a great painter. No matter what else she felt about him, she had to concede that" (103).

The romance plot is marked by versions of the interchanges between Ferdinand and Miranda, made over into a heightened domestic setting. However, where Shakespeare's Prospero forced Ferdinand to perform tasks to prove his love, this Ferdinand figure voluntarily labours around the domestic space. Thus Ferdinand's wood-carrying trial becomes the repair of a "loose board in the step" (Oneal 73) at the entrance to the house, and a dishwashing scene in which: "[h]e hummed as he worked, scraping and rinsing. Kate stacked up the last of the dishes from the table, and started to load the dishwasher's rubberized slots . . . They worked together in a slow, easy rhythm, as if they had worked together for years" (76–77). These moments mark a compatibility between Ian and Kate that convinces Kate she is in love with Ian:

> She knew. She had known for quite a while. It hadn't come to her at any one time or in any special place as she had expected, but so slowly that she hardly recognized its coming at all. It had been there before she gave it a name. Like air, it had been all around her. (117)

She asks Ian to take her away with him, but he declines on the basis that "I'm too old for you right now. I have to go too far away" (Oneal 129). The romance plot is therefore declined, but their relationship, as well as returning her to painting, allows Kate to consciously identify with Miranda: "she thought of Miranda, gazing for the first time on all the shipwrecked men, the first besides her father that she had ever seen" (130). This recognition serves primarily to justify the failed romance with Ian, rather than re-thinking the role of daughter/inheritor to an artist figure. Nonetheless, it is Ian who rekindles her interest in painting, and who convinces her to start painting again. This appears to function as a direct reflection of Miranda's experience in *The Tempest*: moving from the authoritative gaze of a father to that of a lover. Such a connection also challenges the notion of a 'failed' romance between Ian and Kate, for if painting is a coded-sexuality, Ian has literally instigated Kate's sexual development. She returns both to Shakespeare and painting through this temporary lover's influence.

The plot-based appropriation of *The Tempest* offers some useful models for considering Kate's development, but it is in the metafictional appropriation the novel performs that a discursive function may be ascribed to "Shakespeare" in *In Summer Light,* which uses the play's father-daughter relationship at once to structure its own father-daughter relationship, and as a model to 'rewrite' against. Simultaneous to her developing relationship with Ian, Kate is able to observe her father's performance as *father* when her friend Leah visits the island: "[a]ll evening he had been charming, funny, almost poetic, as if nothing at all were on his mind but the pleasure of the moment" (Oneal 52). Kate's memory of Leah's visit is crucial to her own development because it allows her to see the 'tricks' of her father's 'paternity' to a young woman who—unlike Kate herself—is a willing supplicant:

> "I think that you're a believer in magic," Kate's father said, and Leah laughed as though she had never heard anything quite so amusing before . . . He raised his arms, conducting them like an orchestra . . . here he stopped and smiled as though he had conjured up the cafe with the wave of a wand . . ."You know what it makes me think of?" [Leah] said. "It's the way I imagine Prospero's island. Kind of dreamy, you know?" (55–57)

During Leah's visit, Kate articulates her personal history with her father, and in doing so, transcends it. As she returns to painting, Kate also returns to her school paper on *The Tempest.* In a crucial scene, the novel constructs the several competing discourses of reading and authority:

> All afternoon Kate lay flat on her stomach beside the pond reading Shakespeare. She lay reading with her head in her hands, then with her head on her arms, and finally with her chin on the edge of the book. In that position she couldn't see much, but it didn't matter. For half an hour, she hadn't known what she was reading. Her mind kept slipping away from the lines on the page. It was like the lighthouse beacon, pausing on one thought and then on another, but not lingering.

> She wondered whether Shakespeare had ever lived on a real island, or had only imagined one. She wondered what he meant Prospero to represent. In class, some people had said he was meant to represent the artist, creating illusion from reality. Others had said no, the whole play was meant to be political. (83–84)

At this point, Kate is willing to return to Shakespeare, but has no motivation to critique. Just as the arrival of Ian inspires her artistic and literary awakening, his departure inspires her *self-reflexive* reading. This development of literate subjectivity and confidence in her own ideas is reassuring, although it is gendered as masculine. When Kate decides that "she would be comfortable" (95) writing about the play as a political text, she consciously denies the play's resonances with her own life, but this conscious denial comes at the precise time she takes up painting again, therefore *living* a subconscious criticism of Prospero as the all-powerful artist, while technically writing a political critique of the play.

Art itself is resolutely gendered as masculine by the novel, and thus what artistic talent Kate has is identified as something inherited (from the father), which cannot be learned. Throughout the novel, Kate's mother, who has dedicated her life to serving the great artist-husband, is constructed as a moral fable for Kate. Her mother, a painter in her youth, has sacrificed her own career for a family. Initially, this is another point of resentment for Kate toward her father. However, as the novel progresses it is made clear that her mother was not *really* an artist at all, and a last-minute *denouement* reveals that her mother encouraged her father to educate her; Kate's mother then becomes a prompt to Kate's development, rather than a model for it. This is emphasised by an obviously symbolic exchange between Kate and her mother:

> Kate picked up the notebook and looked at the figure her mother had drawn. A person could learn to foreshorten a leg, she thought, to draw a figure that was perfectly adequate. It was the other thing that you couldn't learn, that was simply there, like a present. She knew because she recognized this other thing in her father's work. (Oneal 136)

Kate represents a combination of her father's natural art (he has come to the island to escape professional teaching) and her mother's 'learned' art. In other words, Kate must reject her 'feminine' elements (as daughter and lover) in order to become authoritatively artistic. It is the mental/emotional removal from both her father and Ian which allows Kate's personal artistic development, while also denying her any participation in feminine cultural discourse: Miranda must deny both Prospero and Ferdinand if she is to have autonomy.

In the previous chapter, I was concerned by the discursive linking of "Shakespeare" and/as "romance" in novels aimed at adolescent women. *In Summer Light* demonstrates that simply inverting this model can be as problematic as enforcing romance as the normative goal for young women. While Miranda's engagement to Ferdinand in Shakespeare's *Tempest* has often been constructed as the culmination of her commodification as an exchange-object, Jessica Slights has put forward a more challenging reading of this event in terms of gendered interpretation of the play. She suggests that Miranda's "romance with, and marriage to, Ferdinand is best understood not merely as a political affiliation effected for Prospero's pleasure, but also as a crucial opportunity for Miranda to derive a sense of herself as an agent in the world" (364). If Slights is correct, it must be asked where that leaves Kate's anti-romance trajectory in *In Summer Light*. I believe Oneal reinforces the dominant post-Romantic view of Miranda as passive cipher, while implicitly suggesting that feminine agency can be gained only by rejecting key discourses of femininity (i.e., romance) and taking up the mantle of the father. What Stephens and McCallum praise then, as Oneal offering "the present generation of young female readers reading positions and strategies with which to question textual and social discourses apt to disempower women" ("Discourses" 141) might in fact be read as a capitulation to the male/female binary; an inversion rather than a critique, which never really seeks to provide the young feminine subject with critical *reading* skills, but rather to offer a simplistic alternative based on rejection rather than rethinking. It seems that Kate cannot be both feminine and authoritative.

The link between sexuality and creativity in the novel is read by Stephens and McCallum as masculine:

> Masculinism is implicit in the equation of sex and creativity in Brewer's monologues about painting being 'like making love' and criticism being 'dead from the waist down' . . . Kate's use of her whole body as a brush while painting a rock with clay toward the close of the novel might be read ironically back on these comments. ("Discourses" 138)

As a self-conscious performance by Marcus this is certainly the case, but it is not ironic that Kate temporarily paints back against Marcus's masculinism with her whole body, as her own lived experience confirms the legitimacy of sexuality-creativity. Rather than question the gendering of this equation, Kate becomes symbolically masculine herself. Arguably then, Kate fulfils the Oedipal progression usually ascribed to the male child, where here, rather than finding *sexual* autonomy via the symbolic death of the father, Kate finds *artistic* autonomy upon recognising her father's mortality.

Despite their proclaimed interest in Oneal's novel as an intertextual artefact, Stephens and McCallum do not read Oneal's narrative back against *The Tempest*. In fact, it is their failure to treat *In Summer Light* as a specifically *Shakespearean* intertext that leads to their over-positivist reading of the novel in which they suggest that Kate "comes to recognize the ways in which she has been interpellated and seeks a more personally empowered subject position" ("Discourses" 131). When read against and amongst Shakespeare for children as a genre, *In*

Summer Light actually produces a complex model of gendered subjectivity as mediated by "Shakespeare" which in turn reveals Stephens and McCallum's 'empowered' to be 'masculine'. Kate's development is positive, but it maintains rather than questions the naturalised hierarchy of gendered positions.

The model of reading presented in *In Summer Light* in fact emphasises a kind of idealised Romantic model of finding the self *through* the text, rather than any sense of questioning or challenging it. The cultural capital of Shakespeare, then, is transmitted wholesale, and implicitly Oneal's readers are not encouraged to interrogate the text *they* are presented with. Just as the play provided Kate with a language to express her resentment of her father at the beginning of the novel, her written response to *The Tempest* allows her to perform her forgiveness of him. As she reconciles Shakespeare's play and her own artistic talent, Kate recognises her father's mortality:

> On the step beside her lay her notebook. The paper was finished. A picture of Frances was almost finished. The summer that had seemed so long had shrunk to almost nothing. Her father was old. . . .
>
> "And yet at the end of the play," she wrote, "Prospero has become an old man. His magic powers are nearly gone, and then they are gone entirely. In the Epilogue he asks us to set him free. I think Shakespeare means for us to forgive him. I think he means that if we refuse, we will be trapped like Prospero was, on his island." (Oneal 143)

The articles in this quotation are telling: where Kate has finished 'the' paper, she is working on 'a' picture. The connotation is that for Kate, having resolved a personal crisis through *The Tempest*, Shakespeare will no longer be part of her intellectual activity, whereas the production of visual art will be an ongoing process. Thus, even as she appropriates the Prospero role, the novel never *challenges* the authority of *The Tempest*, nor suggests a developing or dialectic relationship with the Shakespearean text. Kate's forgiveness absolves both Marcus and Prospero, but potentially sanitises the latter in his own play. The conclusion to her essay makes over Prospero into a preoccupied father, rather than any kind of tyrant or inappropriate authority figure: In turn, this sanitisation lessens her victory and reduces the problem of Miranda's subordination in *The Tempest*.

Penni Russon's *Undine* (2004) raises issues via a Miranda figure similar to Oneal's novel, but does so in order to affirm the protagonist's agency and autonomy *from* the father, rather than *through* the father. Like Kate, Undine must learn about her father's discourse of authority (in this case magic), but as opposed to Kate's journey of appropriation, Undine's primary lesson is that this magic was always already hers. Russon's novel invokes two key intertexts of young feminine subjectivity linked with water and/as the supernatural or magic: Shakespeare's *The Tempest* and the folk-tradition of "Undine". However, rather than capitulating to the patriarchal structures inherent to them, Russon rewrites them simultaneously in order to produce a young feminine protagonist who journeys towards maturity on her own terms. That said, the novel nonetheless deploys problematic coding of elements such as sexuality and knowledge as conservatively gendered.

Undine is a sixteen-year-old girl living in Tasmania with her single mother, Lou, and infant brother Jasper. She suddenly finds herself having strange dreams and able to perform 'magic', and goes on a quest to find her father and herself. She must reconcile her new powers, and relationships with her family (her father *and* her mother in different ways) and a variety of males including her friend Trout and two lover figures. In doing so, she symbolically makes the transition from adolescent to adult (or at least an adult in the making).

Undine is the first book of a trilogy that includes *Breathe* (2005) and *Drift* (2007). The sequels effectively abandon intertextual references to *The Tempest* even as they demonstrate a sustained interest in magic. In the first novel, Undine is aware of herself as an intertextual subject in that she feels "like Rapunzel or Juliet, or some other fated and mysterious woman" (Russon 9), but this knowledge is not self-reflexive. As a 'reader', both of self and others, Undine tends to be passive. In terms of the novel's use of Shakespeare (and indeed the narrative tradition of "Undine"), Undine remains either unknowing or uninterested. While the text produces a positive model of feminine development of agency and autonomy, it does so separately from the very cultural capital it uses to add weight *to* that narrative. In short, *The Tempest* is used to structure the plot and deepen the characters, but Undine herself remains oblivious to this fact.[12]

It is indicative of *Undine's* mode of appropriation that Undine initially knows the etymological genealogy of her name but is not aware of the literary-mythological genealogy that is obviously familiar to her friend Trout:

> Her own name was a sea name. The book Lou had bought to choose a name for Jasper, when he was still a restless lump inside her, said *Undine* was Latin, meaning 'of the waves', but Trout had told her Undine was a sea nymph in old mythology. In fact, it was one of the reasons she and Trout had become friends. (Russon 45)

Undine's literary genealogy is one of mermaids for children, and includes Fouqué's *Undine* (1811), Andersen's "The Little Mermaid" (1836), Wilde's "The Fisherman and His Soul" (1891), and possibly Park's *My Sister Sif* (1986).[13] Both Fouqué's and Russon's Undines are "a scaled-down descendant of . . . powerful water deities, a being midway between the supernatural and the human, and midway again between the human and the animal" (Easterlin 258). However, this liminality is signalled not by their physical bodies (they do not have the tail of a fish) but rather by their 'other' spirituality and ability to communicate with and through bodies of water. Both Fouqué's and Russon's Undines experience sexual development literally, rendering the mermaid metaphor unnecessary, but this very sexuality marks them as *unintentionally* dangerous to men, reinforcing a devouring model of feminine sexuality, beyond the control of the female subject. The opening sections of the novel include Undine's ignorance of herself as a sexual subject, as opposed to the visual consumption her male peers perform of her body. The following description is from Trout's perspective:

> Trout did notice Undine's legs, and a lot more besides . . . Funnily enough, no one ever really asked her out. She was possibly too sexy for the average ego of a teenage boy. She was also *too* smart for most high school boys, and despite their big talk he knew most of the boys were a little afraid of her. (Russon 11–12, original emphasis)[14]

Where Fouqué and Andersen's mermaids sought a soul, the quest in Russon's secular novel is not for a soul but for maturity, and Undine temporarily seeks this via relationships with others. *Her* quest commences as she becomes aware of a new power. Although it is never made clear exactly what this power is, it is a form of magic connected with water and sexuality, a natural force that participates in the tradition of mermaid narratives like Fouqué's *Undine.*

Undine's entrance into a new phase of sexual development is marked—in good fairytale fashion—by the spilling of blood, which "pooled from a cut on her hand onto the benchtop" (Russon 26). This wound, caused by broken glass, becomes a site of rupture on Undine's body that marks her connection to the sea: "Undine remembered the sensation of opening the wound and could feel the sand and the shell and the crabs moving—*living*—under her skin" (31). This realisation has been instigated by vivid dreams, voices telling her "*it's time to come home*" (24), and the appearance of dead fish in her bedroom as though from nowhere. Undine unburdens herself of anxiety about these events by reporting them to Trout.

Trout is an alternative focaliser throughout the novel, which not only provides the reader with another perspective on Undine and her life, but establishes his gaze as superior in analysis and understanding. He would like to be a lover figure for Undine, although she views him only as a friend, and he is thus removed to the position of observer throughout. The pattern established early by Trout explaining Undine's name to her is maintained throughout the text, as he sees and understands signs and symbols which Undine cannot or will not examine. A fish that appears in her bedroom has inside it a piece of paper with a quotation from *The Tempest.* It is Trout who finds the paper and recognises the quotation, functioning as an interpreter. In the novel's first direct use of Shakespeare, Undine is literally outside the space where Trout confirms his understanding of the paper by consulting a book:

> Ms. Hague reached up and pulled an enormous book off the shelf. Undine knew which one it was straight away. "Pff, Shakespeare," she breathed aloud,

> dismissively. [Ms. Hague and Trout] were both mad about Shakespeare. No doubt they would be in raptures for the whole period. (Russon 48)

Trout's direct engagement with the Shakespearean text, here and for the remainder of the novel, allows him to interpret Undine's experiences (past and future), as she voluntarily remains ignorant of "Shakespeare" beyond school requirements (53). Having decoded the message, Trout gives the quotation to Undine:

> *Full fathom five thy father lies,*
> *Of his bones are coral made;*
> *Those are pearls that were his eyes;*
> *Nothing of him that doth fade,*
> *But doth suffer a sea-change*
> *Into something rich and strange.*
> *Sea-nymphs hourly ring his knell,*
> *Hark, now I hear them—ding-dong bell.* (52)

Where Trout presumably immediately recognised it as Shakespeare, and then researched its origin, Undine only recognises it as Shakespearean because she has seen Trout reading (as above) and expects him to translate its meaning and source: "why am I reading Shakespeare? What's it from? What does it mean?" (Russon 52). Trout offers an interpretation of the quotation, explaining in a plot-based way that,

> "this bit of the play is when Ariel—he's a spirit—is trying to trick this prince guy, Ferdinand, into *thinking* his father is dead. There was a big storm and they got separated and Ferdinand's stranded on this desert island. Anyway, at the end, Ferdinand's father isn't dead at all. They're reunited." (53–54, original emphasis)

The play is constructed as being about Ferdinand and Alonso, thus privileging patrilineal narratives which arguably are reflected by Trout's insight into Shakespeare as compared with Undine's wilful ignorance. His belief that it signals that Undine's own father is not dead is ultimately borne out by the novel. Importantly, Trout not only provides literary analysis of the quotation, but has 'scientifically' read the paper the quotation is written on, noting watermarks and physical features. For the remainder of the novel, his gaze, when focalised, will be marked by clarity and understanding.

Set against Trout's rational consideration of events are Undine's emotional and bodily responses: She unthinkingly explores her newfound powers (both sexual and supernatural). She is quickly marked as a potential Prospero (to a knowing reader), but one without personal control when she causes a storm in her backyard and is not able to manipulate it:

> Undine was playing the weather like a savage instrument, but it seemed the instrument was becoming the player, performing its own dangerous music.
>
> She swayed. She was losing her control of the storm. She became aware that she was standing in the middle of the garden, though she had no memory of having left her chair. (Russon 58)

The discovery of such powers is explicitly linked with the onset of sexuality when Undine experiences a similar temporary power and subsequent loss of control while sexually experimenting with a 'boyfriend', Trout's brother Richard. This very link, though, means separation from her mother: Undine views Lou through the lens of a feminine sexuality which is set against a model of masculine knowledge. Fundamentally, because Undine herself lives by a model of masculine equals knowledge/feminine equals sexuality, she is unable to recognise her mother as a knower until the end of the novel. As she negotiates her own burgeoning powers and sexuality, Undine explicitly rejects her mother as a negative sexual role-model without knowing any details of her mother's past: "Just because you were stupid enough to get yourself knocked up when you were a teenager . . . just because *you* opened your legs . . . I mean, I'm not like you" (70). The rejection of her mother leads to directionless experimentation, and to her father, but only after she has fallen prey to experimenting with her new powers.

Undine's relationship with Richard is initially a form of escape from the emotional challenges of her new powers: "as they set off making benign small talk, Undine forgot about Trout and Lou, and storms and voices, and fish and feelings, and instead just concentrated on staying upright and mobile at the same time" (Russon 79). This temporary escape in fact leads to an encounter which appears to reify the competition for sexual control in adolescent relationships when, after Undine asks Richard to stop kissing her one night, the novel stages a stereotypical scene of competing narratives of sexual authority and control:

> "God, Undine," he said, and prowled around the couch like a caged animal. "What have you done to me? I've never felt like this before."
>
> It should have been . . . romantic, but it wasn't. He sounded almost angry, as if he really though she had done something. This wasn't how it was supposed to be. Why couldn't he kiss her the way she wanted him to? (113)

It is the fantastic element of the novel, though, which renders this scene *not* as a reified metaphor, but as the *actual* case. Undine *has* exerted a supernatural control over Richard: In constructing feminine power and sexuality as equivalent, Russon reinforces the model of feminine responsibility for sexual maturity in adolescent relationships, and effectively absolves Richard of any responsibility for his behaviour. After Richard has ceased kissing her, Undine then reinitiates sexual activity, but does so as an aggressor:

> Power surged through her hand to his. She was in control, not Richard. She was making this happen. He would do whatever she wanted him to. She pulled him down to sit beside her. She kissed *him*—she kissed him—fiercely. He seemed to dissolve, to surrender, not just his body, but his will. Undine felt it, the same way she had felt tame air pass through her and become transformed by her body into the storm, dangerous and wild. *She* was dangerous, potent, and strong. Richard was weak. She almost, for a moment, despised him. (116, original emphasis)

The novel's constructions of sexuality for its own sake take up the models of consuming femininity present in earlier mermaid texts, but stripped of their moral drives, this model of sexuality is *only* devouring. Undine eventually recognises that she "didn't know enough about her power to make it work for her" (125) and at the moment of recognition "[s]omething—a book—dropped out of the air" (125). Unsurprisingly, the book is *The Tempest*, and its first page has her father's name and address written on it.

The book becomes here, a symbol of superior knowledge—that it is a Shakespearean text surely only adds the weight of cultural capital to this symbolism—and is implicitly handed to Undine as a guide to her experiences and self. Again, however, she does not read the text beyond the address on the flyleaf, which she uses to find her father. In doing so, Undine leaves the realm of her mother, and enters the realm of her father. The recognition and acceptance of this magic thus creates a symbolic island inhabited by herself and her father, who is named, rather heavy-handedly, Prospero Marine, and who lives in a beachfront house with pets he has named after characters from Shakespeare's play: a parrot named Caliban, and a dog named Ariel. By the end of the novel, it is revealed that Prospero has taken his name extremely seriously, and has actively been manipulating events and people to reflect Shakespeare's play. He does not in fact want to marry his Miranda off, but keep her for himself in order to have access to and, ideally, control over, her magical power.

When Prospero discovers that Undine is not a Shakespearean he is "dismayed" (Russon 154) and realises that his carefully constructed intertextual messages to her have not achieved their intended impact:

> Prospero made a deep grumbling sound. "But my note. Full fathom five thy father lies . . ." he intoned. "Don't tell me it had no dramatic effect whatsoever."
>
> "Oh yes, absolutely," Undine assured him. "I had a good interpreter." (155)

The novel itself retains this dependence on Trout as interpreter. Through his knowledge of Shakespeare, and an inherently scientific mind, Trout retains the authoritative gaze as he continues to research Undine's magic. This research marks him not just as the privileged knower of the novel, but is also presented as an alternative to sexuality which is consistently marked as dangerous; his own sexuality is displaced into "a scientist's passion for knowledge" (Russon 191). This literally saves him, as Undine's second lover figure, Grunt, falls victim to her magical powers just as Richard did. Trout also becomes the moral gaze of the novel as he recognises that "power corrupts" (175) just as Undine is unthinkingly embracing power: "[i]t was exhilarating" (178).

Undine (temporarily) believes power is exhilarating because Prospero has been grooming her to hand her power to him. Like Shakespeare's Prospero, he seeks more and more power and can only achieve it by controlling his daughter, telling her "[i]t's not about what we *should* do. It's about what we *can* do. We have enormous power. We can use it. We can do anything we want. Normal laws, normal rules, don't apply to us" (Russon 170, original emphasis). Having established his authority through manipulation and citation of Shakespeare, Prospero now convinces Undine that her power is something inherited patrilineally. Again, the link constructed between power and sexuality is problematic here, particularly given Prospero's thirst for appropriating his daughter's power.

Her magic becomes a defensive weapon when Grunt starts questioning Undine about her relationship with Richard, and although she does not necessarily seek to destroy Grunt, she nonetheless allows herself a tantrum:

> Power welled inside her. She didn't want to fight it. She wanted to destroy something. It was sudden and compelling. It was violent. She felt it surge through her arm . . . she forced her hand away from Grunt, to protect him, and aimed instead at the peppercorn tree.
>
> And then, the tree was gone. She felt a fierce exuberance at this awesome example of her power, Grunt forgotten. She was throwing off the ordinary, the mundane. Like before, with the storm, language left her. Nouns were weak, thin and insubstantial. Verbs and adjectives hung useless in the air. She let them go, she threw them to the four corners of the garden. (Russon 186–87)

Clearly, for the feminine, the embrace of power means the rejection of language and knowledge. Prospero encourages her in this rejection because he wants to appropriate her power and also to convince her to create a world for him to control. He tells her that his section of beach "just wants to disappear, to break off and become an island, a place that can't be left or travelled to" (217). This separation would mark his transition into a *Shakespearean* Prospero: a more attractive model than a 'wannabe' Prospero, although either model is dependent on the exploitation of Miranda as commodity.

In this sense, *Undine* would seem to activate a critique of the father-daughter relationship constructed by Shakespeare's play (and indeed Shakespeare generally), but given Undine's sustained and wilful ignorance of Shakespeare, this critique is logically only available to Prospero and Trout.

I am unsure how effective an 'unknowing' critique can be. An active critique is certainly performed by Undine of Prospero's presumption of authority and appropriation of *her magic* as she recognises that, "'It's not yours to give', she said, marvelling at this new idea. 'It's mine. All the magic, all the power. You're using it, but it's mine'" (Russon 217). In this articulation of ownership (and implicitly therefore responsibility), Undine realises that: "He didn't *love* her. He didn't want a daughter. He simply wanted her power, to possess her magic. Well, she wasn't going to let him have it. It was hers and she would protect it. Instinct. Survival" (219, original emphasis). This recognition of autonomy is linked with the recognition of her power as matrilineal. Undine is assisted in her defeat of Prospero by Trout, but also her mother, who appears unexpectedly at the beach: "a last haze of magic framing her like sunlight, emanating from her—soft, warm, curved, female—was Lou" (229) who is revealed unequivocally as the source of Undine's power. The novel's privileging of matrilineal inheritance certainly challenges the model of education and authority posited by *The Tempest*, and even arguably gives Sycorax a voice in terms of not demonising the magic-woman. Again, however, this privileging is performed to, and approved by, Trout as the rational scientist.

When Undine questions Trout about his opinion, he avoids responding by claiming that he was citing "you know, Shakespeare" (Russon 236), and the reader is made privy to his self-appointed future as protector and watcher of Undine:

> He still felt that pull, that scientific urge to dissect the magic, to analyse its parts. So Trout would still get to protect Undine. He would rescue her a little bit every day, from his own desire, and she would never thank him for it. (237)

Such emphatic inscriptions of the superiority of the masculine gaze, and of rationality over magic (feminine sexuality), render the novel's last revisionary performance of Shakespeare vexed indeed. The final line of the novel is spoken by Undine as Shakespeare's Miranda: "'*O brave*,' Undine said to the wind, '*new world*'" (245). The reader has no way of knowing if this citation is performed *knowingly* of this specific play, or is possibly a random citation in the mind of the character that seems appropriate to the moment. Undine has certainly achieved a separation from (and thus authority over) her father Prospero, but rather than appropriating his Shakespearean knowledge, she bans him from it, telling him "no *Tempest* names" (244) should be used for future pets. *Undine* reinforces the separation of masculine and feminine types of knowledge, rewarding "Shakespeare" to the former, and sexuality to the latter. In doing so, Russon rewrites mermaid and Shakespearean narratives in a celebration of the matrilineal. So, if Russon's appropriation is more empowering to its implied juvenile feminine reader than L'Engle or Oneal, it is made so by this active installation of a matriarchal model of inheritance and authority. Crucially, however, this model is outside Shakespeare; indeed, Shakespearean elements of the novel undermine its privileging. I am not suggesting that *Undine* activates an unequivocally feminist appropriation of these textual traditions; far from it, given the maintenance of unregulated feminine sexuality as dangerous, and the approved rational gaze of a masculine scientist, but Russon comes closer than L'Engle or Oneal to offering the implied feminine reader a position of autonomy like that offered the protagonists (and readers) of Covington and Williams's novels. As with *The Tempest* itself, *Undine* has at its centre a book that suggests "how powerful in effecting purposes and changing reality language might be" (White 11), but also as with the play, that book remains in the realm of the paternal. Shakespearean cultural capital remains the province of patriarchal masculinity.

I look forward to a text which combines feminine autonomy *with* the cultural capital of Shakespeare; a heroine who *knowingly* cites and rewrites 'brave new world'; one who originates, rather than bears the look of, the knowing gaze; who controls her own tempest; who is self-determining rather than self-regulating; and who enjoys a sexuality independent of patriarchal family structures. This may only happen when the emphatically gendered figures of Caliban and Miranda are abandoned in favour, perhaps, of the ambiguously gendered Ariel. That said, the only appropriation to date with Ariel at its centre is Grace Tiffany's *Ariel* (2005), a novel which erases "Shakespeare", obliterates *The Tempest*'s plot, and genders Ariel as feminine and "*childish*" (193) while identifying both categories as negative. Clearly, our cultural production for and about young people is not yet ready to imagine either a non-gendered Shakespearean or a non-policed feminine subject rich in Shakespearean capital.

Conclusions?

> . . . what's past is prologue, what to come
> In yours and mine discharge! (Shakespeare, *Tmp.* 2.1.253–54)

I am hesitant to attribute any form of conclusion, critical or creative, to the field of Shakespeare for children. Given my interest in the construction of gendered child readers (as future adult readers) I would like to agree that intertextual appropriations,

> have a metafictional dimension which causes readers to pay attention to the fabric and artifice of these texts as works of literature, and to the textuality of the world to which they allude; it also causes readers to recognise how they are being (have been) textually constructed in and by this intertextual playground. (Wilkie 136)

However, in the cases of the texts I have read here, rather than making children recognise their own textualisation, the implied child reader is as appropriated as the reader of "Shakespeare". Rather than offering an imaginative space where categories of subjectivity (as discursive constructs) might be contested, appropriations of Shakespeare naturalise normative values, and even make the implied reader complicit in their production. Indeed I firmly believe that the field to date demonstrates an emphatic commitment to patriarchal models of normative gendered subjectivity, but I hope that this may not necessarily be the case in the future.

Failure to take account of alternatives *to* patriarchy can only be sustained finitely; it may be true that "subversion must occur within existing discursive structures" (Salih 59), but the work of thinkers like Judith Butler demonstrates not only that subversion is possible, but may even be originated by any presumption of comprehensive discourse. Thus, the emphatic inscription of an hierarchical patriarchal cultural order necessarily demonstrates its failures at the moment of inscription, and creates a site of potential resistance. The inherently circular logic of "Shakespeare", and its attendant cultural capital, produces the conditions for its own potential subversion. Such possibilities should form a cultural agenda of writing for children, and in turn for the cultural imagining of subjectivity itself.

I have demonstrated that contemporary children's literature consistently appropriates Shakespeare the man as ideal father to boys, and absent father to girls; *Macbeth* as a (masculine) cautionary tale, or (feminine) model of self-policing; *A Midsummer Night's Dream* as a (masculine) liberatory narrative or (feminine) sexual morality tale; and *The Tempest* as a model of (masculine) future authority, but (feminine) future limitation. Further, such texts are in a sense performative, in that they call-into-being that which they name: a "Shakespeare" available to children. Importantly, this "Shakespeare" is then used to validate discourses of identity: the implied child reader learns not just the name of the author, but the 'name' of themselves as the reader of that author. Indeed, within such texts, ways of reading become ways of being, linked to, and shaped by, a *gendered* model of subjectivity. The genre thus reveals itself to be operating discursively, producing a series of statements springing from a particular ideological position. Although I believe that the rendering of such literary strategies visible to the critical reader is crucial, more important than this is finding ways of rendering them visible (and thus contestable) to the 'actual' reader; in this sense, I am accepting the genre's own category of value in relation to the child-subject: the child as future adult.

In the ideal case then, "Shakespeare" would be circulated in such a way as to render Foucault's 'new questions' redundant:

> "What are the modes of existence of this discourse?"
> "Where does it come from; how is it circulated; who controls it?"
> "What placements are determined for possible subjects?"
> "Who can fulfil these diverse functions of the subject?" (138)

The reality of Shakespeare for children means that, while I have attempted to answer the first three questions of the genre in the course of this book, the fourth question is unanswerable. The ideally gendered subjects named by the discourse can not and should not exist to fulfil the demands of prescriptive patriarchy. That the genre consistently constructs a self-policing feminine juvenile subject, as the future ideal feminine adult, obviously indicates the continuing persuasiveness of patriarchal values, but also indicates the extent to which these values are artificial.

If contemporary culture insists upon constructing the juvenile subject as the reader of "Shakespeare", then I can only hope that these constructions evolve to presenting alternative models of production, circulation, and reception of texts; of reading, politics, and identities; not just in relation to "Shakespeare", but of all constructs. The shifting of discursive norms of

Shakespeare for children (and thus necessarily of gendered readership and subjectivity) must be enacted in at least two ways: the first being the willingness to admit the pluralities inherent in the Shakespearean text into appropriations *of* the plays; the second being the re-construction of children as *critical* readers rather than *gendered* readers.

Notes

Notes to the Introduction

1. Stam's description of the commonly imposed hierarchy of literary over visual form could also be applied to the distinctions drawn between "Shakespeare" and "children's literature", a genre itself "regarded as a sub-literature and as a field of study that proves incapable of sustaining high orders of academic or intellectual engagement". Stephen Slemon and Jo-Ann Wallace, "Into the Heart of Darkness?: Teaching Children's Literature as a Problem in Theory," *Canadian Children's Literature* 63 (1991) 7.
2. Bourdieu's initial articulations of cultural capital emerged from extended sociological studies of cultural inheritance. Bourdieu's theoretical frameworks do not spring from literary studies, but nonetheless offer useful models for discussing the mechanisms by which cultural values are inculcated and normalised within literature. The initial research "sought to determine the social and scholastic factors in the success of pedagogic communication by analysing the variations in the efficiency of the communications relative to the social and scholastic characteristics of the receivers". Pierre Bourdieu and Jean-Claude Passeron, *Reproduction in Education, Society and Culture*, trans. Richard Nice (London: SAGE Publications, 1977) 71. However, the results of this research have enabled a broad application of the concept of cultural capital beyond the borders of the classroom. For a clear discussion of the variety of concepts that 'cultural capital' encompasses, see David Swartz *Culture & Power: The Sociology of Power* (Chicago: U of Chicago P, 1997) 75–82.
3. Smith is (perhaps unknowingly) implying a model that Wall describes as "double address" which occurs in work by writers for whom "the fact that there is unavoidably a double audience [of adults and children] to be considered results in the highly self-conscious cultivation of two distinct and separate audiences". Barbara Wall, *The Narrator's Voice: The Dilemma of Children's Fiction* (New York: St. Martin's Press, 1991) 20–21. However, I am more interested in the function of the *Hamlet* plot for the implied child audience. *The Lion King* can be read directly through the lens of

Bourdieu insofar as it "functions as a form of symbolic violence" that works "to encourage or dispose viewers to make a connection between the divisions that apply in the animal 'kingdom', and the social divisions that apply in their own culture". Jen Webb, Tony Schirato and Geoff Danaher, *Understanding Bourdieu* (Crows Nest, NSW: Allen & Unwin, 2002) 117. Further, the film alters the conclusion of *Hamlet's* plot to reflect a hetero-happy ending in keeping with Disney's cultural politics.

4. Although my own critical focus is gender, I accept quite readily that both reader and author are inherently gendered *and* nationed subjects in Romantic discourse. The issue of national identity is significant because the mode of writing and reading—one both privileged and performed by the Romantics—emphasised the 'organic' or natural one that exemplifies "a Burkean attitude to evolutionary English political institutions, as opposed to revolutionary French systems". Jonathan Bate, *The Romantics on Shakespeare* (Harmondsworth: Penguin, 1997) 17. Within such a context, Shakespeare as *English* poet is paramount. That such an issue is never openly addressed in nineteenth-century children's texts may be a telling absence. The nineteenth-century texts under consideration here are all clearly English in their origin and intent; they seek to steep their juvenile reader in a mode of cultural capital linked to notions of national as well as gendered identity. These texts do not just shape the English child but the British child, as English texts for children were routinely distributed throughout the Commonwealth and the United States. In the Twentieth Century, children's literature as a genre and Shakespeare for children within this genre shifted to local production and publication. Interest in national identity thus often operates alongside interest in gendered identity where the Nineteenth-Century texts assume a national identity for readers. I have discussed the contemporary production of explicitly *nationed* child readers of Shakespeare in "Shakespeare as National Discourse in Contemporary Children's Literature," *Papers: Explorations into Children's Literature* 13.1 (2003).
5. Quiller-Couch is a central figure in the professionalisation of English Studies as the second King Edward VII professor of English literature at Cambridge University and as the founder of an autonomous English faculty at that institution. A prolific critical and creative author, Quiller-Couch marked his interest in Shakespeare in his introductions to fourteen Shakespeare comedies for the "New Shakespeare Series" (Cambridge, 1921–1931). His adaptations of Shakespeare for children focussed, as the title states, on *Historical Tales.*
6. This is not to suggest that "children's literature" has now evolved to a previously unknown high-point. Assumptions of contemporary excellence participate in what can be a dangerous teleology: "The main problem with the standard narrative of modern literary history is precisely its narrative features: a distinct origin, a series of causally connected events in a linear

sequence, a teleological progression culminating in the present". Brian Richardson, "Remapping the Present: The Master Narrative of Modern Literary History and the Lost Forms of Twentieth-Century History," *Twentieth Century Literature* 43.3 (1997) 292.

7. The scope of this book is such that there is not room to cover all plays (nor indeed Shakespearean poetry). Similarly, given the methods of adaptation dominant in the nineteenth century (prose narratives for older children) I have excluded picture books, comics, 'straight' retellings, films, animation, audio-books and so on. Obviously there is valuable work to be done in analysing groups of appropriations of other plays in the Shakespearean canon, as all adaptations and appropriations contribute to the history of "Shakespeare": "the production of a new Shakespeare version or citation tends to imagine itself as breaking with the old, with tradition, it also always creates an archive making it continuous with past versions". Richard Burt, *Unspeakable ShaXXXspeares: Queer Theory & American Kiddie Culture* (New York: St. Martin's Press, 1998) 20.

Notes to Chapter 1

1. That all three texts are produced by women might lead one to identify the genre as a site of proto-feminist cultural production. It is true that nineteenth-century women writers were bound up in negotiations between gender and authority, but this very point makes it difficult to presume anachronistic politics on their part. If appropriations offer a mode of critical response to Shakespeare, and women writers are excluded from dominant critical discourse, then the consistently feminine authorship of these children's Shakespeare texts may in fact point to the 'taking over' of a space in which women can offer interpretive responses to Shakespeare in a culturally endorsed manner. However, it may be that these women writers mark the *potential* for rebellion rather than rebellion itself: "[m]any women asserted that they wrote for a general audience and, in the process, denied any claim to high-flown status. Such assertions must be seen in the context of their need to find publishers and acceptance with both reviewers and readers." Gill Perry, Anne Laurence, and Joan Bellamy, "Introduction: Gender and Women's History," *Women, Scholarship and Criticism: Gender and Knowledge c.1790–1900*, eds. Bellamy, Laurence and Perry (Manchester: MUP, 2000) 10.
2. I am emphasising *English* cultural contexts in this chapter, for although publishing history bears out that while England in the early nineteenth century saw a rash of Shakespearean texts for children, which were distributed throughout the English-speaking world, the American reception of Shakespeare offers a different range of critical questions. If we are to believe de Tocqueville, America seems content to circulate an unmediated Shakespeare as a family text: "[s]carcely a single pioneer's cabin is without a few

odd volumes of Shakespeare". Alexis de Tocqueville, *Democracy in America & Two Essays on America,* trans. Gerald E. Bevan, ed. Isaac Kramnick (Harmondsworth: Penguin, 2003) 544. In comparison, when considering Shakespeare specifically for children, Heman Humphrey (an academic clergyman of Amherst College, Massachusetts) wrote in 1840, "I am sorry that most of his plays were ever written. I believe it will appear in the Great Day, that they have done more harm than good . . . It is scarcely possible they should pass through the youthful mind and imagination, without leaving a stain behind". Cited in Gillian Avery, *Behold the Child: American Children and Their Books 1621–1922* (London: The Bodley Head, 1994) 26. A cultural history of Shakespeare for children in America would in all probability reveal fascinating comparisons with the English trajectory I am reading in this chapter.

3. Wordsworth expresses throughout the *Preface* a clear preference for poetry over prose as the true mode for literary art. However, history reveals that as the Romantic ideologies were tempered by social realism, many of the great Romantics themselves found prose, particularly the essay form, an appropriate outlet for their ideas. Even further, the Romantic 'definition' of the poetic moved beyond questions of form; Coleridge argued that poetry "is a species of composition, opposed to science, as having intellectual pleasure for its object, and as attaining its end by the use of language natural to us in a state of excitement—but distinguished from other species of composition, not excluded by the former criterion, by permitting a pleasure from the whole consistent with a consciousness of pleasure from the component parts". *The Literary Remains of Samuel Taylor Coleridge,* ed. Henry Nelson Coleridge, vol. II. (New York: AMS Press, Inc., 1967) 8–9.
4. John Milton offered a similarly attractive forebear to the Romantics, as the author of epic poetry and (perhaps more importantly) as a poet whose biography and politics were widely known. The absence of concrete knowledge about Shakespeare's life and beliefs is obviously empowering to anyone wishing to construct a version of the playwright, but when looking for an antecedent it can prove problematic. If one is ultimately convinced that the Romantics 'found' rather than 'interpolated' their poetic/political values in precursor poets, then one might readily privilege Milton's influence over Shakespeare's on the Romantic movement:

    Shakespeare proved to possess too much "philosophic impartiality"—be too much of a chameleon—to bring the Romantics out philosophically, to prod them into taking a definite stance that clearly revealed their critical attitudes and theory. To be sure, Shakespeare provided the Romantics with their concepts of poetic objectivity and negative capability, with their idea of the poet as a Proteus. But it was Milton in whom they found ideas resembling their own. It was Milton who defined for them the complex relationship between theology, ethics, philosophy, psychology, and poetry; it was Milton who provided them with their basic analogies for the poet and his poem and with the main tenets of their poetical theory. Joseph Anthony Wittreich Jr., *The Romantics on Milton: Formal Essays and Critical Asides* (Cleveland: The P of Case Western Reserve U, 1970) 13.

5. As Eagleton explains of Romantic authorship: "[s]ince we ourselves are post-Romantics, in the sense of being products of that epoch rather than confidently posterior to it, it is hard for us to grasp just what a curious historically particular idea this is". Terry Eagleton, *Literary Theory: An Introduction*, 2nd ed. (Cambridge, Mass.: Blackwell, 1996) 16. It is thus important to remember that curious, particular Romantic ideas have become transhistorical, 'natural', and even invisible in contemporary constructions of Shakespeare.
6. Within quotations I have retained the spellings of Shakespeare's name as they appear in the original; I have standardised spellings in my own writing.
7. John Wesley, founder of the Methodist church, believed that children were born with sin that had to be expunged. He argued a symbolic model wherein children owed obedience to their parents as a domestic version of the obedience owed to God. In "Sermon 96: On Obedience to Parents" (1784), Wesley produced a model unlikely to attract Romantics, when he advised parents:

   > Why, disobedience is as certain a way to damnation as cursing and swearing. Stop him, stop him at first, in the name of God. Do not 'spare the rod, and spoil the child'. If you have not the heart of a tiger, do not give up your child to his own will, that is, to the devil. Though it be pain to yourself, yet pluck your offspring out of the lion's teeth. Make them submit, that they may not perish. Break their will, that you may save their soul. John Wesley, *The Works of John Wesley*, ed. Albert C. Outler, vol. 3: Sermons III (Nashville: Abingdon Press, 1986) 367.

8. Beyond the obvious cases of Lamb, Hazlitt, and Wollstonecraft, Richard Edgeworth co-wrote with Maria Edgeworth, *Practical Education* (1798); Erasmus Darwin wrote about education in *A Plan for the Conduct of Female Education, in Boarding Schools* (1797); Thomas Day published *The History of Little Jack* (1787), and of course, *Sandford and Merton* (1783–1789). For a brief discussion of such thinkers' participation in children's literary culture, see Gillian Avery and Margaret Kinnell, "Morality and Levity: 1780–1820," *Children's Literature: An Illustrated History*, ed. Peter Hunt (Oxford: OUP, 1995) 55–57.
9. Charles Lamb remains one of the notable Romantic critics of Shakespeare who privileged the read play text over the performed, he wrote in 1811 of his confusion over "how people should come thus unaccountably to confound the power of originating poetical images and conception with the faculty of

being able to read or recite the same when put into words; or what connection that absolute mastery over the heart and soul of man, which a great dramatic poet possesses, has with those low tricks upon the eye and ear, which a player by observing a few general effects . . . can so easily compass". Charles Lamb, "On the Tragedies of Shakspeare; Considered with Reference to Their Fitness for Stage Representation," *Charles Lamb: Selected Prose*, ed. Adam Phillips (Harmondsworth: Penguin, 1985) 45–46.

10. Similarly, Tyler Hitchcock suggests of the *Tales* that "[n]o doubt one commented on the writing of the other, back and forth, a sort of two-heads-are-better-than-one mutual authorship that resulted in a book authentically written by the two of them together". Susan Tyler Hitchcock, *Mad Mary Lamb: Lunacy and Murder in Literary London* (New York: W. W. Norton & Company, 2005) 160. Mary Lamb is also the focus of Kathy Watson's *The Devil Kissed Her: The Story of Mary Lamb* (2004), and even of Peter Ackroyd's recent novel, *The Lambs of London* (2004), which imagines a romance between Mary Lamb and William Ireland the notorious Shakespeare forger, and which renders Mary as an avid consumer of Shakespeare.
11. Comparatively, another tradition of Mary Lamb life-writing suggests that her madness was little-known beyond her immediate acquaintance: "[t]he silence that surrounded the facts of Lamb's madness until after she died in 1847 was partially grounded in what Katherine Anthony calls a "conspiracy" by the Lamb family and literary friends to repress, for Lamb's sake, the gruesome events of that afternoon of 22 September 1796 when she stabbed her mother Elizabeth to death with a carving knife". Bonnie Woodbery, "The Mad Body as the Text of Culture in the Writings of Mary Lamb," *Studies in English Literature, 1500–1900,* 39.4 (1999) 659. Woodbery also notes that this silence is also possibly related to "a general silencing of madness as recommended by early-nineteenth-century medical manuals" (661). It also seems to have been the case amongst the Lamb circle at least that Mary was the source of the majority of the *Tales.*
12. There are some problematic discrepancies in a variety of sources regarding the preface to the first edition of Bowdler's *Shakespeare.* I am using a copy of the fifth edition which purports to reprint the preface from the first edition. However, in this case, 'first edition' may in fact refer to the 1818 edition rather than Henrietta's 1807 edition.
13. Franklin reads this as a message from Henrietta herself, arguing that it "cannot be Thomas's note, because he had died in 1825. Henrietta, who lived until 1830, seems in old age to here-asserting [sic] her position as the one responsible for the start of this whole enterprise". Colin Franklin, "The Bowdlers and Their Family Shakespeare," *The Book Collector* 49.2 (2000) 242. If Franklin is correct, I believe this adds weight to the authoritative position ascribed to fathers in the Bowdler model of Shakespearean education, in that it would demonstrate further marginalisation of Henrietta within the paratext.

14. Cowden Clarke dedicates each of her tales to a prominent Shakespearean of her acquaintance. These dedications seem to mark an authorial preference for a 'living' or acted Shakespeare, as opposed to an academic or critical Shakespeare. For example, her version of *Macbeth* is dedicated to William Macready, perhaps England's best-known nineteenth-century player of Macbeth. Cowden Clarke herself acted in Shakespearean productions, and clearly did not share the Romantic 'suspicion' of staged Shakespeare.
15. Aitchison notes that Fordun's *Chronicle* is important in a genealogy of Macbeth-narratives because in it, "Macbeth emerges for the first time as a murderer, usurper, and tyrant . . . Fordun is the first medieval chronicler to accuse Macbeth of murdering Duncan". Nick Aitchison, *Macbeth: Man and Myth* (Gloucestershire: Sutton Publishing Ltd., 2000) 107. It has also been suggested that Fenella provides a narrative basis for Shakespeare's Lady Macbeth; see R. Erskine of Marr, "Lady Macbeth and Finella," *The Month* 142 (July, 1923). It is possible then that this use of Fenella functions as an example of the ways in which creative appropriation performs critical interpretation of its pre-text.
16. That Cowden Clarke understands such oral transmission as a form of symbolic (matrilineal) reading is made clear by the fact that the Cowden Clarkes conjured up such an image for William Shakespeare himself in their preface to the *Works*:

    > We see him . . . fidgeting at his mother's knee . . . with his child's restlessness and eager eyes upturned towards her face, telling one of those wondrous Winter tales that bewitched his young imagination even then; and which, in his after-telling became unfading summer stories for mankind. Charles Cowden Clarke and Mary Cowden Clarke, eds., *The Works of William Shakespeare* (London: Bickers & Son, 1883) iv.

17. Nesbit's importance in marking paradigm shifts in the genre is effaced by the recent OUP reprint for "The Opie Library". This version reprints Nesbit's 1897 preface, and selects ten stories, conflating tales from the 1897 and 1907 editions, producing a deceptively hybrid text. Iona Opie's introduction makes no mention of this, preferring to nostalgically praise Nesbit's "plain speaking" as "the perfect antidote to the prevailing reverential attitude to Shakespeare's plays, which kills them dead" (7). Peter Hunt's afterword contains several factual errors regarding the publication history of Nesbit's stories, leading to the absence of an accurate provenance in the edition, and the misdating of the first publication of the Lambs' *Tales* as 1808. See Edith Nesbit, *The Best of Shakespeare: Retelling of 10 Classic Plays* (Oxford: OUP, 1997).

Notes to Chapter 2

1. A common strategy for initiating this journey is sending a child of the late twentieth century—contemporaneous with the implied reader—back in time to meet Shakespeare, as in Avril Rowlands's *The Shakespeare*

Connection (1994), Susan Cooper's *King of Shadows* (1999), Mary Pope Osborne's *Stage Fright on a Summer Night* (2002), or Lynne Kositsky's *A Question of Will* (2000). Kositsky's novel is a somewhat unusual example in that it features a female protagonist, and thematises the Authorship debate in order to suggest that the Shakespeare canon was written by Edward de Vere. Oxfordian agendas also appear in Norma Howe's *Blue Avenger Cracks the Code* (2002), or Elise Broach's *Shakespeare's Secret* (2005). Given Hollindale's claim that the "time-slip story is the equivalent of theater-in-the-round, where the audience is far more intimate with the action and may be recruited into it", it may not be surprising that often the protagonist of a Shakespearean time-slip novel becomes involved in a theatrical production, usually of *A Midsummer Night's Dream* (discussed in Chapter 4), but always develops an interpersonal relationship with William Shakespeare. Peter Hollindale, "'Children of Eyam': The Dramatization of History," *Children's Literature in Education* 28.4 (1997) 207. As in other juvenile time-travel narratives, "time itself becomes the mirror in which the children seek their reflection, looking back into the past to give depth and dimension to their impoverished sense of self". Carole Scott, "A Century of Dislocated Time: Time Travel, Magic and the Search for the Self," *Papers: Explorations Into Children's Literature* 6.2 (1996) 18.

2. Bright is a genuine historical figure, who did write *Characterie*, but is best remembered for *A Treatise on Melancholie* (1586). Blackwood has cited these texts as inspiration ("Speaks" 77) and in the novel, Widge personifies a relationship between Bright and Shakespeare that has been noted as historically possible. Bright's *Melancholie* is perceived by some critics as having influenced Shakespeare's construction of melancholy in *Hamlet*. See Mary Isabelle O'Sullivan, "Hamlet and Dr. Timothy Bright," *PMLA* 36 (1926). Blackwood also points to this textual relationship; indeed, an actor in *Stealer* tells Widge that "Mr. Shakespeare has found [Bright's] book invaluable. As you may have noticed, Hamlet is a very master of melancholy" (56).
3. As with *Stealer* Blackwood explicitly draws on and responds both to Nicholas Rowe's 1709 biography of Shakespeare, and Heminge and Condell's preface to the first *Folio* (1623). Here, the preface is intertextually invoked directly: "His mind and hand went together: And what he thought, he uttered with that easinesse, that wee have scarse received from him a blot in his papers". John Heminge and Henrie Condell, "To the Great Variety of Readers" *Mr. William Shakespeares Comedies, Histories & Tragedies* (London: Isaac Jaggard, and Ed. Blount, 1623).
4. As Blackwood points out in his foreword "Shakespeare did have a younger brother, Edmund" (*Scribe* n.p.); however, there is little historical data extant about him. Schoenbaum notes that "Edmund seems to have taken after his playwright brother; for, when he was old enough, he followed William to London, and became a professional actor, with which company is not recorded. In his profession he does not seem to have achieved

any special eminence, but he was only twenty-eight when he died". S. Schoenbaum, *William Shakespeare: A Documentary Life* (Oxford: Clarendon, 1975) 26.

5. It is this sense of performance's capacity to become performative (albeit exclusively for male subjects), which distinguishes Blackwood's trilogy as relatively complex when compared with J. B. Cheaney's *The Playmaker* (2000) and its sequel *The True Prince* (2002). Richard Malory, the orphan protagonist of these novels, also forms a symbolically filial relationship with Shakespeare, but the novels display a deep anxiety about performance generally. Richard notes of Shakespeare's words that, "once learned they were not easily forgotten" (*True* 183) and routinely uses Shakespearean quotations to illuminate his own life. In comparison, the novels ultimately affirm that, "Acting has its place, but that place is the theater [. . . else] the player may lose himself" (*Playmaker* 103) if not vigilant about protecting their "essential selves" (*True* 81). This is perhaps unsurprising given Cheaney's own view that, "here is where Shakespeare can be particularly valuable to young people today. No subject fascinates them more than themselves. Their world is truly a stage, and they and their peers the players: testing values, trying on attitudes, discovering the roles they can play, and those they can't" ("Players" 85). If adolescence is viewed primarily as a time of disciplining or policing the self, Shakespeare must be mobilised as a figure of such discipline rather than experimentation or ideological elasticity. Thus Shakespeare is made the *author* of instructional texts, but is distanced whenever possible from the image of the source of theatrical performance.
6. Hassinger is perhaps best-known popularly as one of the authors who attempted to sue Miramax over the content of the screenplay for *Shakespeare in Love.* See "Shakespeare Film Studios 'Face Trial'," *BBC News*, October 11, 2004.

Notes to Chapter 3

1. The *OED* describes tanistry as a "system of life-tenure among the ancient Irish and Gaels, whereby the succession to an estate or dignity was conferred by election upon the 'eldest and worthiest' among the surviving kinsmen of the deceased lord". "tanistry," *OED*, eds. A. J. Simpson and E. S. C. Weiner, 2nd ed. (Oxford: Clarendon, 1989). In Scotland, the tanist system favoured alternating cousins. Aitchison notes that of "the twenty-three Scottish kings who reigned between 843 and 1097, nineteen were the offspring of previous kings but did not, under the system of alternating kingship, succeed their fathers in the kingship immediately". Aitchison, *Macbeth: Man and Myth* (Gloucestershire: Sutton Publishing Ltd., 2000) 13.
2. My discussion here is an abridgement of my extended discussion of *Macbeth* for boys in "Shakespeare's Macbeth: Poster-Boy for Contemporary Masculinity?," *Journal of Interdisciplinary Gender Studies* 9.2 (2004).

3. In comparison to this approach, in 2002 Pearson Longman (British educational publishers) released a "New Century Readers" edition of *MacB* intended for use in lower high-school classes. The commentaries and questions provided by Macey explicitly address the Shakespearean connection, and in fact advise the reader before they have begun the story, that "[t]he novel *MacB* is a modern reworking of the play *Macbeth* by William Shakespeare. Find out about the plot of *Macbeth.* You could watch the BBC's Animated Tales of the play or read a summary of it. Try to note down the main events in *Macbeth*, as you will need to refer to them as you read the book". Julie Macey, ed., *MacB* (Harlow: Pearson Longman, 2002) 8.
4. This is significant because the supernatural is one force that remains entirely in the domain of the feminine in Shakespeare's play. Although the audience may not necessarily believe in the reality of these elements, they nonetheless offer an otherwise disenfranchised sector of the culture access to a privileged discourse of power and knowledge. Although the supernatural remains contingent in *Macbeth*, it forms an important site of resistance to patriarchal authority. Arksey offers the feminine no such opportunity.
5. The unwieldy title identifies the obstacles (or at least some of them) that stand between Jennifer and Elizabeth throughout most of the text. Hecate and *Macbeth* invoke their conceptualisation of witchcraft and narrative, where William McKinley—the president for whom their school is named—is symbolic of the social and cultural mores of a White patriarchy being forced on them within institutions.
6. A similar development based on race may be found in Sharon Draper's *Tears of a Tiger* (1994), in which Andy, a young African-American man, commits suicide in the wake of a dangerous identification with Lady Macbeth. As with this discussion of Konigsburg, Draper's novel is discussed in my " African American Children as 'Readers' of Shakespeare: Cultural Politics and Race in Shakespearean Children's Literature." *To See the Wizard: Politics and the Literature of Childhood.* Ed. Laurie Ousley (Newcastle upon Tyne: Cambridge Scholars Publishing, 2007).
7. Cast members realise that "A French-versus-English version will shake up the critics" (Katz 34), and indeed it does, as Jeneva's staging invokes a key event in Quebecois history: the "battle on the Plains of Abraham between the French forces of Montcalm and the British forces of Wolfe". Ellen Donovan, "Narrative Voices in Francis Parkman's *Montcalm and Wolfe*," *CLIO: A Journal of Literature, History, and the Philosophy of History* 18.3 (1989) 278. This battle was 'won' by the French who successfully held Quebec, hence French-Canadian culture dominating Quebec today. The authoritative text is Francis Parkman's *Montcalm and Wolfe* (1884). Although 'casting' Macbeth as Montcalm is undoubtedly a significant gesture on the part of Jeneva, in that it suggests that Franco rule in Quebec is illegitimate and implicitly temporary, I cannot presume to know what

level of reader competence can be presumed for non-Canadian child readers on this issue. It may be that the resonances of this interpretation are felt only in Canada.

8. In a remarkably heavy-handed moment, Kinny realises: "Until recently she had thought that great actors were great because they could impose themselves on a part and make it work. Now she knew that it was something very different. What made great acting was a self-effacing search for the truth of the character being played, and a decision to speak that truth for the character. It wasn't the Hag's kind of possession, it was more cooperative than that, but it was possession all the same". Welwyn W. Katz, *Come Like Shadows* (Sakatchewan: Coteau Books, 2000) 315–16.

Notes to Chapter 4

1. The infamous lines from Theseus early in the play, "Hippolyta, I woo'd thee with my sword, / And won thy love doing thee injuries" (*MND* 1.1.16–17), which refer to the mythological background of these figures, and Theseus's rape of the Amazon, would disrupt the heteronormative construction of the play for children.
2. The fairies of *Dream* have proved useful narrative fodder for authors writing fantasy for adult readers as well. See, for example, Sarah Hoyt's *Ill Met By Moonlight* (2001) and *All Night Awake* (2002) which use characters from the play as well as William Shakespeare and Christopher Marlowe in their narratives; Gary Kilworth's *A Midsummer's Nightmare* (1996) which combines Celtic and Arthurian mythology with the fairies of Shakespeare's *Dream* to construct an environmentalist narrative; and Terry Pratchett's *Lords and Ladies* (1992) which interpolates Shakespearean content into Pratchett's 'Discworld' (the setting for the majority of his prolific output). These novels, although possibly of interest to an older adolescent readership, have been excluded from this chapter, as due to elements of content and register I do not believe they are addressed to an implied juvenile reading audience.
3. Aspects of the discussion of Cooper's novel here have previously been published in my "Shakespeare as National Discourse in Contemporary Children's Literature," *Papers: Explorations into Children's Literature* 13.1 (2003).
4. *Tattercoats* is an English variant of the "Cinderella" narrative. The story has survived primarily due to the work of Joseph Jacobs who in 1890 and 1894 published *English Fairy Tales* and *More English Fairy Tales* in an attempt to become "a kind of English Grimm" (144). *Tattercoats* appeared in the latter volume, and Jacobs believed it to be "of interest chiefly as being without any 'fairy' or supernatural elements, unless the magic pipe can be so considered" (328) which seems opposed to Masson's use of the tale. See Joseph Jacobs, *English Fairy Tales: Being the Two collection English*

Fairy Tales & More English Fairy Tales, 3rd ed. (London: The Bodley Head, 1975).

5. The text is worth considering given John Updike's status in contemporary literary culture. While criticism of his work is extensive, few Updike critics bother analysing his *Bottom's Dream*, treating it as a juvenile aberration, rather than as a more extended critical project on Updike's part to test and refigure literary history. But, in addition to *Bottom's Dream* Updike has also published a children's adaptation of Mozart's *The Magic Flute* (1962), Wagner's *The Ring* (1964) and *A Children's Calendar* (1965). This output demonstrates, I believe, a strong investment in the rewarding of juvenile audiences with cultural capital that combines musical and literary heritage. Updike has also appropriated Shakespeare for an adult audience in his novel, *Gertrude and Claudius* (2000), a reimagining of Shakespeare's *Hamlet.*
6. Gilead unsurprisingly identifies Maurice Sendak's *Where the Wild Things Are* (1963) as exemplary of this type. Sendak's picture-book closes with Max abandoning his psychic wilderness and returning "into the night of his very own room where he found his supper waiting for him / and it was still hot". Maurice Sendak, *Where the Wild Things Are* (London: Random House Children's Books, 2000).
7. Romance fiction is always already problematic for gender critics, as the genre appears to depend on a vision of femininity as passivity; "[t]he enormous popularity of romantic fiction with women has always presented a problem for feminism. It is an empirical given that pre-eminently signifies some of the limits of feminist understanding and effectivity". Ien Ang, "Living Room Wars: Rethinking Audiences for a Postmodern World," *The Audience Studies Reader,* eds. Will Brooker and Deborah Jermyn (London: Routledge, 2003) 227.

Notes to Chapter 5

1. This model is not without problematic consequences: "[c]rucially, the trope of 'child as colonised' elides those discourses of race which constitute one group of people as inherently inferior to another, much as the tropes of 'woman as victim' and 'woman as dependent' within feminist work have sometimes elided colonialism and its privileging of whiteness". Clare Bradford, *Reading Race: Aboriginality in Australian Children's Literature* (Melbourne: Melbourne UP, 2001) 12.
2. Indeed, the play provided the central model for Mannoni's influential reading of colonialism in Madagascar, in which he read *The Tempest* as a psychoanalytic metaphor for the colonial subject who "must learn to accept himself as he is and to accept others as they are, even if they happen to be called Caliban". O. Mannoni, *Prospero and Caliban: The Psychology of Colonization*, trans. Pamela Powesland, 2nd ed. (New York: Frederick A. Praeger, 1964) 105.

3. For his influential study, Bloom explicitly drew on the Freudian "family romance" (8) to describe the "[b]attle between strong equals, father and son as mighty opposites, Laius and Oedipus at the cross roads". Harold Bloom, *The Anxiety of Influence: A Theory of Poetry*, 2nd ed. (Oxford: OUP, 1997) 11.
4. For a summary of psychoanalytic approaches to the play see Holland, who notes that three major points tend to appear across such readings: Ariel, Caliban, and Sycorax read as projections of Prospero's unconscious mind; the father-daughter relationship; and the play as allegory of transformation of mind (usually Prospero's). Norman N. Holland, *Psychoanalysis and Shakespeare* (New York: McGraw-Hill Book Co., 1964) 269–74. The focus on Prospero as psychoanalytic subject in such readings clearly participates in the extended nineteenth-century model of Prospero as/for Shakespeare.
5. This discussion of Covington's novel appears in an extended form in my "African American Children as 'Readers' of Shakespeare: Cultural Politics and Race in Shakespearean Children's Literature," *To See the Wizard: Politics and the Literature of Childhood*, ed. Laurie Ousley (Newcastle upon Tyne: Cambridge Scholars Publishing, 2007).
6. For a discussion of *JFK*'s extended citations of "Shakespeare", see Marjorie Garber, "Character Assassination: Shakespeare, Anita Hill, and *JFK*," *Media Spectacles*, eds. Marjorie Garber, Jann Matlock and Rebecca L. Walkowitz (London: Routledge, 1993) 33–37.
7. Birmingham, Alabama is a crucial site (physically and historically) in the history of the Civil Rights movement in the United States: "Birmingham events [protests, arrests, and abuses] represent an historic watershed in U.S. politics as the political movement unleashed in Alabama in the spring of 1963 culminated in the demise of the decades-old institution of de jure segregation and discrimination that marked the failure of Radical Reconstruction in the South following the Civil War". John Walton Cotman, *Birmingham, JFK and the Civil Rights Act of 1963: Implication for Elite Theory* (New York: Peter Lang, 1989) 8.

   Later in 1963, the event briefly invoked by Covington galvanised the Civil Rights movement even further:

   > On Sunday morning, 15 September [1963], a dynamite blast ripped through the Sixteenth Street Baptist Church, wounding twenty-one and killing four defenseless black girls—Addie Mae Collins, Denise McNair, Carole Robertson, and Cynthia Wesley—who had just completed a lesson on 'The Love That Forgives'. Cynthia, the Wesleys' only child, had been decapitated. Denise's sobbing grandfather stumbled across her white dress shoe amid the debris. Bruce J. Dierenfield, *The Civil Rights Movement* (Harlow: Pearson Education Limited, 2004) 89.

   Moore believes that *Lizard*'s mention of this event would allow teachers to bring in Dudley Randall's "Ballad of Birmingham" as a "poetic intertext" for students, but does not consider how the historical context might be dealt with *as* historical context. In other words, to deal only with representations of events is not equal to engaging directly with events. John Noell Moore, "Intertextualities: *The Tempest* in *Morning Girl*, *Lizard*, and *In Summer Light*," *Adolescent Literature as a Complement to the Classics*, ed. Joan F. Kaywell, vol. 3 (Norwood, MA: Christopher-Gordon Publishers, Inc., 1997) 84.

Randall's poem uses the figure of the Black girl-child to embody the tragedy and aftermath of the bombing. The final lines of the poem inscribe Dierenfield's focus on the symbolic empty white shoe: "O, here's a shoe, but where's the foot, / And, baby, where are you?". Dudley Randall, "Ballad of Birmingham (1966)," *Black Literature in America*, ed. Houston A. Baker Jr. (New York: McGraw-Hill Book Company, 1971) ll.31–32.

8. On the topic of Shakespeare in Alabama, Sallie says that "Shakespeare invites a kind of snobbishness, even in places where there's nothing to be snobbish about" (Covington 145). In an extratextual irony, this novel was adapted by Covington as a stage play, commissioned by the Alabama Shakespeare Festival (ASF). After being performed at the ASF in 1994, it was showcased in the Olympic Arts Festival in Atlanta, 1996. The plays performed at this festival were chosen to explore "the diverse cultural experiences of Atlanta, the State of Georgia and the American South" (69), although one reviewer of the festival noted that most "productions seemed parochial and safe" (74). Given that *Lizard* is mentioned specifically in the review (in the context of plays "written and directed from a white Southern perspective" [69]). I am assuming that the political conservatism evident in the novel has been maintained in the stageplay. See Yvonne Singh, "Performance Review: 1996 Olympic Arts Festival," *Theatre Journal* 49.1 (1997).
9. Zabus does at least note that Giulietta "may have fallen with both feet in a new trap of domesticity and childbearing with a Caliban-turned-Prospero orchestrating for her a life of lying", but is nonetheless in favour of the novel as an anti-colonial text despite its sustained investment in patriarchal models of gender relations. Chantal Zabus, *Tempests After Shakespeare* (New York: Routledge, 2002) 220.
10. Sedgwick draws this phrase from Heidi Hartmann's definition of patriarchy as "a set of social relations between men, which have a material base, and which, though hierarchical, establish or create interdependence and solidarity among men that enable them to dominate women". Heidi Hartmann, "The Unhappy Marriage of Marxism and Feminism: Towards a More Progressive Union," *Women and Revolution: A Discussion of the Unhappy Marriage of Marxism and Feminism*, ed. Lydia Sargent (Boston: South End, 1981) 14. Sedgwick designates the triangle, particularly the erotic triangle, as the most useful figure for analysing the "intellectual tradition [that] schematizes erotic relations" (21), ultimately arguing that

this triangle—so readily applicable to *The Tempest*—functions critically as "a sensitive register precisely for delineating relationships of power and meaning, and for making graphically intelligible the play of desire and identification by which individuals negotiate with their societies for empowerment." Eve Kosofsky Sedgwick, *Between Men: English Literature and Male Homosocial Desire* (New York: Columbia UP, 1985) 27.

11. *A Wrinkle in Time* cites *The Tempest* within the genre of science fiction, much like the well-known 1956 film *Forbidden Planet* which recast the play as interstellar travel. The film draws directly on Freudian theory, positing the 'Caliban' as a "monster from the id", a projection of the Prospero figure, Dr Morbius (Walter Pidgeon). Fred M. Wilcox, *Forbidden Planet* (MGM, 1956).
12. For an extended discussion of Russon's novel in relation to both the Shakespearean and mermaid traditions referred to here, see my, "Of Tails and Tempests: Feminine Sexuality and Shakespearean Children's Texts," *Borrowers and Lenders: The Journal of Shakespeare and Appropriation* 2.1 (2006).
13. Park's *My Sister Sif* is well-known in Australia, and features a female protagonist, Riko, who is half mermaid and half human. Her journey is one of reconciling this genealogy, and ultimately committing herself to environmentalist causes (the didactic focus of the novel overall). The novel includes an authoritative masculine, scientific gaze in the figure of Henry Jacka. I believe this model is replicated by Russon's novel. Ruth Park, *My Sister Sif* (Ringwood: Puffin, 1987).
14. Trout's unrequited sexual interest may mark him, at least temporarily, as a Caliban figure. His fishy name would certainly lend support to such a claim. If so, Trout's Shakespearean competence may contribute to his self-regulation of sexual interest in Undine: knowing Caliban's fate when marked as unwanted sexual aggressor could serve a cautionary function.

Bibliography

Aaron, Jane. *A Double Singleness: Gender and the Writings of Charles and Mary Lamb.* Oxford: Clarendon, 1991.

Adelman, Janet. "'Born of Woman': Fantasies of Maternal Power in *Macbeth*." *Shakespearean Tragedy and Gender.* Eds. S. N. Garner and M. Sprengnether. Indianapolis: Indiana UP, 1996. 105–34.

Aitchison, Nick. *Macbeth: Man and Myth.* 1999. Gloucestershire: Sutton Publishing Ltd., 2000.

Altick, Richard D. *The Cowden Clarkes.* London: OUP, 1948.

Ang, Ien. "Living Room Wars: Rethinking Audiences for a Postmodern World." *The Audience Studies Reader.* Eds. Will Brooker and Deborah Jermyn. London: Routledge, 2003. 226–34.

Aristotle. *Poetics.* Trans. Malcolm Heath. Ed. Malcolm Heath. Harmondsworth: Penguin, 1996.

Arksey, Neil. *MacB.* Harmondsworth: Puffin Books, 1999.

Auerbach, Nina. *Woman and the Demon: The Life of a Victorian Myth.* Cambridge: Harvard UP, 1982.

"Author and Shakespeare Scholar Grace Tiffany." *Grace Tiffany Website* 29 Nov. 2004 http://www.gracetiffany.com.

Avery, Gillian. *Behold the Child: American Children and Their Books 1621–1922.* London: The Bodley Head, 1994.

Avery, Gillian, and Margaret, Kinnell. "Morality and Levity: 1780–1820." *Children's Literature: An Illustrated History.* Ed. Peter Hunt. Oxford: OUP, 1995. 46–76.

Barker, Francis, and Peter Hulme. "Nymphs and Reapers Heavily Vanish: The Discursive Con-Texts of *The Tempest*." *The Tempest.* Ed. R. S. White. Hampshire: Macmillan Press Ltd, 1999. 32–48.

Barthes, Roland. "The Death of the Author." Trans. Stephen Heath. *Image, Music, Text.* London: Fontana, 1977. 142–48.

———. "From Work to Text." Trans. Stephen Heath. *Image, Music, Text.* London: Fontana, 1977. 155–164.

Bate, Jonathan. *The Romantics on Shakespeare.* 1992. Harmondsworth: Penguin, 1997.

———. *Shakespeare and the English Romantic Imagination.* Oxford: Clarendon, 1986.

Bevan, Clare. *A Midsummer Night's Dream.* The Shakespeare Collection. London: Hodder Children's Books, 2000.

Blackburn, William. "Madeline L'Engle's *A Wrinkle in Time:* Seeking the Original Face." *Touchstones: Reflections on the Best in Children's Literature.* Ed. Perry Nodelman. Vol. 1. West Lafayette, IN: Children's Literature Association, 1985. 123–31.

Blackwood, Gary. "Shakespeare Speaks: Getting the Language Right." *Reimagining Shakespeare for Children and Young Adults.* Ed. Naomi J. Miller. London: Routledge, 2003. 74–80.

———. *The Shakespeare Stealer.* 1998. New York: Puffin Books, 2000.

———. *Shakespeare's Scribe.* New York: Dutton Children's Books, 2000.

———. *Shakespeare's Spy.* New York: Dutton Children's Books, 2003.

Bloom, Harold. *The Anxiety of Influence: A Theory of Poetry.* 1973. 2nd ed. Oxford: OUP, 1997.

Boehrer, Bruce. "Economies of Desire in *A Midsummer Night's Dream*." *Shakespeare Studies* 32 (2004): 99–117.

Boose, Lynda E, and Richard Burt. "Totally Clueless?: Shakespeare Goes Hollywood in the 1990s." *Shakespeare the Movie: Popularizing the Plays on Film, TV and Video.* Eds. Lynda E. Boose and Richard Burt. London: Routledge, 1997. 8–22.

Bottoms, Janet. "Familiar Shakespeare." *Where Texts and Children Meet.* Eds. Eve Bearne and Victor Watson. London: Routledge, 2000. 11–25.

———. "Of *Tales* and *Tempests.*" *Children's Literature in Education* 27.2 (1996): 73–86.

———. "'to Read Aright': Representations of Shakespeare for Children." *Children's Literature* 32 (2004): 1–14.

Bourdieu, Pierre, and Jean-Claude Passeron. *Reproduction in Education, Society and Culture.* 1970. Trans. Richard Nice. London: SAGE Publications, 1977.

Bourdieu, Pierre. *Distinction: A Social Critique of the Judgement of Taste.* Trans. Richard Nice. Cambridge: Harvard UP, 1984.

———. "The Forms of Capital." Trans. Richard Nice. *Handbook of Theory and Research for the Sociology of Education.* Ed. John G. Richardson. New York: Greenwood, 1986. 241–258.

Bowdler, Thomas. *The Family Shakspeare.* 1807. Fifth ed. Vol. 1. London: Longman, Rees, Orme, Brown, and Green, 1827. 8 vols.

"bowdlerize." *Oxford English Dictionary.* Eds. A. J. Simpson and E. S. C. Weiner. 2nd ed. Oxford: Clarendon, 1989.

Bradford, Clare. *Reading Race: Aboriginality in Australian Children's Literature.* Melbourne: Melbourne UP, 2001.

Bradley, A. C. *Shakespearean Tragedy: Lectures on Hamlet, Othello, King Lear, Macbeth.* 1904. London: Macmillan & Co, 1957.

Briggs, Julia. *A Woman of Passion: The Life of E. Nesbit, 1858–1924.* London: Hutchinson, 1987.

Broach, Elise. *Shakespeare's Secret.* New York: Henry Holt, 2005.

Brook, Peter. *The Empty Space.* London: MacGibbon & Kee Ltd., 1968.

Brooks, Harold F. "Introduction." *A Midsummer Night's Dream.* 1979. Ed. Harold F. Brooks. The Arden Shakespeare. London: Thomson Learning, 2003. xxi–cxliii.

Burnett, Mark Thornton. ""Fancy's Images": Reinventing Shakespeare in Christine Edzard's *The Children's Midsummer Night's Dream.*" *Literature/Film Quarterly* 20.3 (2002): 166–70.

———. "The 'Fiend-Like Queen': Rewriting Lady Macbeth." *Parergon* 11.1 (1993): 1–19.

Burt, Richard. *Unspeakable ShaXXXspeares: Queer Theory & American Kiddie Culture.* New York: St. Martin's Press, 1998.

Butler, Judith. "Burning Acts: Injurious Speech." *Performativity and Performance.* Eds. Andrew Parker and Eve Kosofsky Sedgwick. London: Routledge, 1995. 197–227.

———. *Gender Trouble: Feminism and the Subversion of Identity.* 1990. 2nd ed. New York: Routledge, 1999.

Butts, Dennis. "The Beginnings of Victorianism: c.1820–1850." *Children's Literature: An Illustrated History.* Ed. Peter Hunt. Oxford: OUP, 1995. 77–101.

Calder, Charlotte. *Cupid Painted Blind.* Sydney: Pan Macmillan Australia, 2002.

Callaghan, Dympna. "Wicked Women in *Macbeth*: A Study of Power, Ideology and the Production of Motherhood." *Reconsidering the Renaissance: Papers from the Twenty-First Annual Conference.* Ed. Mario Di Cesare. New York: Medieval & Renaissance Texts and Studies, 1992.

Cartelli, Thomas. *Repositioning Shakespeare: National Formations, Postcolonial Appropriations.* London: Routledge, 1999.

Chambers, Aidan. "The Reader in the Book." *The Signal Approach to Children's Books.* Ed. Nancy Chambers. Harmondsworth: Kestrel Books, 1980. 250–75.

Charnes, Linda. "Dismember Me: Shakespeare, Paranoia, and the Logic of Mass Culture." *Shakespeare Quarterly* 48.1 (1997): 1–16.

———. "What's Love Got to Do with It? Reading the Liberal Humanist Romance in Shakespeare's *Antony and Cleopatra.*" *Textual Practice* 6.1 (1992): 1–16.

Cheaney, J. B. "The Players, the Playmaker, and Us." *Reimagining Shakespeare for Children and Young Adults.* Ed. Naomi J. Miller. London: Routledge, 2003. 81–86.

———. *The Playmaker.* New York: Dell Yearling, 2000.

———. *The True Prince.* New York: Dell Yearling, 2002.

Chedgzoy, Kate, Susanne Greenhalgh and Robert Shaughnessy (eds). *Shakespeare and Childhood.* Cambridge: CUP, 2007.

"The Children's Midsummer Night's Dream". *Sands Films.* 2001. 31 Jan. 2004 http://www.sandsfilms.co.uk/midsummer/midsummer.htm.

Cleverley, John, and D. C. Phillips. *Visions of Childhood: Influential Models from Locke to Spock.* 1976. Revised ed. New York: Teachers College, Columbia University, 1986.

Coiro, Ann Baynes. "Writing in Service: Sexual Politics and Class Position in the Poetry of Aemilia Lanyer and Ben Jonson." *Criticism* 35.3 (1993): 357–76.

Coleridge, Samuel Taylor. *Lectures 1808–1819 on Literature*. The Collected Words of Samuel Taylor Coleridge. Ed. R. A. Foakes. Vol. 5, pt 1. Princeton: Princeton UP, 1987.

———. *The Literary Remains of Samuel Taylor Coleridge*. 1836. Ed. Henry Nelson Coleridge. Vol. II. New York: AMS Press, Inc., 1967.

Connell, R. W. *Masculinities*. St. Leonards, NSW: Allen & Unwin, 1995.

Cooke, Katharine. *A. C. Bradley and His Influence on Twentieth-Century Shakespeare Criticism*. Oxford: Clarendon, 1972.

Cooney, Caroline B. *Enter Three Witches: A Story of Macbeth*. New York: Scholastic, 2007.

Cooper, Susan. *King of Shadows*. 1999. Harmondsworth: Puffin Books, 2000.

Cotman, John Walton. *Birmingham, JFK and the Civil Rights Act of 1963: Implications for Elite Theory*. New York: Peter Lang, 1989.

Coville, Bruce. *William Shakespeare's A Midsummer Night's Dream*. Ill. Dennis Nolan. New York: Puffin Books, 1996.

Covington, Dennis. *Lizard*. 1991. London: Bloomsbury, 1996.

Cowden Clarke, Charles, and Mary Cowden Clarke. *Recollections of Writers*. 1878. Fontwell, Sussex: Centaur Press Ltd, 1969.

———, eds. *The Works of William Shakespeare*. 1860, 1864. London: Bickers & Son, 1883.

Cowden Clarke, Mary. *The Complete Concordance to Shakespeare*. 1881. 2nd ed. London: Bickers & Son, Ltd., 1924.

———. *The Girlhood of Shakespeare's Heroines: In a Series of Fifteen Tales*. 3 vols. London: W H Smith & Son, 1850–51.

———. "Shakespeare as the Girl's Friend." *The Girl's Own Paper* 8 (1887): 562–64.

Craven, Peter. "More Than a Bard Dream." *The Age* July 31 2004, sec. Review: R8.

de Tocqueville, Alexis. *Democracy in America & Two Essays on America*. 1835. Trans. Gerald E. Bevan. Ed. Isaac Kramnick. Harmondsworth: Penguin, 2003.

Dierenfield, Bruce J. *The Civil Rights Movement*. Harlow: Pearson Education Limited, 2004.

Dobson, Michael. *The Making of the National Poet: Shakespeare, Adaptation and Authorship, 1660–1769*. Oxford: Clarendon, 1992.

Dobson, Michael, and Stanley Wells, eds. *The Oxford Companion to Shakespeare*. Oxford: OUP, 2001.

Donkin, Andrew. *William Shakespeare and His Dramatic Acts*. London: Scholastic Children's Books, 2004.

Donovan, Ellen. "Narrative Voices in Francis Parkman's *Montcalm and Wolfe*." *CLIO: A Journal of Literature, History, and the Philosophy of History* 18.3 (1989): 275–90.

Draper, Sharon M. *Tears of a Tiger*. 1994. New York: Simon & Schuster, 1996.

Dubosarsky, Ursula. *How to Be a Great Detective*. Camberwell, Vic: Puffin, 2004.

Durband, Alan. *The Tempest: Modern English Version Side-by-Side with Full Original Text*. Shakespeare Made Easy. New York: Barron's Educational Series, Inc., 1985.

Eagleton, Terry. *Literary Theory: An Introduction*. 2nd ed. Cambridge, Mass.: Blackwell, 1996.

Easterlin, Nancy. "Hans Christian Andersen's Fish out of Water." *Philosophy and Literature* 25.2 (2001): 251–77.

Erskine of Marr, R. "Lady Macbeth and Finella." *The Month* 142 (July, 1923): 55–59.

Fiedler, Leslie. "Caliban or Hamlet: A Study in Literary Anthropology." *Friendship's Garland: Essays Presented to Mario Praz on His Seventieth Birthday*. Ed. Vittorio Gabrieli. Vol. II. Roma: Edizioni di Storia e Letteratura, 1966. 401–11.

Finkelstein, Richard. "Disney Cites Shakespeare: The Limits of Appropriation." *Shakespeare and Appropriation*. Eds. Christy Desmet and Robert Sawyer. London: Routledge, 1999. 179–96.

Fordun, John of. *Chronicle of the Scottish Nation*. 1872. Trans. Felix J. H. Skene. Ed. William F. Skene. Vol. 1. Lampeter, Dyfed: Llanerch Publishers, 1993.

Foucault, Michel. "What Is an Author?" Trans. Donald F Bouchard and Sherry Simon. *Language, Counter- Memory, Practice: Selected Essays and Interviews*. 1969. Ed. Donald F. Bouchard. Ithaca: Cornell UP, 1977. 113–38.

Fowler, Bridget. *Pierre Bourdieu and Cultural Theory*. London: SAGE Publications, 1997.

Franklin, Colin. "The Bowdlers and Their Family Shakespeare." *The Book Collector* 49.2 (2000): 227–43.

Freedman, Barbara. "Misrecognizing Shakespeare." *Shakespeare's Personality*. Eds. Norman N. Holland, Sidney Homan and Bernard J. Paris. Berkeley: U of California P, 1989. 244–60.

French, Jackie. *Macbeth and Son*. Sydney: Angus and Robertson, 2006.

Frey, Charles H. "A Brief History of Shakespeare as Children's Literature." *The New Review of Children's Literature and Librarianship* 7 (2001): 147–56.

Garber, Marjorie. "Character Assassination: Shakespeare, Anita Hill, and *JFK*." *Media Spectacles*. Eds. Marjorie Garber, Jann Matlock and Rebecca L. Walkowitz. London: Routledge, 1993. 23–39.

Gilead, Sarah. "Magic Abjured: Closure in Children's Fantasy Fiction." *PMLA* 106.2 (1991): 277–93.

Gilmore, Kate. *Enter Three Witches*. Boston: Houghton Mifflin Company, 1990.

Grady, Hugh. "Shakespeare Criticism, 1600–1900." *The Cambridge Companion to Shakespeare*. Eds. Margreta de Grazia and Stanley Wells. Cambridge: CUP, 2001. 265–78.

Greenhalgh, Susanne. "Introduction: Reinventing Shakespearean Childhoods." *Shakespeare and Childhood*. Eds. Kate Chedgzoy, Susanne Greenhalgh and Robert Shaughnessy. Cambridge: CUP, 2007. 117–136.

Hamilton, Sharon. *Shakespeare's Daughters*. London: McFarland & Company, Inc., 2003.

Han, Younglim. *Romantic Shakespeare: From Stage to Page*. London: Associated UP 2001.

Hartmann, Heidi. "The Unhappy Marriage of Marxism and Feminism: Towards a More Progressive Union." *Women and Revolution: A Discussion of the Unhappy Marriage of Marxism and Feminism*. Ed. Lydia Sargent. Boston: South End, 1981. 1–41.

Hassinger, Peter W. *Shakespeare's Daughter*. New York: HarperCollins, 2004.

Hateley, Erica. "African American Children as 'Readers' of Shakespeare: Cultural Politics and Race in Shakespearean Children's Literature." *To See the Wizard: Politics and the Literature of Childhood*. Ed. Laurie Ousley. Newcastle upon Tyne: Cambridge Scholars Publishing, 2007. 41–66.

———. "Of Tails and Tempests: Feminine Sexuality and Shakespearean Children's Texts." *Borrowers and Lenders: The Journal of Shakespeare and Appropriation* 2.1 (2006): n.p.

———. "Shakespeare as National Discourse in Contemporary Children's Literature." *Papers: Explorations into Children's Literature* 13.1 (2003): 11–24.

———. "Shakespeare's Macbeth: Poster-Boy for Contemporary Masculinity?" *Journal of Interdisciplinary Gender Studies* 9.2 (2004): 80–92.

Hazlitt, William. *Characters of Shakespeare's Plays*. 1817. London: OUP, 1970.

Heminge, John, and Henrie Condell. "To the Great Variety of Readers." *Mr. William Shakespeares Comedies, Histories & Tragedies*. London: Isaac Jaggard, and Ed. Blount, 1623.

Holbrook, David. *Images of Women in Literature*. New York: New York UP, 1989.

Holland, Norman N. *Psychoanalysis and Shakespeare*. New York: McGraw-Hill Book Co., 1964.

Hollindale, Peter. "'Children of Eyam': The Dramatization of History." *Children's Literature in Education* 28.4 (1997): 205–218.

Horowitz, Anthony. *The Devil and his Boy*. 1998. London: Walker, 2004.

Howe, Norma. *Blue Avenger Cracks the Code*. 2000. New York: HarperTempest, 2002.

Hoyt, Sarah A. *All Night Awake*. 2002. New York: Ace Books, 2003.

———. *Ill Met by Moonlight*. 2001. New York: Ace Books, 2002.

Hutcheon, Linda. *A Theory of Parody: The Teachings of Twentieth-Century Art Forms*. 1985. Urbana: U of Illinois P, 2000.

Isaac, Megan Lynn. *Heirs to Shakespeare: Reinventing the Bard in Young Adult Literature*. Portsmouth NH: Heinemann, 2000.

Jacobs, Joseph. *English Fairy Tales: Being the Two Collections English Fairy Tales & More English Fairy Tales*. 1890, 1898. 3rd ed. London: The Bodley Head, 1975.

Jenkinson, Dave. "Portraits: Welwyn Winton Katz." *Emergency Librarian* 21.2 (1993): 61–65.

"Judith." *The Holy Bible: A Translation from the Latin Vulgate in the Light of the Hebrew and Greek Originals*. London: Burns & Oates, 1956.

Katz, Welwyn W. *Come Like Shadows*. 1993. Saskatchewan: Coteau Books, 2000.

Kilworth, Garry. *A Midsummer's Nightmare*. 1996. London: Corgi Books, 1997.

Kingsley-Smith, Jane E. "Shakespearean Authorship in Popular British Cinema." *Literature/Film Quarterly* 30.3 (2002): 158–65.

Kipling, Rudyard. *Puck of Pook's Hill*. London: Macmillan and Co., Ltd., 1906.

Klein, Robin. *Penny Pollard's Diary*. Ill. Ann James. Oxford: OUP, 1983.

Konigsburg, E. L. *Jennifer, Hecate, Macbeth, William McKinley, and Me, Elizabeth*. 1967. New York: Bantam Doubleday Dell Books, 1985.

Kositsky, Lynne. *A Question of Will*. Montreal: Roussan Publishers Inc, 2000.

Lamb, Charles. "On the Tragedies of Shakspeare; Considered with Reference to Their Fitness for Stage Representation." *Charles Lamb, Selected Prose*. 1811. Ed. Adam Phillips. Harmondsworth: Penguin, 1985. 45–60.

Lamb, Charles, and Mary Lamb. *The Letters of Charles and Mary Anne Lamb*. Ed. Edwin W. Marrs. Vol. II: 1801–1809. Ithaca: Cornell UP, 1976.

———. *Tales from Shakespeare*. 1807. Ed. Martin Armstrong. London: Collins, 1953.

Lamb, Mary Ellen. "Taken by the Fairies: Fairy Practices and the Production of Popular Culture in a Midsummer Night's Dream." *Shakespeare Quarterly* 51.3 (2000): 277–312.

Lancaster, Kurt. "Neil Gaiman's 'A Midsummer Night's Dream': Shakespeare Integrated into Popular Culture." *Journal of American and Comparative Cultures* 23.3 (2000): 69–77.

Lane, Pam. "'Something Rich and Strange': Shakespeare for the Very Young." *Orana: Journal of School and Children's Librarianship* 37.2 (2001): 4–11.

Lanier, Douglas. *Shakespeare and Modern Popular Culture*. Oxford: OUP, 2002.

———. "Shakespeare™: Myth and Biographical Fiction." *The Cambridge Companion to Shakespeare and Popular Culture*. Ed. Robert Shaughnessy. Cambridge: CUP, 2007. 93–113.

Lanyer, Aemilia. "Salve Deus Rex Judaeorum." *Renaissance Women: The Plays of Elizabeth Cary, The Poems of Aemilia Lanyer*. 1611. Ed. Diane Purkiss. London: William Pickering, 1994. 239–333.

L'Engle, Madeleine. "Childlike Wonder and the Truths of Science Fiction." *Children's Literature* 10 (1982): 102–10.

———. *A Wrinkle in Time*. 1962. London: Puffin, 1995.

Lesko, Nancy. *Act Your Age!: A Cultural Construction of Adolescence*. New York: Routledge Falmer, 2001.

Levin, Harry. "Critical Approaches to Shakespeare from 1660 to 1904." *The Cambridge Companion to Shakespeare Studies*. 1986. Ed. Stanley Wells. Cambridge: CUP, 2000. 213–29.

Lindblad, Ishrat. "In the Company of Shakespeare." *Signal: Approaches to Children's Books* 34.100 (2003): 127–34.

Locke, John. *Some Thoughts Concerning Education*. 1693. Eds. John W. Yolton and Jean S. Yolton. New York: OUP, 1989.

Lootens, Tricia. *Lost Saints: Silence, Gender, and Victorian Literary Canonization*. Charlottesville: UP of Virginia, 1996.

Macey, Julie, ed. *MacB*. Harlow: Pearson Longman, 2002.

MacPhail, Catherine. *Another Me*. London: Bloomsbury, 2003.

Mannoni, O. *Prospero and Caliban: The Psychology of Colonization*. 1950. Trans. Pamela Powesland. 2nd ed. New York: Frederick A. Praeger, 1964.

Marchitello, Howard. "Descending Shakespeare: Toward a Theory of Adaptation of Children." *Reimagining Shakespeare for Children and Young Adults*. Ed. Naomi J. Miller. London: Routledge, 2003. 180–89.

Marsden, Jean I. "Shakespeare for Girls: Mary Lamb and *Tales from Shakespeare*." *Children's Literature* 17 (1989): 47–63.

Masson, Sophie. *Cold Iron, Clementine, Carabas*. 1998. Sydney: Hodder Children's Books, 2000.

———. *The Tempestuous Voyage of Hopewell Shakespeare*. London: Hodder Children's Books, 2003.

———. "That Merry Wanderer of the Night; or, How I Learnt to Stop Worrying and Enjoy Plundering the Fantastic Works of the Bard!" *Locus Online*. 22 Aug. 2002. 26 Aug. 2002. http://www.locusmag.com/2002/Reviews/Masson08.html.

Mathur, Amy. "Promoting the Original: Perspectives on Balancing Authenticity and Creativity in Adaptations of *The Tempest*." *Reimagining Shakespeare for Children and Young Adults*. Ed. Naomi J. Miller. London: Routledge, 2003. 147–52.

Mayo, Sarah. "'A Shakespeare for the People'?: Negotiating the Popular in *Shakespeare in Love* and Michael Hoffman's *A Midsummer Night's Dream*." *Textual Practice* 17.2 (2003): 295–315.

Meacham, Margaret. *A Mid-Semester Night's Dream*. New York: Holiday House, 2004.

Messner, Michael A. *Power at Play: Sports and the Problem of Masculinity*. Boston: Beacon Press, 1992.

Micros, Marianne. "'My Books Are My Children': An Interview with Welwyn Wilton Katz." *Canadian Children's Literature* 24.2 (1998): 51–65.

Miller, Naomi J. "'What's in a Name?': Collaborating with Shakespeare at the Millennium." *Reimagining Shakespeare for Children and Young Adults*. Ed. Naomi J. Miller. London: Routledge, 2003. 1–9.

Moi, Toril. "Appropriating Bourdieu: Feminist Theory and Pierre Bourdieu's Sociology of Culture." *New Literary History*. 22.4 (1991): 1017–49.

Montrose, Louis Adrian. "'Shaping Fantasies': Figurations of Gender and Power in Elizabethan Culture." *A Midsummer Night's Dream*. Ed. Richard Dutton. New York: St. Martin's Press, 1996. 101–38.

Moore, John Noell. "Intertextualities: *The Tempest* in *Morning Girl, Lizard*, and *In Summer Light*." *Adolescent Literature as a Complement to the Classics*. Ed. Joan F. Kaywell. Vol. 3. Norwood, MA: Christopher-Gordon Publishers, Inc., 1997. 71–92.

Morse, Ruth. "Children's Hours: Shakespeare, the Lambs, and French Education." *Shifting the Scene: Shakespeare in European Culture*. Eds. Ladina Bezzola Lambert and Balz Engler. Newark: U Delaware P, 2004. 193–204.

Moss, Elaine. "Afterword." *A Wrinkle in Time*. London: Puffin, 1995. 214–18.

Mowat, Barbara. "The Problem of Shakespeare's Text(s)." *Textual Formations and Reformations*. Eds. Laurie E. Maguire and Thomas L. Berger. Newark: U of Delaware P, 1998. 131–48.

Neill, Michael. "Post-Colonial Shakespeare? Writing Away from the Centre." *Post-Colonial Shakespeares*. Eds. Ania Loomba and Martin Orkin. London: Routledge, 1998. 164–85.

Nelson, Robert J. *Play within a Play, the Dramatist's Conception of His Art: Shakespeare to Anouilh*. New Haven: Yale UP, 1958.

Nesbit, Edith. *The Best of Shakespeare: Retellings of 10 Classic Plays*. The Opie Library. Oxford: OUP, 1997.

———. *The Children's Shakespeare*. Ed. Edric Vredenburg. Ill. Frances Brundage. London: Raphael Tuck & Sons, 1897.

———. *Twenty Beautiful Stories from Shakespeare: A Home Study Course*. Ed. E. T. Roe. Chicago: D. E. Cunningham & Co, 1907.

Nikolajeva, Maria. *Children's Literature Comes of Age: Toward a New Aesthetic*. New York: Garland Publishing, Inc., 1996.

"norm." *Oxford English Dictionary*. Eds. A. J. Simpson and E. S. C. Weiner. 2nd ed. Oxford: Clarendon, 1989.

Oneal, Zibby. *In Summer Light*. 1985. London: Victor Gollancz Ltd, 1986.

Orgel, Stephen. *Impersonations: Performance of Gender in Shakespeare's England*. Cambridge: CUP, 1996.

Osborne, Laurie E. "Harlequin Presents: That '70s Shakespeare and Beyond." *Shakespeare after Mass Media*. Ed. Richard Burt. New York: Palgrave, 2002. 127–50.

———. "Romancing the Bard." *Shakespeare and Appropriation*. Eds. Christy Desmet and Robert Sawyer. London: Routledge, 1999. 47–64.

Osborne, Mary Pope. *Stage Fright on a Summer Night*. Magic Tree House. Vol. 25. New York: Random House, Inc, 2002.

O'Sullivan, Emer. *Comparative Children's Literature*. Trans. Anthea Bell. London: Routledge, 2005.

O'Sullivan, Mary Isabelle. "Hamlet and Dr. Timothy Bright." *PMLA* 36 (1926): 667–79.

Ovid. *Metamorphoses: A New Verse Translation*. AD 8. Trans. David Raeburn. Ed. Denis Feeney. Harmondsworth: Penguin, 2004.

Park, Ruth. *My Sister Sif*. 1986. Ringwood: Puffin, 1987.

Parkman, Francis. *Montcalm and Wolfe*. 1884. Bristol: Purnell & Sons, 1964.

Perantoni, Cynthia. "First One I and Then the Other: Identity and Intertextuality in Shakespeare's Caliban and Covington's Lizard." *Reimagining Shakespeare for Children and Young Adults*. Ed. Naomi J. Miller. London: Routledge, 2003. 153–61.

Perrin, Noel. *Dr. Bowdler's Legacy: A History of Expurgated Books in England and America*. London: Macmillan, 1969.

Perry, Gill, Anne Laurence, and Joan Bellamy. "Introduction: Gender and Women's History." *Women, Scholarship and Criticism: Gender and Knowledge c. 1790–1900*. Eds. Joan Bellamy, Anne Laurence and Gill Perry. Manchester: MUP, 2000. 1–15.

Pinsent, Pat. "'Not for an Age but for All Time': The Depiction of Shakespeare in a Selection of Children's Fiction." *New Review of Children's Literature and Librarianship* 10.2 (2004): 115–26.

Polowetzky, Michael. *Prominent Sisters: Mary Lamb, Dorothy Wordsworth, and Sarah Disraeli*. London: Praeger, 1996.

Pratchett, Terry. *Lords and Ladies*. 1992. London: Corgi, 1993.

Price, Leah. "The Poetics of Pedantry from Thomas Bowdler to Susan Ferrier." *Women's Writing* 7.1 (2000): 75–88.

Purkiss, Diane, ed. *Renaissance Women: The Plays of Elizabeth Cary, the Poems of Aemilia Lanyer*. London: William Pickering, 1994.

———. *Troublesome Things: A History of Fairies and Fairy Stories.* 2000. Harmondsworth: Penguin, 2001.

Quiller-Couch, A. T. *Historical Tales from Shakespeare.* London: Edward Arnold, 1899.

Randall, Dudley. "Ballad of Birmingham (1966)." *Black Literature in America.* Ed. Houston A. Baker Jr. New York: McGraw-Hill, 1971. 337–38.

Rasmussen, Eric. "Fathers and Sons in *Hamlet.*" *Shakespeare Quarterly* 35.4 (1984): 463.

Rausen, Ruth. "An Interview with Madeleine L'Engle." *Children's Literature in Education.* 19 (1975): 198–206.

Richardson, Brian. "Remapping the Present: The Master Narrative of Modern Literary History and the Lost Forms of Twentieth-Century History." *Twentieth Century Literature* 43.3 (1997): 291–309.

Rosen, Michael. *Shakespeare: His Work & His World.* London: Walker Books, 2001.

Rousseau, Jean-Jacques. *Emile, or, On Education.* Trans. Allan Bloom. New York: Basic Books, 1979.

Rowlands, Avril. *The Shakespeare Connection.* Oxford: OUP, 1994.

Rowse, A. L. *Homosexuals in History: A Study of Ambivalence in Society, Literature and the Arts.* London: Wiedenfeld and Nicolson, 1977.

———. *Shakespeare's Sonnets: The Problems Solved.* 1964. 2nd ed. London: Macmillan, 1973.

Rozett, Martha Tuck. *Talking Back to Shakespeare.* Newark: U of Delaware P, 1994.

Russon, Penni. *Undine.* Milsons Point, NSW: Random House, 2004.

Salih, Sara. *Judith Butler.* London: Routledge, 2002.

Sanders, Julie. *Novel Shakespeares: Twentieth-Century Women Novelists and Appropriation.* Manchester: MUP, 2001.

Schiffer, James. "Macbeth and the Bearded Women." *In Another Country: Feminist Perspectives on Renaissance Drama.* Eds. Dorothea Kehler and Susan Baker. Metuchen NJ: Scarecrow, 1991. 205–217.

Schoenbaum, S. *William Shakespeare: A Documentary Life.* Oxford: Clarendon, 1975.

Schwebel, Sara L. "Historical Fiction and the Classroom: History and Myth in Elizabeth George Speare's *The Witch of Blackbird Pond.*" *Children's Literature in Education* 34.3 (2003): 195–218.

Scott, Carole. "A Century of Dislocated Time: Time Travel, Magic and the Search for Self." *Papers: Explorations into Children's Literature* 6.2 (1996): 14–20.

Seamer, Mary. *Shakespeare's Stories Simply Told.* New York: Thomas Nelson and Sons, 1899.

Sedgwick, Eve Kosofsky. *Between Men: English Literature and Male Homosocial Desire.* New York: Columbia UP, 1985.

Sendak, Maurice. *Where the Wild Things Are.* 1963. London: Random House Children's Books, 2000.

"Shakespeare Film Studios 'Face Trial'". *BBC News.* 4 Oct. 2001. 11 Oct. 2004 http://news.bbc.co.uk/1/hi/entertainment/film/1579443.stm.

Shakespeare, William. *All's Well That Ends Well.* The Arden Shakespeare. Ed. G. K. Hunter. London: Methuen & Co Ltd, 1959.

———. *Macbeth.* 1962, 1984. The Arden Shakespeare. Ed. Kenneth Muir. London: Thomson Learning, 2001.

———. *A Midsummer Night's Dream.* 1979. The Arden Shakespeare. Ed. Harold F. Brooks. London: Thomson Learning, 2003.

———. *The Tempest.* The Arden Shakespeare. Eds. Virginia Mason Vaughan and Alden T. Vaughan. London: Thomson Learning, 1999.

———. *Timon of Athens.* The Arden Shakespeare. Ed. H. J. Oliver. London: Methuen & Co Ltd, 1963.

———. *Twelfth Night.* 1975. The Arden Shakespeare. Eds. J. M. Lothian and T. W. Craik. London: Thomson Learning, 2000.

Singer, Marilyn. *The Course of True Love Never Did Run Smooth.* New York: Harper & Row, 1983.

Singh, Jyotsna G. "Caliban Versus Miranda: Race and Gender Conflicts in Postcolonial Rewritings of *The Tempest.*" *Shakespeare's Romances.* Ed. Alison Thorne. London: Palgrave Macmillan, 2003. 205–25.

Singh, Yvonne. "Performance Review: 1996 Olympic Arts Festival." *Theatre Journal* 49.1 (1997): 69–74.

Skeggs, Beverley. "Context and Background: Pierre Bourdieu's Analysis of Class, Gender and Sexuality." *Feminism After Bourdieu.* Eds. Lisa Adkins and Beverley Skeggs. Oxford: Blackwell/Sociological Review, 2004. 19–33.

Skura, Meredith Anne. "Discourse and the Individual: The Case of Colonialism in *the Tempest*." *Critical Essays on Shakespeare's The Tempest*. Eds. Alden T. Vaughan and Virginia Mason Vaughan. New York: G K Hall & Co., 1998. 60–90.

Slemon, Stephen, and Jo-Ann Wallace. "Into the Heart of Darkness?: Teaching Children's Literature as a Problem in Theory." *Canadian Children's Literature*. 63 (1991): 6–23.

Slights, Jessica. "Rape and the Romanticization of Shakespeare's Miranda." *Studies in English Literature* 41.2 (2001): 357–79.

Smith, Kay H. "'*Hamlet, Part Eight, the Revenge*' or, Sampling Shakespeare in a Postmodern World." *College Literature* 31.4 (2004): 135–49.

Stallybrass, Peter. "'Macbeth' and Witchcraft." *Macbeth*. Ed. Alan Sinfield. Hampshire: Macmillan, 1992. 25–38.

Stam, Robert. "Beyond Fidelity: The Dialogics of Adaptation." *Film Adaptation*. Ed. James Naremore. London: The Athlone Press, 2000. 54–76.

Stephens, John. "Gender, Genre, and Children's Literature." *Signal* 79 (1996): 17–30.

———. *Language and Ideology in Children's Fiction*. London: Longman Group Ltd., 1992.

———. "Not Unadjacent to a Play About a Scottish King: Terry Pratchett Remakes *Macbeth*." *Papers: Explorations into Children's Literature* 7.2 (1997): 29–37.

———. "'A Page Just Waiting to Be Written on': Masculinity Schemata and the Dynamics of Subjective Agency in Junior Fiction." *Ways of Being Male: Representing Masculinities in Children's Literature and Film*. Ed. John Stephens. London: Routledge, 2002. 38–54.

Stephens, John, and Robyn McCallum. "Discourses of Femininity and the Intertextual Construction of Feminist Reading Positions." *Girls, Boys, Books, Toys: Gender in Children's Literature and Culture*. Eds. Beverly Lyon Clark and Margaret R. Higonnet. Baltimore: Johns Hopkins UP, 1999. 130–41.

———. *Retelling Stories, Framing Culture: Traditional Story and Metanarratives in Children's Literature*. New York: Garland Publishing, 1998.

Stone, Oliver (dir). *JFK*. Perf. Kevin Costner, Gary Oldman, Tommy Lee Jones. Warner Bros, 1991.

Swartz, David. *Culture & Power: The Sociology of Power*. Chicago: U of Chicago P, 1997.

"tanistry." *Oxford English Dictionary*. Eds. A. J. Simpson and E. S. C. Weiner. 2nd ed. Oxford: Clarendon, 1989.

Taylor, Gary. *Reinventing Shakespeare: A Cultural History from the Restoration to the Present*. 1989. London: The Hogarth Press, 1990.

Taylor, Michael. *Shakespeare Criticism in the Twentieth Century*. Oxford: OUP, 2001.

Thacker, Deborah Cogan, and Jean Webb. *Introducing Children's Literature: From Romanticism to Postmodernism*. London: Routledge, 2002.

Thompson, Ann, and Sasha Roberts, eds. *Women Reading Shakespeare 1660–1900: An Anthology of Criticism*. Manchester: MUP, 1997.

Thomson, J. C. *Bibliography of the Writings of Charles and Mary Lamb*. Hull: J R Tutin, 1908.

Tiffany, Grace. *Ariel*. New York: Laura Geringer Books, 2005.

———. *My Father Had a Daughter: Judith Shakespeare's Tale*. New York: Berkley Books, 2003.

Trease, Geoffrey. *Cue for Treason*. 1940. Harmondsworth: Puffin, 2002.

Tyler Hitchcock, Susan. *Mad Mary Lamb: Lunacy and Murder in Literary London*. New York: W. W. Norton & Company, 2005.

Updike, John. *Bottom's Dream: Adapted from William Shakespeare's A Midsummer Night's Dream*. New York: Alfred A. Knopf, 1969.

Vaughan, Alden T. and Virginia Mason Vaughan. *Shakespeare's Caliban: A Cultural History*. Cambridge: CUP, 1991.

Wall, Barbara. *The Narrator's Voice: The Dilemma of Children's Fiction*. New York: St. Martin's Press, 1991.

Warner, Marina. *From the Beast to the Blonde: On Fairy Tales and Their Tellers*. 1994. London: Vintage, 1995.

———. "Introduction." *Tales From Shakespeare*. Harmondsworth: Penguin, 2007.

Webb, Jen, Tony Schirato, and Geoff Danaher. *Understanding Bourdieu*. Crows Nest, NSW: Allen & Unwin, 2002.

Weir, Peter (dir). *Dead Poets Society*. Perf. Robin Williams, Robert Sean Leonard, Ethan Hawke. Touchstone Pictures, 1989.

Wesley, John. *The Works of John Wesley*. Ed. Albert C. Outler. Vol. 3: Sermons III. Nashville: Abingdon Press, 1986.

White, R. S. "Introduction: Prospero 2000." *The Tempest*. Ed. R. S. White. Hampshire: Macmillan Press Ltd, 1999. 1–14.

Wilcox, Fred M. (dir). *Forbidden Planet.* Perf. Walter Pidgeon, Anne Francis, Leslie Nielsen. MGM, 1956.
Wilkie, Christine. "Relating Texts: Intertextuality." *Understanding Children's Literature: Key Essays from the International Companion Encyclopedia of Children's Literature.* Ed. Peter Hunt. London: Routledge, 1999. 130–37.
Williams, Marcia. "Bravo, Mr. William Shakespeare!" *Reimagining Shakespeare for Children and Young Adults.* Ed. Naomi J. Miller. London: Routledge, 2003. 29–38.
———. *Mr. William Shakespeare's Plays.* London: Walker Books, 1998.
Williams, Tad. *Caliban's Hour.* London: Legend Books, 1994.
Williamson, Marilyn L. "Violence and Gender Ideology in *Coriolanus* and *Macbeth.*" *Shakespeare Left and Right.* Ed. Ivo Kamps. New York: Routledge, 1991. 147–60.
Wilson, Jean. *The Shakespeare Legacy: The Material Legacy of Shakespeare's Theatre.* Godalming, Surrey: Bramley Books, 1995.
Wittreich Jr., Joseph Anthony. *The Romantics on Milton: Formal Essays and Critical Asides.* Cleveland: The P of Case Western Reserve U, 1970.
Wolfson, Susan J. "Explaining to Her Sisters: Mary Lamb's *Tales from Shakespear.*" *Women's Re-Visions of Shakespeare: On Responses of Dickinson, Woolf, Rich, H.D., George Eliot, and Others.* Ed. Marianne Novy. Urbana: U of Illinois P, 1990. 16–40.
———. "Shakespeare and the Romantic Girl Reader." *Nineteenth-Century Contexts* 21.2 (1999): 191–234.
Woodbery, Bonnie. "The Mad Body as the Text of Culture in the Writings of Mary Lamb." *Studies in English Literature, 1500–1900.* 39.4 (1999): 659–74.
Woolf, Virginia. *A Room of One's Own, Three Guineas.* Ed. Morag Schiach. Oxford: OUP, 1992.
Wordsworth, William. *Lyrical Ballads.* 1802. Ed. Michael Mason. New York: Longman, 1992.
Yoshimoto, Mitsuhiro. *Kurosawa: Film Studies and Japanese Cinema.* Durham, NC: Duke UP, 2000.
Zabus, Chantal. *Tempests After Shakespeare.* New York: Routledge, 2002.
Ziegler, Georgiana. "Accommodating the Virago: Nineteenth-Century Representations of Lady Macbeth." *Shakespeare and Appropriation.* Eds. Christy Desmet and Robert Sawyer. London: Routledge, 1999. 119–41.

Index

For Product Safety Concerns and Information please contact our EU representative GPSR@taylorandfrancis.com
Taylor & Francis Verlag GmbH, Kaufingerstraße 24, 80331 München, Germany

www.ingramcontent.com/pod-product-compliance
Lightning Source LLC
Chambersburg PA
CBHW071524110726
47908CB00003B/945
* 9 7 8 0 4 1 5 8 8 8 8 8 2 *